Reengineering Corporate Training

Reengineering Corporate Training

Intellectual Capital and Transfer of Learning

Robert E. Haskell

QUORUM BOOKS
Westport, Connecticut • London

Library of Congress Cataloging-in-Publication Data

Haskell, Robert E.
    Reengineering corporate training : intellectual capital and
transfer of learning / Robert E. Haskell.
        p.   cm.
    Includes bibliographical references and index.
    ISBN 1–56720–148–2 (alk. paper)
        1. Employees—Training of.   2. Transfer of training.   3. Learning,
Psychology of.   4. Corporate culture.   I. Title.
HF5549.5.T7H335   1998
658.3'124—dc21   97–22746

British Library Cataloguing in Publication Data is available.

Library of Congress Catalog Card Number: 97–22746
ISBN: 1–56720–148–2

First published in 1998

Quorum Books, 88 Post Road West, Westport, CT 06881
An imprint of Greenwood Publishing Group, Inc.

Printed in the United States of America

The paper used in this book complies with the
Permanent Paper Standard issued by the National
Information Standards Organization (Z39.48–1984).

10   9   8   7   6   5   4   3   2   1

Copyright Acknowledgments

The author and publisher are grateful for permission to reproduce portions of the following
copyrighted material:
    Figures B.1–B.6. Screen shots reprinted with permission from Microsoft Corporation.
    Kenneth Brown, *Inventors at Work: Interviews with 16 Notable American Inventors*, Tempus Books (Redmond, WA: Microsoft Press, 1988).
    A. Fisher, "The Ever-Bigger Boom in Consulting," *Fortune* (April 24, 1989), p. 130.
Copyright 1989 Time, Inc. All rights reserved.
    I. L. Goldstein, *Training in Organizations: Needs Assessment, Development, and Evaluation*
(Pacific Grove, CA: Brooks/Cole Publishing Company, 1993).
    Brian O'Reilly, "What's Killing the Business School Deans of America?" *Fortune* (August
8, 1994), p. 64. Copyright 1994 Time, Inc. All rights reserved.
    John H. Zenger, "Then: The Painful Turnabout in Training; Now: A Retrospective," *Training and Development* 50(1) (January 1996), p. 48. Reprinted from *Training and Development*.
Copyright January 1996, the American Society for Training and Development. Reprinted with
permission. All rights reserved.

Contents

Introduction

It continues to be widely recognized that transfer of training for employees is crucial to performance in business and industry. Transfer of learning—a.k.a. transfer of *training*—is the use of our past learning in our learning of something new and in our *application* of that learning to both similar and quite dissimilar situations; transfer of learning is the very foundation of learning, thinking, and problem solving. In short, it's the goal of all training programs. Moreover, the downsizing of our workforce requires increasing efficiency and payoff in training functions. The financial significance of transfer of learning is that American companies spend upwards of 70 billion high-gloss dollars on training hardware, materials, seminars, conferences, and consultants. Of all human resource development (HRD) programs, training is one of the most expensive.

The research shows that transfer of learning in formal learning situations doesn't have a good track record. I maintain this is because instructional and training programs have neither systematically made use of the available information nor developed specific frameworks for transfer of learning. Despite these findings, the transfer of learning, while requiring hard work, is not difficult. To varying degrees of success, transfer of learning occurs spontaneously in informal learning situations every day by everyone, regardless of ability. If it didn't, we couldn't learn about, or adapt to, anything.

For the busy executive, manager, and corporate HRD professional, the job of deciding on an effective instructional program is no small matter. Despite current "how-to" trendy offerings of "accelerated" or immediate learning outcomes, there's little evidence demonstrating that most of these training programs work very well. In fact, the evidence is clear: They don't. At least they don't on any but the most superficial level (see Chapter 2).

So why are executives, managers, and corporate HRD professionals spending billions of dollars each year on instructional programs in which at least 50 percent of the training doesn't transfer, representing a loss of at least $35 billion a year? The answer is that it is probably for the same reasons why many educational institutions have continued to adopt trendy educational methods. Trendy methods offer apparent quick fixes, they seem experientially and intuitively valid, and they feel good. But they don't work.

The crucial piece in the corporate training puzzle is missing. That piece is *how* to achieve transfer of learning in training programs. Corporate training needs to be reengineered radically. Let me say right up front, however, that this is not a traditional "how-to cookbook" for achieving transfer of learning unless by *how-to* we mean the understanding of a clear set of principles for how to achieve transfer of learning—in which case, this is a how-to book.

In this book, I'll present a set of eleven principles for this expensive problem. The prescriptions I'll offer, however, are not a typical series of concrete, quick-and-dirty how-to's, nor are they a set of shortcut skills or simple learning strategies. The reality of transfer of learning, corporate or otherwise, isn't that simple. There are, however, learning strategies that can augment these principles.

For the modern organization, a reengineering requires a shift from a *training* orientation to a *learning* orientation. This shift requires more than a list of how-to's and other simple instructional techniques; it requires considerable understanding of the prescriptions and why they are important to this shift. Again, there are no magic bullets or quick and easy shorts. If you and your company are not ready to spend some time thinking about what you're about to read, to transform what you currently think is required for effective training, and to implement the eleven principles of transfer seriously, then you might as well not read any further.

The issue of "transferable skills" is a serious one for the relationship between business and the public schools. Recently, the United Kingdom funded the Pegasus Program for transferring skills learned in the schools to the workplace. The initial funding level was £20 million. More recently, the U.S. government has launched a similar school-based transfer program. With recent federal programs created to facilitate the transfer of school learning to the workplace, the figure will increase significantly. Bryan, Beaudin, and Greene, writing in the *Journal of Vocational and Technical Education*, note that as "the number of coordinated training programs between corporations and schools increase, accountability and transfer to the work environment becomes increasingly important."[1] Second, of the estimated $70 billion a year spent for training in organizations, at least half of this amount is wasted because training is not being transferred and maintained on the job.

This book addresses two significant concerns that are part of an emerging shift in corporate culture. First, to compete in a global market, there is an increasing emphasis on a high-performance workforce that's increasingly dependent on the rapid acquiring and processing of knowledge. Indeed, knowledge is being viewed as a form of capital investment—as value added. It's crucial to know how this *intellectual capital* is managed (see Chapter 4). Transfer of learning is fundamental to this management.

From my years of instructional design of workshops, teaching college and university psychology courses to all ages, including many ethnic groups, and my ongoing reviews of the research findings on the transfer of learning, there are three things I've clearly learned: (1) There are no easy shortcuts to learning, (2) learning is hard work (which doesn't mean it can't be enjoyable), and (3) the transfer of formally presented instructional content seldom transfers to the workplace.

Based on my previous work in reviewing the transfer of learning research,[2] here is what I've concluded that's required in order to achieve significant instructional payoff:

1. Acquire a large primary knowledge base in the area in which transfer is required.

2. Seek some level of knowledge base in subjects outside the primary area (see Chapter 8).

3. Obtain an understanding of the history in the area(s) that you want to transfer.

4. Acquire motivation or, more specifically, a "spirit of transfer" (see Chapter 7).

5. Understand what transfer of learning is and how it works.

6. Strive toward an orientation to think and encode learning in transfer of learning terms (see Chapter 9).

7. Create cultures of transfer or support systems (see Chapter 7).

8. Understand the theory underlying the area(s) you want to transfer (see Chapter 8).

9. Engage in hours of practice and drill (see Chapter 8).

10. Allow time for the learning to incubate.

11. Observe and read the works of people who are exemplars of transfer thinking (see Chapter 6).

While transfer of learning research dates back to at least 1901 to the classic work of psychologist Edward Thorndike, until recently, interest in transfer of learning within the fields of instructional psychology and education has waned. There is now considerable rigorous research on transfer, with most of the research coming from the field of cognitive psychology. It is generally agreed that transfer of learning is the most fundamental concept in education and training—and the most elusive to demonstrate. Transfer of learning is the key to all effective instruction.

The new model of "embedded" training, that is, training that takes place in the work situation, also requires transfer of learning. The recent prediction of the demise of the "transfer model" by some training professionals who advocate an embedded model of training as opposed to a classroom setting is based on a misunderstanding of transfer in the training field. Transfer of learning encompasses a great deal more than just applying what one learns in a classroom situation and physically transferring that learning to the workplace. Transfer of learning is not a technique; it is a way of thinking and perceiving. Thus, the transfer of learning is crucial to corporations being reengineered into intelligent or learning organizations. The reason is that all effective instructional or training programs are built on a transfer of learning foundation.

While this book outlines the cognitive foundations for organizations that learn, it's not only about "learning" or "learning organizations"; it's about transfer of learning *for* organizations. This is an important distinction for two reasons. The first is that while transfer of learning is a necessary condition for learning organizations, it's not sufficient. There are, for example, group and organizational structures that are required. Second, it means that I'll not be primarily covering material that most other books on instruction or books on learning organizations cover. In short, it's not my intent to cover material on *learning*. Similarly, I'll not present an outline on what constitutes a learning organization. Rather, I'll be presenting something much more fundamental: the cognitive foundations upon which all learning and learning organizations must be based. In a fundamental sense, transfer of learning *is learning*; it *is* thinking.

My goal, then, is to lay the foundations for transfer of learning in the corporate training function. In order to lay such a foundation, I have reviewed the research findings on transfer of learning. They are voluminous and complex. So what I have had to do is to act as a translator, translating specialized findings into everyday terms. In this translation, I have had to interpret, generalize, and coalesce complex and provisional findings. There are of course dangers to this, just as there are dangers in translating a poem into a different language: Something is always lost in the translation.

I can speak not only from an academic research perspective but from personal experience on the use and importance of transfer of learning and its being accessible to everyone. This book is not only based on my years of teaching; it's based on a review of the transfer of learning research for the past 95 years. After completing this review of the 95 years of research on transfer of learning, I was profoundly affected. The literature confirmed my own classroom experience that students were not transferring what they learned. I looked for educational materials on teaching methods, but most were to no avail. There seemed to be nowhere to turn for help. So I decided to write a book myself, one that, though based on my previous research publications, was an applied book, a book that trainers could use.

I had concerns, however, with the traditional notion of *training* and how I was going to tailor the true implications of transfer of *learning*, instead of the "coin of the realm" term *training*, to the corporate environment. Historically, there has existed a split between what is called *transfer of training* in business and industry and *transfer of learning* in education. Training is a more narrow and constricted form of learning. It's clear, however, in an information age, an age of the learning organization, requires a shift from a training orientation to a learning orientation. This shift is one that I not only feel more comfortable with; it's one that *requires* a transfer of learning approach to corporate training.

I have managed a department in a learning environment, as chair of a social and behavioral sciences department. Moreover, having taught social psychology for many years, I have a working knowledge of the fields of industrial and organizational psychology and have served as a consultant. I was thus aware that outside academia there's another university: the corporate "virtual" university with millions of students engaged in serious and applied learning every day, a university of adult learners and managers of learning. Unlike the teachers and learners in this corporate university, most faculty and students in academia don't function under the bottom-line and application constraints that those in the corporate university do and thus, quite frankly, don't have the motivation needed for acquiring transfer of learning skills.

Transfer of learning is something that everyone can master. I began my career with a poor educational background and history. When I started college at age 24, only a community college would admit me. I now hold a doctorate in psychology and social relations from the Pennsylvania State University and have published four academic books and many research papers. I am convinced my early interest in transfer of learning was a spontaneous survival strategy for me that enabled me to achieve my educational goal. In any event, the point is that the transfer of learning is crucial for all those who would be learners, teachers, and designers of instructional programs at any level.

My work in transfer of learning originated many years ago as an undergraduate. I then came to the subject by way of an interest in thinking and teaching with analogies and metaphors when both were considered just "literary" devices. I wrote my senior thesis and later my master's thesis on it, have published theoretical and applied papers extending the concept of transfer, and have developed transfer of learning exercises for my lecture courses and experiential small group classes, where students learn about groups by actually functioning as a team. Since then, research in cognitive psychology has recognized the importance of what has become known as analogical reasoning and analogical transfer. Considerable work has been done in these areas.

Let me point out what I consider to be the uniqueness of this book. Actually, its uniqueness is sevenfold: First, it provides the missing cognitive foundations for all training and learning; second, it's based on a review of the research findings on the transfer of learning for the past 95 years, including the "new look" at the issue of transfer of learning coming out of the research in cognitive psychology and other related fields; third, it presents a framework for integrating workplace systems; fourth, it shows how transfer of learning is important to mental models, archetypes, and generic thinking in workplace learning; fifth, contrary to current trends suggesting that transfer can only be taught by how-to cookbook techniques, this book provides a general framework for how to learn to think in transfer terms; sixth, it provides a practical framework for solving the unsolved problem of how we can access transfer processes; and seventh, it provides a framework to unite the various names by which transfer is known. This book will practice what it preaches: It will demonstrate transfer of learning in the act of explaining it. In the more modern vernacular, it will "walk the talk."

In a trivial sense, all books that purport to offer effective training programs are about transfer. There are only two books on the market, however—past or present—directly addressing the transfer of learning in business, industrial, and other organizations. The first, by Mary Broad and John Newstrom, is entitled *Transfer of Training: Action-Packed Strategies to Ensure High Payoff from Training Investments*;[3] the second, by Farhad Analoui, is entitled *Training and Transfer of Learning*.[4] Both books view transfer of training from an organizational perspective. More specifically, they detail the organizational support systems needed to ensure and maintain the transfer of training once the trainee is back in the workplace or is applying what he or she has just learned on the job. While these are excellent, well-executed, and important books for human resource development training, they offer an entirely different approach to transfer of learning than is being proposed here. These books take a management support systems approach to transfer of learning. Unlike most HRD books and virtually all training publications, this book primarily addresses individual mental processes that make transfer of learning possible. These two approaches, however, complement one another. In fact, they are two sides of a single coin.

A prominent feature of this book is that I'll be making extensive use of short quotes by respected HRD practitioners and researchers. I do this for a number of reasons. First, quotations bring a contextual meaning and flavor to findings that are frequently lost in paraphrasing. Second, quotations emphasize the fact that the material being read isn't just the opinion of a single author but is solidly based on the works of many others. Thus, the quotations also act as a kind of shorthand documentation and everyday database for the reader. There is no shortage of books on book stands, in education, psychology, and business, that are based on unsupported personal experience and subjective opinions.

In addition, these citations are important for a book such as this one that owes so much to the dedication, and often tedious pursuit, of many scientific researchers. Accordingly, the chapters in this book are designed to demonstrate some of the complexity of the subject matter of each particular chapter. It's not enough to simply accept, for example, that knowledge base is important for transfer; it's necessary to understand *why* knowledge base is important to transfer and *how* it works.

I am going to speak frankly throughout this book about the widespread problems and misconceptions about what is possible and what is not possible to impart with HRD training programs. I do this knowing that it's not the popular thing to do. It is, however, necessary if corporate training is to be cost-effective. I can speak frankly for two reasons. The first is that I think the fiscal times are right executives, managers, and trainers want to know—indeed, *must* know—what is hype and what is not. The second reason that I can speak frankly is that I still have my "day job."

Robert E. Haskell
Old Orchard Beach, Maine, 1997
E-mail: rhaskell@javanet.com
web page: http://www.javanet.com/~rhaskell

NOTES

1. J. M. Bryan, B. P. Beaudin, and D. S. Green, "Increasing Self-Efficacy Expectations and Outcome Expectations: A Model to Facilitate Transfer of Training," *Journal of Vocational and Technical Education* 9 (1993), p. 24.

2. See R. E. Haskell, *The Future of Education and Transfer of Learning: Cognition, Learning, and Instruction for the 21st Century* (forthcoming).

3. M. L. Broad and J. Newstrom, *Transfer of Training: Action-Packed Strategies to Ensure High Payoff from Training Investments* (New York: Addison-Wesley, 1992).

4. Farhad Analoui, *Training and Transfer of Learning* (Brookfield, VT: Avebury, 1993).

Reengineering Corporate Training

1

Why Corporate Transfer of Learning Isn't Only Nice but Absolutely Necessary: The Documented Failure of HRD Training Programs

For . . . organizations to remain competitive in the global marketplace, and to develop the highly skilled workforce that can contribute to solutions for the world's pressing problems, improving transfer of training must become HRD's top priority.

Mary Broad and John Newstrom, *Transfer of Training*[1]

In this chapter, I find myself in the unfortunate, but necessary, role of the bearer of bad news about corporate training programs. In this necessary role as naysayer, I can only trust that I won't be the recipient of the age-old reaction to the messenger. Nevertheless, I need to open this chapter with the bad news for two reasons. First, I think that this bad news will put into unequivocal relief the importance of transfer of learning for increasing the effectiveness of corporate training. Second, the bad news is necessary in order to get to the good news. The bad news is this: There is every reason to doubt seriously the effectiveness of most corporate training programs beyond the most minimal level. And this is at best. At the worst, training programs can be counterproductive. Now for the good news.

Despite the evidence showing the past and current failure of corporate training programs to deliver on their claims, the good news is that I'm not pessimistic about the future of corporate training—at least in principle. To carefully document the ineffectiveness of most training programs is important for two reasons: The first is that with the billions of dollars being spent it may perhaps be difficult for many managers and trainers to believe that their training dollar is largely misspent; the second is to demonstrate the crucial importance of understanding transfer of learning for corporate training payoff. Let me say, however, that the failure of corporate training is not unique; as I have documented elsewhere,[2] education programs in the schools have also failed to show transfer of learning beyond the most minimal of levels. The failure of corporate training is thus but a subset of a much larger instructional problem.

Let me say, too, that in documenting HRD training failures many trainers will undoubtedly wince. Indeed, they must; they make their living on such training programs, a multi-billion-dollar high-gloss living, I might add. Some may even cry foul. As we will see, however, there's no factual basis for doing so. The evidence is there to be examined by all. Let me also say that I'm not trainer bashing. While some are clearly quacks, most are not. Most have serious intentions. But good intentions are not enough. Corporate training is badly in need of reengineering.

Although all human resource development training programs aspire, assume, indeed claim—either implicitly or explicitly—the transfer of their training to the job and to increased performance, precious few programs actually deliver on their promises. Again, at the risk of sounding like a naysayer, if some programs do deliver a positive outcome—beyond the most minimal of results—the evidence suggests it's in spite of the program, not because of transfer-based instruction and program design.

Is the claim that corporate training has largely been a failure my own opinion? The answer is clearly no. Is this claim based on academic or ivory-tower hairsplitting? Again, the answer is clearly no. In demonstrating the failure of corporate training, I'll be quoting the conclusions of many respected HRD practitioners that I have gleaned from the training literature. So what does the HRD evaluation evidence show?

REMEMBRANCE OF THINGS THEN AND NOW: THE GENERAL FAILURE OF CORPORATE TRAINING

Let me begin by quoting John H. Zenger, chairman of the Times Mirror Training Group, whom I'm going to cite at some length. I cite this one HRD professional at length for reasons that will become clear in a moment. Zenger begins his article by lamenting: "Researchers who rigorously evaluate training have said that demonstrable changes following training are hard to find. Kenneth Andrews in his study of the efficacy of executive-development programs concluded that companies should expect no dramatic change in the behavior of people sent to such programs."[3] Zenger goes on to quote two other training specialists who maintain that "[o]ur research adds additional confirmation to what most practitioners and academicians have long suspected: For management as a whole, training produces only minor changes."[4] He then says, "Management training, with such high-potential, has missed something and fallen short of its task. Why? . . . The failure of management and supervisory training can be traced to the fact that it has been operating on shaky assumptions, using inappropriate methodology, relying on untested theories, following fads, ignoring evaluation research, and not defining the behavior changes we seek."[5] And this is just for openers.

Continuing his assessment of corporate training, Zenger says, "We followed fads that affected both content and methodology, including such content fads as human relations, motivation, assertiveness, negotiation, group dynamics, and power. Methodology fads include case study, programmed instruction, buzz groups, structured exercises, role play, sensitivity training, and simulation."[6] Finally, he concludes, "We ignored evaluation research. We haven't sought assessment studies or real measurements of behavior change. Instead, we've relied on participant reactions and anecdotes."[7] Certainly a telling indictment of corporate training.

I would now like to point out that these quotes from Zenger are from a reprinted article in the 1996 fiftieth anniversary issue of *Training and Development*, perhaps the premier practitioner journal that is published by the American Society for Training and Development. Zenger wrote these words in the journal in 1980, over seventeen years ago. An immediate and typical response to Zenger's article may be that these findings are seventeen years old and that as HRD trainers we have learned a lot since then. Have we? Printed beside his 1980 article, however, Zenger wrote an update to his earlier piece. Let's see what he says.

Zenger begins his 1996 article thusly: "It's eerie to reread," he says, "an article one wrote 16 years ago. You wonder whether you'll be embarrassed by silly predictions or by points of view that have turned out to be totally incorrect. Fortunately, that isn't the case," he says. *"I still agree with all of it"* (italics added).[8] He further points out, "We continue to violate the research that shows spaced learning to be far superior to massed. Yes, having a three-day seminar is convenient and cuts down on travel. But that doesn't change the evidence." He concludes, *"Despite our strides, much of our training content is not grounded in good research"*[9] (italics added). But this is only one man's opinion, right? Again, the answer is a clear no.

So let's see what others have to say. In a similar then-and-now review of the management training effectiveness literature, Goldstein, in the 1993 edition of his book *Training in Organizations: Needs Assessments, Development, and Evaluation*, notes, "At this time, the 1961 and 1971 comments . . . continue to provide an accurate description of the vast number of business games. . . . [T]he most recent Annual Review . . . reach[es] the general conclusion that there is little evidence to indicate that these kinds of simulations result in any long-term improvement in management effectiveness."[10] Apparently, time doesn't heal our training wounds; it simply marches on—like inertial motion.

Yet another practitioner concludes that while "millions of dollars are spent on training in the public sector . . . there is little empirical evidence linking training to improved job behavior or employee attitude."[11] It is well known in HRD training that valid program evaluation research is rare, and when it does occur, as well-known trainer Mary Broad, in her article "Management Actions to Support Transfer of Training," points out, "most evaluations of training find little measurable behavioral change on the job."[12] Further, Robert Bretz and Robert Thompsett note that "training program evaluation is rare, and *rigorous evaluation* is virtually nonexistent" (italics added).[13]

Further still, Robert Smither, author of the comprehensive text *The Psychology of Work and Human Performance*, observes that "many researchers have concerns about the quality of evaluation in the OD [Organizational Development] field. One unfortunate aspect of OD evaluation is the fact that virtually all published cases report the success of the intervention." The facts are, however, says Smither, that most training "programs do not work very well."[14] Yet other then-and-now findings conclude similarly.

At least since the 1970s there has been an emphasis in vocational education and training on teaching what are called *core skills*. A core skills approach is one that emphasizes general skills that are not restricted to specific work situations and contexts but that will apply to a range of work situations. For example, figuring the area of a rectangle should automatically transfer to calculating how much flooring is needed for a room. Again, research from both then and now shows that it doesn't. Nearly 20 years ago in 1978, Frank Pratzner in his monograph *Occupational Adaptability and Transferable Skills*, published by the National Center for Research in Vocational Education, noted that the "literature and research in this area provides little explicit guidance, and few recommendations for practice can be made with confidence. . . . Occupational adaptability or skill transfer is, at best, a serendipitous outcome of most educational programs."[15] That was then. What about now?

In 1984 and 1986, field research evaluation studies by Fotheringhame,[16] clearly demonstrated that there is little evidence to support the core skills approaches to transfer of learning on the job. Fotheringhame examined skills training in the use of measurement gauges, expecting that motor vehicle servicing trainees that were instructed in the use of micrometers should be able to transfer this skill to other similar instruments. The results demonstrated that the performance of the trainees in using a height gauge was no better than that of other trainees not trained in the use of micrometers. Transfer of learning only occurred when trainees were either explicitly taught the principles of measurement gauges or given practice on a wide range of similar instruments.

More recently, in 1992, British researcher Carole Myers, in her article "Research Core Skills and Transfer in the Youth Training Schemes: A Field

Study of Trainee Motor Mechanics," observes, "The growing popularity of broad-based approaches to training has raised important new practical and theoretical questions about how to train for transfer." She concludes, "[I]t is not clear how these aims can be achieved."[17] Citing field research findings, she suggests that there is "little directly relevant evidence on the core skills approach." Such core skills training programs are underpinned by erroneous belief about transfer of learning. It is believed that if the same skill occurs in several contexts, then there should be transfer of learning of those skills across the different situations. Mixing concrete and mixing a cake, for example, can both be described in terms of their core measuring and mixing skills. Hence, a person already trained to mix concrete can be expected to be more successful in his or her initial attempt to mix a cake than is a person not skilled in mixing or measuring at all. The main difficulty is that while numerous activities can be conceptually described in a similar way, they do not necessarily involve sufficiently *similar* psychological and motor processes to transfer the learning.

The difficulty with a core skills approach, says Myers, is

that while many activities may be described in the same way, they need not involve the same psychological processes. Consider the example of mixing cakes and concrete; the demands on the individual in terms of the scale of the operation, judgments made, motor skills used, operation of equipment, use of tools, and so on are very different in the two tasks. While they can be described in similar terms, this similarity may occur at such a high level of abstraction that it serves no practical purpose.[18]

Thus, the core skills approach to transfer of learning, while intuitively appealing, says Myers,

is inadequate in promoting occupational flexibility. Although its aim to promote the recognition of similarities across skills is admirable, it is by no means obvious which aspects of tasks need to be similar for transfer of learning to take place. While the core skills list uses common descriptions for tasks and jobs these are not based on any coherent theory of the relationships of skills' and jobs and are of unknown validity.

Moreover, says Myers, "[s]uch an approach lacks theoretical support and there is little empirical evidence to say if it can be successful."[19] As it was then, so it is now.

What Frank Pratzner concluded nearly 20 years ago is equally true today: "[T]here is," he said, "little definitive information or explicit guidance to offer either the course developer, the curriculum builder or the media specialist."[20] In a 1996 article in *Training and Development* by Jack Phillips entitled "Was It the Training?" he opens the article with: "It's a common scenario. After a major training program, there's a boost in trainee work performance. Clearly the two events are linked. But then a manager asks the dreaded question: 'How much of the improvement was caused by the training?' This familiar inquiry is rarely answered with much accuracy or credibility."[21] There's still more.

SPECIFIC FAILURES OF CORPORATE TRAINING

Having cited the general findings of corporate training failure, at the risk of adding insult to injury, I would now like to cite additional research on specific kinds of training programs and their effectiveness—or more precisely, their general lack of effectiveness.

A current and widespread corporate practice is teamwork. In many organizations, teams are used throughout the various levels of production and management. The use of teams is becoming so prevalent that perhaps this practice is more aptly described not simply as a practice but as a new principle of corporate organization and functioning. Because most people do not know how to work in small groups effectively, this team mode of organizational functioning has virtually spawned a separate training industry within the HRD training profession. I might add that small groups and teamwork is an area dear to my heart. I've been conducting small-group courses and training for over 20 years. I would like to say that I have the greatest confidence that training in small-group functioning is very effective. But I can't. Although I've had a few former students write to me 10 years later, saying that it was the most helpful course they had taken in their entire college career, the hard evidence isn't there.

Jerald Greenberg and Robert A. Baron, in their well-received book *Behavior in Organizations*, observe, "Understanding the true effectiveness of teams is a tricky business, at best. This difficulty has been fueled in recent years by cover stories in the top business periodicals touting the success of teams."[22] They go on to ask how much of the hype on teams stems from the latest management fad and how much of the hype should be accepted as rigorous evidence for the effectiveness of teams? After reviewing two relatively rigorous studies, they conclude, "These two studies do not paint a clear and convincing case for the overall effectiveness of teams. Although teams are generally well received—that is, people enjoy working in them—it is not yet apparent that they are responsible for making individuals any more productive."[23] Whatever effectiveness teams may have, say Greenberg and Baron, teams appear to be a way of eliminating layers of management. Certainly a benefit in itself, if it works.

Many training programs not only advertise positive outcomes; there are an increasing number of what can be called "miracle methods," programs offering not only positive outcomes but nearly instant transfer success, all with an added bonus of a high entertainment quotient thrown in for higher smile sheet scores. An example of these miracle methods is the recent notoriety surrounding what is generally termed "accelerated, integrative, or superlearning" programs. Although accelerated learning programs have been in use for about ten years, they appear to be the current fad in a long history of trendy training methods purporting to exhibit superior transfer of training.

Accelerated learning programs have been used in Fortune 500 companies, in government agencies, and in public school systems on a large scale. Such programs are actually a mix of a number of traditional and nontraditional instructional components, including playing baroque music, reciting poetry, and using mental imaging techniques. Most of the evaluation research conducted on such superlearning programs has been fraught with numerous and the most serious of methodological problems, however. A recent and superbly executed study on accelerated learning, conducted at Eastman Kodak by Robert Bretz and Robert Thompsett and reported in the *Journal of Applied Psychology*, found no evidence for the superior learning or transfer of learning attributable to accelerated learning methods over standard training methods.[24]

Goldstein has reviewed the HRD training effectiveness literature for a number of areas. I will cite his findings extensively here. One area receiving considerable training attention over the years is programmed instruction (PI). Like most thoroughly reviewed studies, they are divided into two categories: (1) the reasonably well controlled methodologically and (2) the not-so-well-controlled studies. While some studies did find that programmed instruction was fairly effective, it is instructive to note that Goldstein observes that "the studies that did find that PI resulted in superior achievement levels were [the] less effectively controlled studies."[25] Thus, there are serious questions about the effectiveness of training with programmed instruction.

This distinction between well-controlled studies and not-so-well-controlled studies is a crucial one. But not all studies are created equal, and we must learn to evaluate which studies are the valid ones. Not understanding this distinction leads many to conclude in frustration, "Oh, you can always find studies to support what you want." The logical implication of such untutored thinking is: Anything goes; every opinion is equal—in which case we might as well roll the dice for what training program is to be implemented. Not a profitable state of affairs. Gambling only pays off if you're the House. With this said, let me continue.

With regard to training using business games, simulation, and case studies, Goldstein says, "Unfortunately, efforts to examine business games are few and far between, and efficacy of the technique is typically based on the proponents' hard-sell verbal approach. This has led some investigators to suggest that it was time to stop assuming that learning would occur automatically as a result of the use of business games."[26] Goldstein goes on to quote other reviewers who have concluded, "For all we know, at this time, there may be a negative or zero relationship between the kinds of behavior developed by business game training and the kinds of behavior required to operate a business successfully."[27] Goldstein himself concludes that since these authors stated their findings, other investigators have expressed concern about the cost of business gaming and the continued lack of rigorous research in HRD training.

Citing specific pieces of research from 1961 and 1971, Goldstein says things haven't changed, that the early research showing training ineffectiveness continues to provide an accurate description of the vast number of business games. Moreover, in the 1992 *Annual Review of Psychology*, Tannenbaum and Yukl conclude that there is little evidence indicating that these kinds of business simulations result in any long-term improvement in management effectiveness.[28] Similarly, there have been almost no recent rigorous studies into the effectiveness of problem-solving and decision-making skills despite the fact that there are a number of strategies for developing such skills.

Role-playing is yet another widely practiced training method. Relatively few research efforts on role-playing exist. One reason for this lack is that role-playing tends to be used as a part of other techniques such as behavioral role-modeling. Once again, there is little evidence showing that role-playing or role-modeling "is more cost-effective than other methods."[29] Yet other training areas are motivation training for increasing individual achievement and the newer method of computer-assisted instruction (CAI). With regard to these areas, at worst, the research suggests that "[t]he achievement data appear to parallel PI analyses."[30] At best, while some studies indicate that with CAI students perform better than traditionally educated students, "[t]he largest number of investigations, however, found no significant difference between the two groups."[31]

A method that has received considerable popular "bad press" in recent years is the old and ostensibly outmoded lecture method. This bad press about the lecture method may, however, be premature. As Goldstein points out, "Unfortunately, few studies have examined lecture courses that are specifically designed as part of a training program . . . [and] the lecture technique is viewed with disdain without much empirical evidence." The lecture as a method of delivering information is still widely used, despite proponents who excitedly proclaim the superiority of other—more costly—techniques "with little, if any, empirical evidence."[32] And so it goes.

Finally, in reviewing the training literature on management training techniques such as sensitivity training, a method called meta-analysis has been used. Meta-analysis enables the examination of statistical effects across many studies by combining the data from these studies. Such analyses don't typically find much support for the effectiveness of management training programs, especially as they relate to changes on the job. Typically, many researchers express serious concern about the criterion measures being used to evaluate such programs. They note that, in too many cases, "observers were simply asked to report changes in behavior without determining whether it actually affected job performance. In other cases, the measures were unconfirmed self-report measures."[33] In other words, smile sheet research.

SMILE SHEET RESEARCH

When training effectiveness is evaluated, it's more often than not conducted with the infamous smile sheet, those subjective recordings of participants' evaluation of the training program. Clearly, as Bretz and Thompsett point out, when training is evaluated, much of the evaluation research is conducted with the infamous so-called smile sheets, participants' *perceptions* of their training.[34] As Robert Smither has observed, "Although many OD programs do undertake an evaluation, such evaluations are typically focused more on process variables—how workers *felt* after the intervention—than on harder criteria such as turnover, absenteeism, sales volume, and so on" (italics added).[35] The typical response to all the above solid research showing the absence of effectiveness is that those receiving the training should be the best judge of how much and how well they learned. Sounds good. The question remains, however, Are participants' subjective judgments about their learning correct?

Sue Faerman and Carolyn Ban, in their 1993 article "Trainee Satisfaction and Training Impact," conclude that we may assume all we like that "to the extent that training participants feel positively about their experience and report its relevance to their work environment, they are likely to transfer their learnings to the work environment, thus resulting in the enhancement of both individual and organizational performance." The facts are, say Faerman and Ban, evaluation research "has failed to find a clear linkage between course satisfaction and change in work behaviors."[36] The participants and their supervisors in the accelerated learning Kodak program (mentioned earlier) enjoyed the training and firmly believed they had learned more than from traditional training methods. Without going into the excellent methodological detail of the study, suffice it to say that using an experimental and control group design Bretz and Thompsett found no evidence for the superior learning or transfer of learning attributable to accelerated learning methods over standard training methods.

Now it might be asked: If participants enjoyed the program, and perhaps learned as much as from more traditional methods, why not use accelerated learning? The answer is quite simple: The cost of many of these feel-good programs is much more than the cost of the typical training program. For example, in the Kodak study, the trainer/student ratio for the accelerated learning approach was approximately 1:10, as compared to a 1:44 trainer/student ratio for the traditional approach—plus other equipment costs.

Most smile sheet evaluations that show training is effective are at best like some medical placebo effects or what is now called the Hawthorne Effect in organizational research. The Hawthorne Effect is the result of Elton W. Mayo's classic research. Mayo was an organizational researcher and consultant and is generally considered the founder of what is called the human relations movement.[37] In 1927 Mayo began his studies at Western Electric's Hawthorne Works near Chicago. Mayo and his colleagues examined the effects of a variety of variables on morale and productivity. Among them were the length of rest pauses, the duration of the workday and workweek, the presence or absence of a free midmorning snack, and the effects of illumination. To cut a long story down to size, Mayo constantly found an increase in morale and productivity due to these variables, only to later have them both fall to preintervention levels. In the end, the increase in morale and productivity was found to be the consequence of workers' being given personal attention while the research was being conducted. The increase in morale and productivity that was thought to be the result of the intervention variables but that, in fact, was due to "human relations factors" is now called the Hawthorne Effect. Unfortunately, all too often, if training makes participants feel good, then it's considered effective.

The reasons for this expensive state of affairs in HRD training are complex, including time pressures, costs of evaluation research, and a short-run orientation. Moreover, notes Goldstein:

Top management does not emphasize training evaluation. Although top management is usually interested in evaluating all aspects of business practice, they don't tend to apply the same pressure on training management to evaluate their products. Some people feel that is because top management's fervor in emphasizing the importance of training and career development results in their accepting training on the basis of faith in its value.[38]

Obviously, a faith misplaced. Faith is for religion, not for doing business.

But the reasons go even deeper. For years, surveys have shown that there is a widespread absence of understanding in the general population about scientific methods of investigation—and it seems to be getting worse. Indeed, there is a large antiscience segment in the general population and in the HRD profession. Both in the general population and in the HRD profession, there are many who uncritically accept all manner of "New Age" hocus-pocus. At a recent international training conference that I attended stood an expensive, high-gloss customer booth advertising training in tarot card reading for more effective management. The tarot trainer was obviously making a decent living at it. (If the White House, under two different administrations, sets the tone for employing fortune-tellers, well . . .)

Aside from keeping the troops happy, as it were, considering smile sheet research as truly reflecting effectiveness is derived from our elevation of *personal experience* to an epistemological principle; knowledge gained through personal experience is the secular analog of received knowledge through divine revelation. We live in a society where the cult of personal experience reigns supreme. But let's not forget that every day our personal experience reveals to us that the sun goes around the earth—after all, we see with our own eyes the sun "rise" in the East and "set" in the West.

Now, I don't intend to argue whether personal experience, religion, astrology, or tarot card readings are real (though I certainly don't think they are). It's important, however, to point out one fact for those who do think they are real. That fact is: Even if they are real, they are notoriously unreliable forms of knowing. Without valid knowledge, training is not only ineffective; it can even be downright counterproductive.

COUNTERINTUITIVE AND NEGATIVE EFFECTS OF TRAINING

Being ineffective is one thing. Being counterproductive is quite another. Goldstein cites a counterproductive study that investigated the role-playing training outcome on the attitudes of police officers. He says:

As part of their academy training, both white and black police officers role-played sensitive racial situations. Attitude-change scores indicate that black officers became more positive in their views of whites. However, white officers, while becoming more sensitized to the presence of black-white problems, became more prejudiced toward blacks. The author's interpretation of these results indicates that white officers had the perception that the program was intended for the benefit of blacks rather than whites. Independent of the interpretation the results underscore the importance of examining the outcomes of our interventions rather than simply assuming that all is well.[39]

As Goldstein notes, many programs simply assume their success.

Similar counterproductive effects have been found in other areas of education and therapeutic interventions.[40] It's thus important that we know what we are doing before we do it. We shouldn't just do something because we think it's good to do. I recall an old cover of the magazine *Psychology Today* that depicted the statue of a Buddha. The caption read: Don't just do something, stand there.

Because on a basic level transfer of learning appears so simple and commonsensical, we may all too often do the opposite of what appears to be obvious. We saw this in the case above of training police to be sensitive to racial issues. What appears to be logical, or reasonable, or just plain commonsense, however, is all too often counterintuitive.[41] As a consequence, in the absence of valid knowledge of transfer of learning, negative transfer may—and often does—occur. Negative transfer of learning can occur when previous learning interferes with new learning either (1) because some part of the previous learning is different from the new learning, (2) because previous learning is superficially applied to a new situation, or (3) due to a lack of sufficient knowledge or depth of knowledge. Insufficient knowledge base, or expertise, however, is one of the most important factors in lack of transfer of learning and in negative transfer.

The identical elements model of transfer of learning, for example, predicts that the degree of positive transfer depends on the degree to which the training program is identical to the on-the-job task; that is, the more similar the training situation is to the real job situation, the more transfer of learning will occur. This model seems to make intuitive sense (there are also years of research that seem to back it up). Most industrial simulators, from simulated flight training to mock nuclear power plants, are constructed to be as identical as possible to the real operating situation. There is increasing research, however, indicating that simulators constructed on the basis of identical elements can lead to negative transfer as well.[42]

As technology develops, transfer of learning research on control and display equipment takes on increasing importance. The only antidote for counterintuitive predictions and negative transfer is knowledge of the transfer of learning research.

There is ample research to demonstrate the instructional consequences of an inadequate knowledge base on transfer of learning and the ensuing counterintuitive effects: For example, it's generally the case that immediate feedback during learning results in more efficient learning. It therefore seems to logically follow that immediate feedback during learning would result in more efficient transfer of learning. Recent findings, however, indicate that under certain conditions *delayed* feedback is more efficient. Other examples point out the difference between understanding typical learning principles, on the one hand, and principles of transfer of learning, on the other. Increasing the frequency of information about errors to learners during practice improves their performance. It seems reasonable, then, that transfer of learning would also be improved. The fact is that increasing the frequency about errors can work in just the opposite manner for long-term retention and for transfer.

Further counterintuitive effects come from research showing that increasing the variability of a task during practice depresses performance during training but may increase transfer of performance after training when conditions are altered from the original training situation.[43] Still other data show that performance on solving a puzzle is virtually perfect with no delay between instruction and application but rapidly declines as the delay is increased (e.g., where periods of delay are two weeks and one, two, three, and four months). In contrast, performance on a similar puzzle was worse than performance on the same puzzle at first but stayed relatively constant over a delay of four months. In other words, the transfer effect was much more persistent than the specific effects of learning a particular puzzle.[44]

These kinds of findings demonstrate the counterintuitive nature of instructing for transfer of learning. At least in terms of the examples given above, not only is counterintuitive instruction for transfer of learning largely due to insufficient knowledge about transfer, but, more important, transfer of learning is *different* from learning (see Chapter 3). In short, the widespread instructional beliefs about learning—that immediate feedback, increased feedback about errors, and decreasing variability during training lead to efficient performance—are counterintuitive with respect to transfer of learning. Contrary to many educational theorists, transfer of learning is not simply a special case of learning; if anything, learning is a special case of transfer of learning.

Something needs to be rectified in HRD training programs. In fact, HRD training methods need a radical reengineering. Clearly, much of the information about HRD training effectiveness belongs more to the category of folklore than to valid knowledge. Can your business continue to afford this?

POSTSCRIPT TO THE FAILURE OF HRD TRAINING

Why the widespread failure of training programs? We have only to look at the years of research on the effectiveness of sensitivity training, counseling, and psychotherapy. There is perhaps no more intensive learning situation than counseling and psychotherapy, yet the payoff findings (i.e., therapeutic change) have never been all that encouraging even under such intense and presumably motivated circumstances. The fact is, however, that most human beings don't change their minds (read: learn, acquire new attitudes, or adapt new behaviors) very easily. This includes transfer of learning, whether it's in university classrooms or in corporate training programs.

Now, lest I be accused of absurdly maintaining that no training programs are effective, let me now back up just a bit and say that assessing the effectiveness of training programs depends on what we meant by *effective*. Certainly, trainees don't come away from programs having learned nothing. The questions, then, are:

1. How much did they learn?
2. What kind and level of learning was it?
3. Was what they learned just due to sheer exposure to the material?
4. Did they learn what they learned in spite of the training?
5. Could they have acquired the learning in other less elaborate and less expensive

ways, like peer teaching or simply giving trainees the material and take-home questions?

It seems reasonably clear that, for whatever reasons, training participants do learn simple, concrete, technical, and procedural material (e.g., how to fill out and use forms). This in itself is, of course, not unimportant learning. Typically, however, this kind of learning is welded to the specific content and context of the situation. This hardly speaks of what I would consider transfer of learning. In the next chapter, I offer a general scheme for distinguishing simple learning from transfer of learning. But for now suffice it to say that "transferring" or applying learning from the classroom to the job is not transfer of learning; it's simply learning, simply applying what has been learned in one *physical* situation to another. Granted, this is important in itself. If we are just talking about specific concrete material being learned and applied to a specific job or specific context, however, then there's not a great problem. There is a great waste, however, as with each slightly different content, or application context, additional resources must be expended.

The problem for learners and training programs, then, is the self-transferring or applying learning to slightly different contexts, to situations that are similar to the original learning (near transfer of learning), and being able to extend and adapt that learning to quite different and new situations (far transfer of learning). Once we leave the training realm of the concrete, the technical, and the procedural and enter the realm of more complex and "fuzzy" material like team functioning, human relations, sales, organizational, and management training, transfer of learning ability becomes ever more crucial and problematic.

So, how do we fix this problem? The short answer is outlined in the next two chapters. The longer answer is what this book is about.

NOTES

1. M. L. Broad and J. Newstrom, *Transfer of Training: Action-Packed Strategies to Ensure High Payoff from Training Investments* (New York: Addison-Wesley, 1992).

2. R. E. Haskell, *The Future of Education and the Transfer of Learning: Cognition, Learning, and Instruction for the 21st Century* (forthcoming).

3. John H. Zenger, "Then: The Painful Turnabout in Training; Now: A Retrospective," *Training and Development* 50(1) (January 1996), p. 48.

4. Ibid., pp. 48–49.

5. Ibid., p. 49.

6. Ibid.

7. Ibid., p. 50.

8. Ibid., p. 48.

9. Ibid., p. 49.

10. I. L. Goldstein, *Training in Organizations: Needs Assessments, Development, and Evaluation* (Pacific Grove, CA: Brooks/Cole Publishing Company, 1993), pp. 279–280.

11. Cited in S. R. Faerman and C. Ban, "Trainee Satisfaction and Training Impact: Issues in Training Evaluation," *Public Productivity & Management Review* 16 (1993), p. 299.

12. M. L. Broad, "Management Actions to Support Transfer of Training," *Training and Development Journal* 36(5) (1982), p. 124.

13. R. D. Bretz and R. E. Thompsett, "Comparing Traditional and Integrative Learning Methods in Organizational Training Programs," *Journal of Applied Psychology* 77(6) (1992), p. 941.

14. R. D. Smither, *The Psychology of Work and Human Performance* (New York: Harper and Row, 1988), p. 277.

15. F. C. Pratzner, *Occupational Adaptability and Transferable Skills* (Information Series No. 129) (Columbus, OH: National Center for Research in Vocational Education, 1978), p. 1.

16. See, for example, J. Fotheringhame, "Transfer of Training: A Field Investigation of Youth Training," *Journal of Occupational Psychology* 57 (1984), pp. 239–248; J. Fotheringhame, "Transfer of Training: A Field Study of Some Training Methods," *Journal of Occupational Psychology* 59 (1986), pp. 59–71.

17. Carole Myers, "Research Core Skills and Transfer in the Youth Training Schemes: A Field Study of Trainee Motor Mechanics," *Journal of Organizational Behavior* 13 (1992), p. 625.

18. Ibid.

19. Ibid., p. 632.

20. Pratzner, *Occupational Adaptability and Transferable Skills*, p. 1.

21. J. Phillips, "Was It the Training?" *Training and Development* (March 1996), p. 28.

22. Jerald Greenberg and Robert A. Baron, *Behavior in Organizations*, 5th ed. (Englewood Cliffs, NJ: Prentice-Hall, 1995), p. 311.

23. Ibid., p. 314.

24. Bretz and Thompsett, "Comparing Traditional and Integrative Learning Methods in Organizational Training Programs."

25. Goldstein, *Training in Organizations*, p. 242.

26. Ibid., p. 280.

27. Ibid., p. 279.

28. S. I. Tannenbaum and G. Yukl, "Training and Development in Work Organizations," in *Annual Review of Psychology* (Palo Alto, CA: Annual Reviews, 1992).

29. Goldstein, *Training in Organizations*, p. 287.

30. Ibid., p. 251.

31. Ibid.

32. Ibid.

33. Ibid., p. 296.

34. Bretz and Thompsett, "Comparing Traditional and Integrative Learning Methods in Organizational Training Programs."

35. Smither, *The Psychology of Work and Human Performance*, p. 277.

36. Faerman and Ban, "Trainee Satisfaction and Training Impact: Issues in Training Evaluation," p. 301.

37. See, for example, E. Mayo, *The Human Problems of an Industrial Civilization* (London: Macmillan, 1933).

38. Goldstein, *Training in Organizations*, p. 148.

39. Ibid., p. 284.

40. D. Hartley, H. B. Roback, and S. I. Abramowitz, "Deterioration Effects in Encounter Groups," *American Psychologist* 31 (1976), pp. 247–255.

41. Jay Forrester, "Counterintuitive Behavior of Social Systems," *Technology Review* (January 1971), pp. 52–68. It was Forrester, I believe, who first pointed out the counterintuitive nature of human behavior.

42. See, for example, E. Baudhuin, "The Design of Industrial and Flight Simulations," in S. M. Cormier and J. D. Hagman (eds.), *Transfer of Learning: Contemporary Research and Application* (New York: Academic Press, 1987), pp. 217–237.

43. R. A. Schmidt and R. A. Bjork, "New Conceptualizations of Practice: Common Principles in Three Paradigms Suggest New Concepts for Training," *Psychological Science* 3 (1992), pp. 207–217.

44. M. K. Singley and J. R. Anderson, *The Transfer of Cognitive Skill* (Cambridge, MA: Harvard University Press, 1989), p. 199.

2

What Transfer of Learning Is and Why It Both Does and Doesn't Occur

As our memory and information-processing powers are limited, it seems natural that the mind should tend to minimize the amount of information stored and maximize the use of that which is already stored.

R. S. Michalski[1]

What does a ballistic missile defense system have to do with correcting the shape of the cornea of our eye? And what does a toy have to do with solving a NASA (National Aeronautics and Space Administration) space station docking problem? Or what do insects have to do with designing heavy earthmoving equipment? Or what kind of learning and thinking made it possible to invent barbed wire or Velcro? The short answer is the transfer of learning; the longer answer, again, is what this book is all about (see Chapter 5). Finding the answers to each of these questions was important economically to business and industry.

WHAT TRANSFER OF LEARNING IS

Transfer of learning involves the problem of how previous learning influences current and future learning and how past or current learning is applied or adapted to similar or new situations so we don't have to constantly learn anew each situation we encounter. Transfer of learning is therefore fundamental to all training and learning. Contrary to some HRD definitions of transfer of training, transfer of learning is not just the simple application of what was learned in a training classroom to the workplace, although it can be seen as that as well. Without transferability we could not engage in our everyday thinking and reasoning processes nor acquire the most basic of motor skills; it's responsible for the simplest of ideas and for the highest achievements of humankind.

Transfer of learning is paradoxical. In one sense, we are all expert in transfer of learning. Yet in another and more important sense, we are all woefully lacking in higher-order transfer of learning skills. The more skilled we are in transfer of learning, the more creative and efficient we are in how we think and how we perform. With corporate and organizational training costs being what they are, this is a matter of cardinal importance. So, more specifically, what is transfer of learning?

It's a deceptively simple concept. For example, when we say: "It's like . . ."; "It's equivalent to . . . for example . . ."; "It's akin to . . . for instance . . ."; "It's the same as . . ."; "By the same token . . ."; "Similarly . . ."; "In the same way . . ."; "It reminds me of . . ."; "It resembles . . ."; "It's comparable to . . ."; or, "It's analogous to . . ." we are engaging in the transfer of learning. Transfer of learning includes our use of analogies, metaphors, mental models, and generic learning. The history of science, invention, technology transfer, and everyday life is replete with people who are good at transfer of learning. Even when I use the word *example* I am engaging in transfer of learning. When I say "For example," I have already decided that the characteristics of the example I am giving are in fact members of the category that I am talking about. So when we say "For example," we have engaged in a form of thinking and reasoning based on transfer of learning. Transfer of learning is thus not so much an instructional technique as it is a way of thinking, perceiving, and processing information.

The Gutenberg printing press, invented by Johanne Gutenberg, was apparently invented by the transfer of two "technologies" that had existed for many years. The idea for individual block letters was transferred from engraved wooden blocks that were used to make an imprint in wax to put an embossed seal on a document. The invention of the printing press itself involved transfer thinking from the wine press. The wine press had a handle that when pulled would lower a mechanism that would squeeze or "press" the juice from grapes. This was adapted to press a piece of paper onto the inked block letters. Put the embossed blocks and the wine press together, and you have a printing press.

Another famous example is the cotton gin ostensibly invented, by many popular accounts, nearly whole cloth—if I may be permitted a (verbal transfer) pun. In fact, the cotton gin was already in wide use at the time Elie Whitney supposedly invented it. The cotton gin had *similar* precursors going back at least to the East Indian gin, or *charka*, with the *charka* itself being modeled on the older sugar cane press. Further, the wire "teeth" in Whitney's gin were fashioned after similar wire teeth used in wool carding "gins."

We typically develop and see new things in terms of past experience, as being *like* something we are already familiar with. When cars were invented, they were initially seen as horseless carriages. Similarly, we now have electronic "mail" sent via our computer terminals. Small laptop computers are called electronic "notepads" in analogy with paper notepads. The development of a technology capable of analyzing the complex structure of our DNA (deoxyribonucleic acid) has found its way into the courtroom. Each person's DNA code is unique to that individual, *like* fingerprints: Thus, we call it DNA fingerprinting—even though the similarity is not all that exact.

A fundamental innovation in management systems was developed by Alfred Sloan, the automobile pioneer, by using transfer of learning. Before we can understand what Sloan did, however, we must understand where he transferred his idea from. Adam Smith, the philosopher and economist, in 1776 published his now-famous *The Wealth of Nations*.[2] In his book, Smith described a new kind of workplace organization. Instead of each artisan making a single item, he said, it would be less expensive if the separate tasks required to make an item were each carried out by a different worker. In short, he described a "division of labor." This division of labor principle soon became commonplace in industrial production systems, as the legacy of Henry Ford attests.

At the risk of oversimplification, what Sloan did was to transfer the ideas of Adam Smith's division of labor to management practices, creating smaller, decentralized managerial units, each with a specialized bureaucratic function. The "new" system evidently saved General Motors from going out of business. While this hierarchical division of labor is currently being changed radically, virtually all management systems are based on Sloan's transfer of Adam Smith's factory model that we now take so much for granted. Does this transfer of learning seem obvious?

One of the deceiving aspects of transfer of learning is that once the transfer is made, the connection may seem obvious. But of course, seeing it as obvious is only possible with the proverbial 20/20 nature of hindsight. If the transfer connection that Sloan made was so obvious, the question, of course, is why was it not seen before and why not by many people? Stanford Ovshinsky, the inventor, observed that many discoveries often seem obvious after they've been invented. That transfer thinking may seem obvious is only after the fact, however—not before. To illustrate the nonobviousness of transfer thinking, consider the following before I define transfer of learning further.

When NASA was designing a satellite that would be tethered to a space station by a thin wire about 60 miles long, it soon realized that the motion caused by reeling in the satellite would create a pendulumlike movement with an increasingly widening arc, resulting in the uncontrollable erratic behavior of the satellite at the end of the 60-mile-long tether. This was a serious problem that had implications of not only science but economics for NASA. The solution is quite simple—deceptively simple—and involves transfer from a child's toy. The solutions will be explained below.

The word *transfer* is derived from the terms *trans*, meaning "across" or "over," and *ferre*, meaning "to bear," thus, "to carry over." In both a trivial and a profound sense, as no situation is ever exactly the same, all learning is transfer of learning. In short, virtually all learning involves our carrying over previous learning to new situations. Failing to carry over previous learning all too frequently leads to rigid patterns of behavior and thinking leading to expensive instructional and personal costs. In psychology, we use the term *functional fixedness* to describe such rigid patterns. For example, say you are in a hotel room and you need to tighten a screw on your computer case, but you don't have a screwdriver. Many people would not think of using (or "seeing") a dime or a fingernail file as a screwdriver.

We constantly transfer previous learning and experience to learn a new skill more quickly and efficiently. A person who plays the piano will learn to play an accordion more quickly and efficiently than a person who has no experience with the piano. Similarly, experience with ice skating should decrease the learning time of a person learning roller skating; or experience with one computer program should facilitate the transfer to a similar program. If everything was different from everything else—which in fact it is to one degree or another—we would be unable to function; we would experience a constant flux. Transfer of learning reduces the world to manageable proportions; it makes the world familiar. Transfer of learning, the seeing of similarities, creates categories and concepts for us. It is responsible for creating what Peter Senge and others call *generic* or general structures of thinking.

Thus, the concept of transfer of learning, while simple, is crucial to all learning from the lowest level of skill to the highest reaches of theoretical thinking. But from the most primitive of life forms to the best and the brightest of humankind, transfer ability varies. The variation is, in part, founded on biological evolution. For example, if a rat is taught to respond to the image of a triangle drawn with solid lines, T_1, if shown a triangle drawn with lines made up of a series of dots, T_2, it is unable to recognize T_1 as the *same* object as T_2. Similarly, a rat trained to respond to a white triangle with a black background will not respond to a black triangle with a white background (see Figure 2.1).

A chimpanzee and a small child, however, will respond to both triangles as the same object; they will transfer their experience. On a different level, when we recognize a familiar melody even though it's played in a new key, or in a different octave, we are engaging in transfer because the new melody is in fact not the *exact same* set of notes that we are familiar with. The capability to perceive "different" melodies, or the transposition of different

Figure 2.1
Equivalence Transformations Are Related to Phylogenetic Level

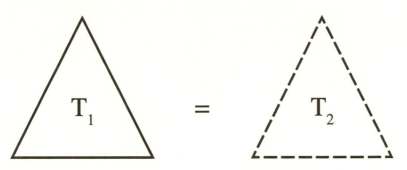

octaves into the same musical experience, appears to be built into single brain cells and hardwired into our neurological pathways.[3] This is important because it means that any discussion about learning must involve a discussion of transfer of learning. One early researcher has noted, "It has long been apparent to . . . myself and to others that transfer is the more general phenomenon and learning a particular case."[4] Since nothing ever repeats itself exactly the same way or in exactly the same context, the essential problem in transfer of learning is: When and how is something perceived as being the *same as* or *equivalent to* something else? This is not a simple problem.

Novices and children—lacking sufficient knowledge—often transfer inappropriately, as when a whale is called a fish, or when a penguin *is not* seen as a bird, or when a bat *is* seen as a bird. In terms of language usage, children's transfer of learning may be logically "appropriate" but actually incorrect: From the point of view of the conjugation of *big, bigger, biggest,* children often transfer their learning and say *good, gooder, goodest.* Although not complex, transfer of learning is not a simple matter.

On another level, language is often troublesome in terms of transfer of learning with clear implications for globalization and multiculturalism. At an international training and development conference near Los Angeles, California, I was sharing a luncheon table with a Latin American woman. I was explaining what transfer of learning was all about when she quickly transferred my explanation to her own consulting business. She had been recently asked by a well-known international consulting firm to retranslate their training material into Spanish. The problem was that the first translation merely translated the material literally. The example she used was the current pithy phrase often used in training literature, "walk the talk," meaning that trainers and managers should demonstrate their instructions by engaging in them themselves. It seems that this phrase cannot be transferred literally or translated into Spanish. If literally translated, it ends up being gibberish. Moreover, she said, "walk the talk" will not transfer into any equivalent pithy phrase. Some things cannot be transferred.

A more serious implication of transfer of learning for an increasingly global, diverse, and multicultural business environment is ethnic and gender prejudice. Its transfer of learning (or training) can result in over-generalization. This "negative transfer" or overgeneralization is the down-side of transfer. When we meet a few members of a minority group who act in a certain way, there is often the tendency to generalize or transfer this learning to other members of the group whom we have not met. This is what prejudice is. As instructional practitioners have pointed out, "A very subtle carry-over from one situation to another is seen in the transfer of attitudes. Prejudices and biases about one ethnic group are likely to transfer (or generalize) to other groups with like characteristics, and other groups that are perceived to have similar characteristics."[5] Such negative transfer of learning may affect both learning and performance. Unfortu-nately, overgeneralization, like generalization itself, is an inherent part of the human (and nonhuman) mental apparatus; the problem is how to man-age it.

Part of the problem of understanding transfer is that it is known by many names. Think of the basic structure of transfer, however, as being like 2 + 2 = 4—that just like we can plug in apples, plums, and pencils, we can also plug in different examples or instances of transfer: abstraction, ana-logical relations, archetypal thinking, classification, generalization, generic thinking, induction, invariance, isomorphic relations, logical inference, and metaphor. If you understand one of these concepts, by transfer thinking, you can generally understand the others. Transfer is thus so fundamental that to explain it is to repeat the *same* thing over and over, using different terms from different fields, in different contexts, on different levels of ab-straction, and in different orders of magnitude. To say that I am repeating the same thing, however, isn't to say that I'm *simply* repeating the *exact* same thing. In mathematics, such repetition is called the *differentiation of an invariant* through its various mathematical forms; it's like counting from 10 to 100, then counting from 100 to 1,000; that is, 1 is to 10 as 10 is to 100 as 100 is to 1,000. In other areas, transfer may be known as variation on a theme. Or it can be seen as different archetypes or proverbs all ex-pressing the *same* meaning.

The research on teaching for transfer clearly shows that for transfer to occur, the original learning must be repeatedly reinforced with multiple examples or similar concepts in multiple contexts. And I would add, on different levels and orders of magnitude. Teaching for transfer, then, in-volves returning again and again to an idea or procedure but on different levels and in different contexts, with apparently different examples. The great psychologist Jean Piaget referred to this method as epigenetic, as a kind of spiral (or matrix series, as I will outline in Chapter 10) where each new turn is a higher-order manifestation of the order below it, just as 2 is to 4 and 4 is to 8. The bare-bones essence of transfer, however, is simple: It's *equivalence*, and it can be summarized by the = sign.

Most of the accessing of our everyday knowledge base cannot occur consciously, if for no other reason than the large size of our knowledge base. The capacity of conscious memory, like your computer's working memory (random-access memory [RAM]), in comparison to nonconscious (computer hard-drive storage) memory is small. Most transfer processes occur nonconsciously, intuitively, automatically (I will discuss nonconscious transfer in more detail in Chapter 11). Most of what we learn in experiential learning and in learning of motor skills occurs by way of nonconscious comparisons or transfer between the new activity and what has been stored in long-term memory.

A GENERAL SCHEME FOR UNDERSTANDING THE LEVELS OF TRANSFER

As I indicated earlier, one of the problems in the transfer literature is the many names for transfer. Another problem is that there exists no adequate definition, classification scheme, or taxonomy for systematically understanding transfer. Having no taxonomy and many names for what is essentially a single phenomenon creates confusion and impedes transfer. Among other things, it creates confusion when assessing whether transfer has occurred. To combat this confusion, I have developed the following rough scheme to understand the multiple levels and kinds of transfer. The scheme is a qualitative one, however, for there doesn't exist a "metric of similarity" by which we can quantitatively distinguish precise degrees of how similar one thing is to another. To recognize that X *is like* Y is one thing; to determine how alike it is, is quite another.

Level 1—nonspecific transfer. Since all learning depends on some connection to past learning, all learning in this sense is transfer. This general level of transfer is typically referred to as nonspecific transfer. Level 1, then, is what is simply called learning but is nevertheless often referred to as transfer.

Level 2—application transfer. Application transfer refers to applying what one has learned to a specific situation—for example, when having learned a word processing system, being able to apply the learning to actually operating the word processor. This level, too, reflects what we typically call simple learning, but like Level 1, it is nevertheless often referred to as transfer.

Level 3—contextual transfer. Contextual transfer refers to applying what one has learned to a slightly different situation. Often, a change in context, although the learned task is exactly the same, may result in lack of transfer. Again, this level is what we usually call simple learning.

Level 4—near transfer. Near transfer refers to recognizing and applying what was learned originally to situations that are similar but that are slightly different from the original learning task and situation. For example, after having learned a specific word processing system, being able to apply the learning to another similar word processor. This level can be seen as an extension of Level 3 and is a low level of transfer.

Level 5—far transfer. Far transfer refers to applying learning to situations that are quite dissimilar, either in substance or contextually, to the original learning. What we ordinarily call metaphorical and analogical reasoning is evident in this kind of transfer.

Level 6—displacement or creative transfer. Displacement transfer refers to transferring past learning in a way that leads to more than the insight that "this is like that." When one discovers a heretofore unrealized similarity and interaction between the old and the new, a new concept is created. This level is often involved in problem solving and other creative endeavors.

In the transfer literature, studies often refer to Level 1 as transfer, Level 2 as near transfer, and Level 3 and above as far transfer. I consider Levels 1 and 2 as essentially simple learning, not transfer at all; Level 3 as the application of learning; Level 4 as near transfer; and Levels 5 and 6 as far transfer. Finally, I would like to note that what I consider to be significant transfer—as opposed to just plain learning and the application of that learning to the same or very similar situations—is transfer that requires the learning of something new in the transfer. Levels 4, 5, and 6 typically require such new learning. Without the requirement of new learning, the transfer is not transfer but simply applying the same learning. The requirement of new learning may apply to Levels 2 and 3 if the learner's application is the consequence of newly recognizing the application.

The striking thing to point out from this transfer scheme is that most instructional research that shows our failure to achieve transfer of learning in fact refers to the very basic Levels 1, 2, and sometimes 3. Conversely, the research showing success at transfer also refers largely to Levels 1, 2, and Level 3. This casts an even more dismal shadow on the problem of transfer. In effect, from the perspective of this transfer scheme, what the majority of studies show—with the possible exception of Level 3—isn't a failure of training participants to achieve transfer but something worse: a failure of learning itself.

In addition, it is useful to understand the different kinds of transfer in order to begin to develop a rudimentary taxonomy or a classification of the different kinds of transfer, like near transfer and far transfer. See Appendix A for a brief initial scheme.

Finally, the six levels of transfer relate directly to levels of instruction in transfer. Not to design transfer programs to be congruent with the level of transfer performance can lead to very unhappy employees. Early in my workshop presentations on transfer, I made the mistake of letting myself be talked into designing a workshop for a Blue Cross and Blue Shield organization on the general nature of transfer and relating it to the idea of the learning organization for a very mixed set of participants. Only three or four of the participants were familiar with the idea of a learning organization; others were trainers who were basically interested in Level 1 and 2 transfer problems. Then there were participants whose job was to teach new employees how to make out forms. It soon became clear to me that if I spoke to either half of the group, I was going to lose the other half. At least half of these people went away from the workshop very unhappy, not understanding how it would help them in their jobs.

THE BASIC PROBLEM OF TRANSFER: HOW TO RECOGNIZE IT

While this entire book is an answer to the question of why transfer doesn't occur, the following will be an introduction to the essential problem of transfer. Accessing transfer involves recognizing that two events are the *same* in important respects or that one thing can be used as a model for another thing. Two people can look at the same object or an array of information but not see the same thing. Many engineers looked at a yo-yo and did not solve the NASA space station docking problem mentioned earlier; many looked at the ballistic missile system and did not see its application to eye surgery. Why? (See Chapter 6).

The answer is not just that other engineers may not have had the knowledge. The answer lies in one word: *access*. Even when a person has the knowledge, he or she often can't access it properly. As I suggested at the opening of this chapter, most engineers had the knowledge to solve the NASA space docking problem but didn't transfer what they knew about the behavior of a yo-yo to the space docking problem.

Stanford scientist Thomas Kane solved the NASA space docking problem by accessing and using the analogy of a yo-yo as a mental transfer model. Anyone who has played with a yo-yo knows that it climbs back up the string into one's hand. But you can't just have a space station tumbling over and over up the tether. So the ingenious—but simple—solution was to get the satellite to climb back up the tether to the space station. This is how he solved the problem: Kane reasoned that a small electric motor on the satellite would allow the satellite to crawl back up the tether to the space station just like a giant yo-yo.

How and why this scientist happened to think of or access the dynamics of a yo-yo only Kane's mind knows. But his thinking process obviously involved transfer thinking. If we knew exactly how the scientist accessed the transfer, then there would be no reason for this book. How a similarity is accessed is the product of the eleven transfer principles that I outline in Chapter 3. Was the yo-yo solution the only solution? Probably not. There are undoubtedly many solutions "out there" somewhere, waiting for someone to discover (or invent) them. Someone good at transfer of learning.

Ever since psychologist Edward Thorndike's influential research in 1901, nearly all explanations of transfer of learning are based on the similarity between an original situation and a new situation. Thorndike maintained that transfer only occurs if two situations are related by identical elements of some kind. This has become known as the "identical elements" theory of transfer. There is little doubt that similarity plays a large role in most transfer. But it's not the whole story. Typically, "identical elements between two situations" has meant surface similarity (although it need not). Surface similarity is an identity between two situations that has no causal role to play between them. Surface similarity is more like a literary metaphor. That a spark is like lightning is not simply based on a surface similarity because there is an underlying causal or theoretical similarity between the two. It's this deep, underlying similarity that constitutes significant transfer.

Surface similarity typically results in a simple analogy. It is based on simple perception, not on deep theoretical, relational, or structural understanding. The example I used earlier of calling a whale a fish derives from a surface and perceptual similarity. Seeing a whale as a fish is an example of *literal transfer*. At best, surface similarity most always leads to only near transfer. Most training programs are based either explicitly or implicitly on surface similarity.

This is not to say that surface similarity should always be avoided. Again, the research shows that for most people surface similarity is the main avenue of access into transfer. We often don't see the surface similarities existing among events, even though they may appear obvious after they are pointed out. Surface similarity, or simple recognition of identical elements, however, tends not to lead to the important kinds of transfer. In short, it does not result in the kinds of transfer in science, technology, and invention that I describe in Chapter 6. This is why traditional *training* programs founded on identical elements theory fail in anything but the simplest of transfer. Training is typically based on surface and perceptual similarity, not on *conceptual* similarity.

Cookbook manuals are doomed to failure because instructions that say "Look over here" and "Look over there" or "Compare Y and Z" assume the trainee has and will be able to access the appropriate mental schema to "see" the similarity in the first place and thus to transfer the similarity to the second place. A schema is a mental structure by which our knowledge is organized and processed. This is the very heart of the transfer problem. Similarity-based and cookbook (or recipe) approaches to transfer in fact implicitly assume that the trainee has the requisite knowledge for accessing and recognizing specific equivalencies. It's like trying to teach children to read when they do not have the requisite knowledge of the alphabet.

Most all accounts and models of transfer in the research literature do not address the basic problem of how we access transfer, of how we recognize a transfer situation. M. K. Singley and J. R. Anderson in their seminal book *The Transfer of Cognitive Skill* note, "Conspicuous by its absence in this discussion is any mention of the . . . mechanisms of generalization and discrimination which create new productions by inductive, syntactic transformations. . . . [The] . . . processes of generalization and discrimination do not figure in our analysis of skill acquisition. . . . [W]e have nothing new to say about this type of transfer in this book."[6] This is largely because we simply do not know how or why one person sees a similarity relation between two things and the other doesn't. While I do not have a complete solution to the transfer problem, I believe that the essential ingredient is the acquisition of a large knowledge base (see Chapter 8).

Accordingly, cookbook approaches or lists of "how-to's" are doomed to failure in leading to significant higher-order transfer. Having disparaged cookbook approaches, let me now say that they can be aids to transfer. But only that. Cookbooks can assist in the initial recognition and access to similarities, archetypes, or generic structures but only if the requisite knowledge base is available. While surface similarity may provide the initial access point into far transfer processes, to recognize deeper relationships requires a rich conceptual and theoretical knowledge base and mental set for generic structures. Training in specific knowledge and identical elements is no longer appropriate in many workplace circumstances. Not only is specific information changing rapidly, but our recognition of what is similar in any situation is constantly changing, based on different information and contexts. In other words—and this is extremely important—similarity is not so much "out there" to see as it is in the mind of the person doing the transfer.

CONCLUSION

The basic transfer of learning question continues to be: What is it that enables a person with specific knowledge, learning, understanding, or skill learned in one area and/or social context to adapt, modify, or extend it in such a way to be able to apply and extend it to other areas? This is the central and long-standing issue this book will continue to address.

NOTES

1. R. S. Michalski, "Two-Tiered Concept Meaning, Inferential Matching, and Conceptual Cohesiveness," in S. Vosniadou and A. Anthony (eds.), *Similarity and Analogical Reasoning* (New York: Cambridge University Press, 1989), p. 125.

2. See Michael Hammer and James Champy, *Reengineering the Corporation* (New York: HarperCollins, 1993).

3. See, for example, R. E. Haskell, "Analogical Transforms: A Cognitive Theory of the Origin and Development of Transformation of Invariance, Part I, II," *Metaphor and Symbolic Activity* 4 (1989), pp. 247–277. See also F. A. Hayek, *The Sensory Order: An Inquiry into the Foundations of Theoretical Psychology* (Chicago: University of Chicago Press, 1952); and L. E. Marks and M. H. Bornstein, "Sensory Similarities: Classes, Characteristics and Cognitive Consequences," in R. E. Haskell (ed.), *Cognitive and Symbolic Structures: The Psychology of Metaphoric Transformation* (Norwood, NJ: Ablex, 1987), pp. 49–65.

4. G. A. Ferguson, "On Transfer and the Abilities of Man," in R. G. Grose and R. C. Birney (eds.), *Transfer of Learning: An Enduring Problem in Psychology* (New York: D. Van Nostrand, 1963), p. 185.

5. F. J. Di Vesta and G. G. Thompson, *Educational Psychology: Instruction and Behavioral Change* (New York: Appleton-Century-Crofts, 1970), p. 257.

6. M. K. Singley and J. R. Anderson, *The Transfer of Cognitive Skill* (Cambridge, MA: Harvard University Press, 1989), pp. 50, 34.

3

The Importance of Corporate Transfer of Learning and How to Fix the Lack of Transfer in HRD Training Programs

The five disciplines now converging appear to comprise a critical mass. . . . [P]erhaps . . . developments emerging in seemingly unlikely places will lead to a wholly new discipline that we cannot even grasp today.
Peter Senge, *The Fifth Discipline*[1]

The demands of our modern civilization make transfer increasingly important. In slow-changing traditional societies, there is much less need for transfer of learning. In our highly complex, ever-changing society, the ability to transfer or generalize from the familiar to the less familiar not only renders our world predictable and understandable but is a necessity for our personal, social, and economic adaptation.

An adaptable worker, says an early report on occupational adaptability and transfer skills, is "one who can generalize, transfer, or form associations so that the skills, attitudes, knowledge, and personal characteristics that have been learned or developed in one context can be readily used in a different context."[2] To the extent that individuals can perceive similarities among jobs and are able to effectively transfer their knowledge and skills is the extent to which the time and costs in training or retraining are drastically reduced, reflecting cost savings to employers. What is more intriguing, and in many ways more central to training, notes one author, "is the identification of what is involved in transferring skills or what it is that enables someone with some knowledge, learning, understanding, or skill gained in one cognitive domain and/or social context to adapt, modify, or extend it in such a way as to be able to apply it in another. It is this area that should receive our full attention."[3] The same is true for organizations that are required to learn constantly in response to technological, social, and global changes.

Those individuals and organizations who develop transfer abilities will be the ones who will be able to best adapt, compete, and survive. For corporations that survive, as consultant and author Peter Block has noted, "[l]earning and performance will become one and the same thing."⁴ Another HRD author notes that the corporate approach to transfer speaks of

aligning training with business needs, designing programs that are job-related, modifying the culture to support new skills, preparing participants' managers to reinforce new behavior, and designing follow-up programs and measures. Such practices are crucial for training to have impact, *but somewhere along the way they leave out a key player: the employee being trained.*⁵

This book is about the mental makeup of those key players.

Peter Senge outlines five disciplines involved in learning organizations: (1) the *personal mastery* of our inner goals and visions, (2) understanding the *mental models* we have in our heads, (3) developing *shared visions* with others, (4) *team learning*, and (5) *systems thinking*.⁶ Systems thinking is learning to recognize relationships and interconnections among phenomena. All five disciplines must work as an ensemble and in an integrative way. This is what makes systems thinking the primary discipline and therefore, as Senge terms it, the fifth discipline. There is a missing piece in the learning organization literature, however: transfer. If systems thinking undergirds the other four disciplines and is therefore the fifth discipline, it is transfer that undergirds all five of these disciplines and is therefore the sixth discipline necessary for working with learning organizations. It is also necessary for developing the individual employee (see Chapters 5 and 7).

Transfer thinking is mental invention and innovation. Transfer of learning is fundamental to technology transfer, where a piece of technology developed for one area is transferred to an area unrelated to the original design. What can a servomechanism control device for regulating the sequential flow of actions of complex industrial machinery be transferred to? The answer is that it has been transferred to an inventory management system in business as well as to other human control, decision-making, and planning functions.⁷ This was accomplished by modeling and mapping (i.e., comparing, transferring) engineering design schematics originally developed for mechanical control of data and flow charts that track the sequential movement of inventory. This kind of technology transfer increases efficiency and therefore productivity.

The importance of transfer for corporate training cannot be overemphasized. One trainer, writing in the HRD journal *Training and Development*, says, "The problem of transfer is a critical concern. This is especially true in a tight economy where payback on investment in em-ployee development is essential."[8] Because all job skills are transferable, transfer in training is of singular and foundational importance. A worker who has learned to transfer is an adaptable worker. An adaptable worker is one who can generalize and form associations so that the skills, attitudes, knowledge, and personal characteristics they have learned in one context can be used easily in a different context.

Understanding transfer is important for personnel changes or promotions to other positions. Adaptation and transition to job changes can be facili-tated by mapping the similarities and differences in the move to a new job. Understanding the similarities can result in positive transfer. Conversely, not understanding the differences can result in negative transfer, interfering with learning the new job. There are other examples of the counterintuitive nature of transfer models. For example, most industrial models of instruc-tion and transfer are based on Edward Thorndike's 1901 simple identical elements theory of transfer.

Studies on transfer in technical domains are being conducted with work-ers in naturalistic settings. A study of U.S. Air Force aviation maintenance jobs where three jobs were being merged into one, requiring adaptiveness by technicians across complex test equipment, found that the less proficient technicians simply tried to adapt by using the very specific knowledge of their experience. The more proficient technicians generalized or transferred their specific knowledge by constructing generalized mental models and mapping them to the new test equipment.

Yet another example of the financial benefit of transferring technology is illustrated in a recent article in *Fortune* magazine describing a division of a large company whose expertise is drilling minute holes in ultrathin plastic rings for fiber-optic connectors. While the drillers are considered the best in the world, allowing the company to make connectors for half the cost of its competitors, the market for fiber-optic connectors was limited. The company wanted to grow. What was it to do?

The company brought in a consultant with expertise in mapping com-pany assets. Mapping is a process that is part of analogical reasoning—systematically comparing two things. In this case, it was comparing mi-crodrilling skills in the fiber-optic industry to possible microdrilling needs in other industries. In mapping the company's skills, the consultant saw that its microdrilling expertise in fiber-optic connectors could be transferred to drilling connectors for fine copper-wiring systems.[9] This transfer required a person who had the knowledge base and the transfer ability to be able to make this mental connection.

Although, psychologically, I would consider this transfer to be only a minor case of near transfer, its benefits were nevertheless of major financial proportions to the company. Transfer of learning is leveraged learning.

A fundamental training task confronting corporations today is the need to continuously acquire and improve skills in the use of computers. Transfer is central to this need. As one computer programmer put it:

Transfer of learning is a problem vexing both users and manufacturers of computer software. Users discover that the skills and expectations that they have developed in the use of one application turn out to be inapplicable or substantially dissimilar to those appropriate to a second application on the same system. Manufacturers find that families of applications, intended to provide a common interface across different environments, nonetheless result in significant difficulties as users move from one instantiation of the system to the next. Both kinds of transfer effects result in user frustration and employer retraining costs.[10]

For example, individuals *trained* in the use of a particular word processing program may know what keys to press to achieve desired results, but if either a revised or a somewhat different program is given to them, they may be lost. They don't see the similarities between the programs or understand that there is often a general structure shared by a given class of programs that if they understood, they could use to learn the new program more efficiently.

Thus, the transfer challenge facing all corporate computer instruction is not merely to teach the keystrokes (training) necessary to perform program tasks but to develop mental models of the underlying structure (learning) of the different user interfaces. Complicating this issue is the problem of having to deal with multiple hardware architectures, operating systems, and user interfaces. But with the trend of moving toward common user interfaces based on graphics such as Microsoft Windows, transfer is accelerated. Just as many countries have been changing language-based road signs to include icons (e.g., signs with the word *Food* are paired with a picture of a dinner plate, connoting a restaurant) to make the information understood by a wider audience, computer software designers have likewise found that pictures or icons can do the same for learning programs. As experience increases, users realize that the underlying structure among apparently different applications is similar. The primary differences reside in terminology (semantics) and keystrokes, while the end result is identical.

One application that is included with the basic Windows program is Notepad, a small miniprogram designed to function like the hard-copy paper notepad. The menu structure in Notepad is simple, with headings for File, Edit, Search, and Help. Once familiar with Notepad, a user can begin using a more complex word processing program such as WordPerfect for Windows and be capable of at least transferring the fundamental tasks of typing and editing text, opening and saving files, printing, and cutting and pasting text from one section to another because WordPerfect also contains File, Edit, and Help menus virtually identical to those in Notepad. Properly instructed, a user should be capable of transferring to an entirely new word processor, spreadsheet, or database program with relative ease.

A final example of transfer is the ability to expand the skill of searching a simple index on a computer to that of scanning and exploring worldwide indexes on the Internet. This example of transfer can be traced back to one's previous ability to use the index in a book. Negative transfer may also occur, however, in the transition from one operating system or program to another, particularly when different terminology and procedures are emphasized.[11]

The development of the Sony Data Discman is another example of transfer. The Discman is an "electronic book" player with 200 megabytes of read-only memory (ROM). The user can search and retrieve visual information as text, graphics, and sound. In its development, one employee saw the Data discman as being *akin* to a portable computer but harnessing the storage capacity of the CD-ROM (compact disc read-only memory) he was working on. A second employee was searching for an application for Sony's CD player, which did not seem to have a good market. Together they combined their ideas and developed a new and—apparently—successful product by transferring components of already existing technologies into a new concept.[12]

Advertising agencies are populated with people who are good at transfer. Take, for example, the television Sprint ad where a pin is shown in slow motion, turning and floating in an empty space. While it's never mentioned explicitly, it appears that the pin represents the monolith from the movie *2001*. A simple and elegant instance of transfer thinking.

TRANSFER OF TRAINING VERSUS TRANSFER OF LEARNING

A central problem in reengineering corporate training involves an important distinction. That distinction is between training and learning. It is learning in the workplace that is of crucial significance to transfer performance, not training. And it's this distinction that distinguishes the industrial age organization from the information age organization. Instruction for the transfer of training is not the same as instruction for the transfer of learning. This difference is coming to be recognized in the HRD field. An article in *Fortune* magazine discussing what corporations must have to compete in a competitive and increasingly complex market, and knowledge-based workplace, says that one of the things companies have to do is "grasp the difference between training and learning."[13] In a global environment of rapid change, both corporate and technological, those who are narrowly trained will be more likely to be unemployed. Many corporate cultures have outgrown the transfer of training model as the primary approach to instruction.

There has been a long-standing distinction in the HRD field between training and learning. As W. J. Heisler and P. O. Benham in their article "The Challenge of Management Development in North America in the 1990s"[14] point out, the terms *learning* and *education* are viewed as more academic, while *training* is viewed as more immediate, practical, and directed specifically at a task. With each view goes a different philosophy and culture of values. Heisler and Benham explain:

Academics concerned with education as the capacity to think tend to see practitioner-trainers as too vocational and narrow in their focus on the job-utility of knowledge. Practitioner-trainers concerned with the capacity to do a job tend to see academics as too ethereal and broad in their focus on the life-utility of knowledge. . . . In management training, the relevance of knowledge is defined more precisely in terms of its direct utility to job performance criteria. For example, in performance appraisal training, the instructor/trainer would emphasize the mechanics of completing a particular form correctly and then using that information and data to justify subsequent personnel actions. A management education program on performance appraisal, however, might focus more broadly on conceptual issues, such as the relative merits of a criterion-referenced versus a norm-referenced system in meeting a variety of design and implementation considerations.[15]

While training is appropriate for some very concrete tasks, it's becoming an increasingly less appropriate mode of instruction for business.

The basic differences between transfer of training and transfer of learning are as follows: Unlike training, learning tends to be

1. more knowledge based,
2. less concrete,
3. less task specific,
4. more long-run oriented,
5. more connected to other knowledge,
6. less rote memorization,
7. more meaningful to the learner,
8. more process than product oriented,
9. less superficial and more depth of understanding oriented,
10. more conceptual and theoretical, and
11. more learner centered than instructional method or technique driven.

Thus, learning tends to be more generative or creative than training. Finally, learning results in a deeper level and a broader scope of transfer than does training; therefore, there is more long-term payoff.

To further illustrate the difference between training and learning: I've a friend in the merchant marine. Years ago he invited me onboard his ship and gave me a tour of the engine room. He introduced me to two engineers. I was informed that one of them was the "operating" engineer, the other, the first engineer. I asked my friend what the difference was. He pointed to a large instrument board with many dials, pressure gauges, and levers. The operating engineer knew what each of the instrument indicators meant, and he knew when and where to adjust valves in response to the readings. But, unlike the first engineer, he did not know what went on behind the instrument panel. He was trained.

Learning in business organizations needs to be viewed from a developmental perspective, just as we view individual growth. In a time when most business tasks were industrial, simple, task specific, concrete, and relatively isolated from each other, training was perhaps appropriate. Now, with corporate structure and individual performance having evolved, and having to respond to ever-increasing complexity as well as deal with more information and knowledge, not to mention having to respond to a more highly competitive, global, and teamwork environment, training alone will no longer suffice; it's knowledge that is needed. Insufficient knowledge base, or expertise, is one of the most important factors in lack of transfer. Seen in this light, the transfer of training model, which has served a specific purpose, is now often inappropriate in the same way that the methods used to instruct children are inappropriate when instructing adults.

The traditional business-training notion of what is known as the "transfer model" of instruction refers to transfer in a classroom that leads to a trainee's increased performance on the job. With recent corporate restructuring, downsizing, and outsourcing of many HRD functions, there is a move to what is called *embedded training*. Embedded training takes place within the actual job situation. Presumably, classroom training will diminish. But the traditional on-the-job training (OJT) approach is beginning to be reconceptualized into on-the-job learning (OJL).[16] On-the-job learning is more structured, more tailored to the learner. It also involves the learner in the design of the on-the-job experience more than the typical OJT approach.

As an article in the fiftieth anniversary issue of *Training and Development* outlining future trends in training suggests, what has been known as the transfer model will "face serious challenges from new models that account for the way people learn—in the context of work."[17] Others, too, have asserted that the transfer model is dead. Presumably, embedded instruction and OJT require much less transfer. They don't. I will clearly and unequivocally demonstrate in the current and following chapters that the transfer model is not dead. Indeed, it is more alive and crucial to corporate and organizational learning than ever before. The view that the transfer model is dead is due to an antiquated and constricted HRD definition of transfer. In this view, transfer is narrowly defined as a *physical* transfer from the classroom to the workplace. Certainly, this is an important aspect of transfer but only its most simple attribute.

The misunderstanding about the state of the transfer model is due not only to a different and restricted view of transfer within the HRD field but to an erroneous understanding of the academic and educational research on transfer. Traditionally for corporate trainers, transfer of training has meant the transfer of material from the classroom to performance in the workplace; trainers have tended to hold the view that "[I]n educational theory . . . it refers to the effect of knowledge or abilities acquired in one area on a person's subsequent ability to acquire knowledge or skills in other areas"[18]—for example, from psychology to sociology or anthropology. This statement reflects only a partial understanding of transfer in educational research.

In fact, research on transfer tends to classify the HRD-type notion of transfer on the lower end of a learning continuum and the transfer of knowledge toward the higher end of the continuum, with the transfer of higher-order thinking and reasoning at the extreme end. Since all learning and training programs are (or should be) based on transfer principles and strategies, the transfer model—in this primary sense—remains pertinent to any training situation.

Business can no longer afford the performance losses and long-term costs of the misuse of information and knowledge. All too often, training *is like* strip-mining information and knowledge. While with training the immediate costs may be lower, and the rate of initial learning faster, the use of the information is severely restricted and the long-term losses are greater. The successful reengineering of the traditional organization into the information age, then, requires more learning and less training.

Finally, I should point out that the move toward learning and transfer of learning doesn't necessarily mean that training has become antiquated, as some may suggest. There is a downside to the shift from a training model to a learning model. As in social movements, or during large-scale shifts in our ways of thinking or models for doing things, we often overreact and view everything in the old model as outdated. New theories or paradigms, however, don't always completely replace old ones. Quantum mechanics, for example, didn't replace Newtonian physics; both are recognized as applicable to different levels of reality. Similarly, learning will not completely replace training. There are situations where time constraints, task specifications, trainee ability, short-run needs and goals, and financial constraints will make training the instructional method of choice.

THE TRANSFER MODEL: A CORPORATE AND ACADEMIC MERGER

A more positive note is that while the HRD model of transfer has been a conceptually restricted one and lacking a research base, it has one extremely important characteristic that has been missing from the more academic instructional model of transfer. In contrast to the HRD model of transfer, virtually nonexistent in either academic instruction or research is a recognition of the organizational or social support systems for facilitating or sustaining transfer—if and when it should occur.[19] It was somewhat of a revelation to me when reviewing the HRD literature to find that, with few exceptions,[20] the literature almost exclusively focused on organizational support of transfer and not on cognitive and instructional methods from the psychological research. This organizational approach is exemplified most systematically by Mary Broad and John Newstrom's book *Transfer of Training*. They approach transfer almost exclusively as a managerial and organizational problem. Unfortunately, however, it appears that most organizations still don't translate Broad and Newstrom's organizational support systems approach to transfer into everyday practice.

Mainstream academic instruction, with its emphasis on (1) the individual, (2) internal mental processes, and (3) instructional methods that seldom extend beyond the small-group learning environment, has virtually ignored the social or cultural context or social support components to learning (see Chapter 7). In short, academic instruction typically doesn't take what in effect is a systems view of learning. In large measure, this state of affairs has been historically and socially conditioned. First, learning is considered a property of the individual psyche; second, the classroom is an isolated environment; third, transfer has historically been assumed to occur naturally; fourth, learners in the academic environment have not traditionally had a context of application since they are not employed; and fifth, dormitories on most U.S. campuses are considered places for socializing, not for extending and supporting learning.

Students in most academic settings have no context of support to facilitate transfer. In fact, their student-life context is often counterproductive to transfer. In contrast, learners in corporate training environments have a built-in context of application: their job. The idea of organizational support to facilitate and sustain transfer is crucial. A great deal of the failure to find transfer after instruction is often not due to a lack of learning but to a lack of organizational, social, and contextual support. With the increase in adult learners in academic settings, the context of transfer will take on increasing importance. As a consequence, the flow of ideas on learning may reverse its traditional direction from academia to business. There are signs this is already occurring in continuing and adult educational programs.

Any instructional program has four basic levels of potential transfer: (1) simply learning the material (based on instructional transfer methods); (2) applying or transferring the learned material to a specific job or task; (3) being able to transfer the learned material to similar but significantly different job contexts; and (4) using the learning for problem solving, creative thinking, and innovation. Taken together, these levels of transfer constitute what I call leveraged learning (see Chapter 9). Leveraged learning is getting the maximum use out of information. The loss of any one of these levels is costly.

HOW TO FIX THE LACK OF TRANSFER IN HRD TRAINING PROGRAMS

As I indicated in Chapter 1, currently there is little to offer the HRD trainer that will increase the payoff for the training dollar. As T. Oates, writing in *Education, Training and Technology International*, observed, "[T]here is a 'gap' between our technical knowledge about transfer and our aspirations about enhancing and promoting it en masse in general education and vocational education and training."[21] Similarly, HRD trainers Philip Hallinger and Ruth Greenblatt in their article "Designing Professional Development for Transfer of Learning" lament, "As staff developers, we . . . have been guilty—more often than we would like to admit—of providing . . . programs that offered interesting content and engaging speakers, but that failed to provide conditions that maximize the transfer of knowledge, skills and attitudes to the workplace."[22] Zemke and Gunkler also note, "We know of nothing you can rub on, administer, do or say to your trainees that is guaranteed to make transfer from training to the job a lead-pipe cinch."[23] Why this failure is in fact the case for most training is because there hasn't been—and doesn't currently exist—a clear understanding of transfer or a set of transfer tools for trainers to build into the design of their programs.[24] Here's a brief look at how to reengineer training programs.

In brief, these eleven principles are required to promote transfer of learning. The following chapters will elaborate on these principles. Participants in training programs:

1. *Need to master a large primary knowledge base or a high level of expertise in the performance area of transfer.* To some, this requirement may not seem to be any great news. But it is clear that either by design or by default simple learning strategies have been *in* and that requiring learners to master a large knowledge base has been *out* for quite some time in both education and training philosophy (see Chapter 8). Instruction has tended to reflect our technological society. Somehow, learning a number of skills, procedures, and simple facts is supposed to add up to significant knowledge and transfer. It doesn't.

2. *Need to acquire some level of knowledge base in subjects outside the primary performance area* (see Chapter 8). It's peripheral or oblique knowledge that often provides important links to a primary area of knowledge and makes it possible to engage in transfer.

3. *Need to acquire an understanding of the history of the transfer area(s).* Without at least a general grasp of the history of an area, transfer may be incorrect or inadequate (see Chapter 6).

4. *Need to acquire motivation or, more specifically, a spirit of transfer* (see Chapter 7). Without this affective or emotion/feeling-based foundation, the impetus to transfer is unlikely to occur.

5. *Need to understand what transfer of learning is and how it works.*

6. *Need to acquire an orientation to think and encode learning in transfer terms* (see Chapter 9). How we encode new information determines how we retrieve and apply it.

7. *Need cultures of transfer to be created* (see Chapter 7). To one degree or another, transfer is supported or inhibited by the group or culture in which learning takes place. Accordingly, we need to develop what are called cultures of transfer.

8. *Need to acquire an understanding of the theory underlying the transfer area.* It's grasping the theory that underlies a subject that allows us to see and to make the appropriate transfer (see Chapter 8).

9. *Need to engage in hours of practice and drill* (see Chapter 8). This in turn requires hours of self-conscious learning and discipline. Fundamentals have to be learned thoroughly before significant and creative transfer can occur.

10. *Need significant time for transfer to incubate.* It tends not to occur instantaneously. In our society, we typically transmit to students expectations of instant knowledge and success. Expecting such instant results and gratification, learners often quit trying to transfer.

11. *Need to observe and read the works of people, both in and out of their performance fields, who are exemplars of transfer thinking.* This means reading accounts of scientific discoveries, of invention, of innovation (see Chapter 6), and, in Senge's terms, of systems thinkers (see Chapter 10), for it is systems thinkers who exhibit transfer to a significant degree.

Contrary to much of current wisdom, the secret of transfer is to immerse yourself in examples of transfer. I have used many examples throughout this book, and Chapter 6 is entirely about examples of technological transfer. Immersion does two basic things to foster transfer. First, it makes it possible for us to develop mental schemas that include the abstracting of patterns from a diverse array of information. It's from these schemas that transfer is generated. Second, it allows nonconscious processes to do their work of cross-correlating and integrating these patterns (see Chapter 11). This is the incubation process that creativity requires. Most of our transfer work is done prior to conscious recognition. Our conscious recognition of similarity is the end product to the transfer process, not its beginning. In the absence of engaging in these eleven principles, significant transfer will not occur.

INSTRUCTING FOR GENERAL TRANSFER

In keeping with my review of the 95 years of research on transfer of learning, I have come to certain conclusions about how people best acquire proficiency in general transfer of their learning. Based on this research, I have developed an approach to transfer that generally goes against the grain of most of my colleagues as well as most of the thinking in the business training literature.

My review of the transfer literature has convinced me of the importance of approaching some kinds of transfer in a more holistic manner. The view I am about to advocate is based largely on the eleven principles I have outlined above, especially acquiring a large knowledge base and expertise in your speciality area or job; acquiring a knowledge base in subjects outside your primary area; developing an orientation to think in transfer terms; developing the spirit of transfer (see Chapter 7); thinking and encoding new learning in generic terms; and reading works and observing people who are examples of transfer thinking. In short, immersing yourself in transfer thinking.

Let me explain why I am convinced that the approach to transfer that I've outlined is the only course of action open to us if we are to ensure transfer. It has been assumed by most educational researchers and practitioners—including myself—that instructional methods should be designed on the *basis of the detailed findings* from research. I now have serious reservations about this assumption, at least for most instructional purposes and especially for achieving general transfer. To be informed by research findings is one thing; to build instructional models based on research details is often inappropriate. The implications of not basing a theory of instruction directly on the details of research, however, is dangerous business.

The implications of such an approach are dangerous because not directly basing instructional design on research findings can lead all too easily to an anything-goes philosophy of education—tarot cards included. There is, however, precedent for my general approach. In 1963, well-known educational psychologists L. J. Cronbach, E. R. Hilgard, and W. B. Spalding maintained "Formal psychological theory is not, and may never be, able to calculate a prescription for teaching; its service is to point out factors requiring adjustment and to suggest provisional tries."[25] In 1964, another educational researcher noted that "it is not to be assumed that the architectonics of knowledge is necessarily the same as the architectonics of instruction,"[26] which is to say that the structures of our cognitive processes are not necessarily the appropriate structures on which to base a theory of instruction.

Often, a more naturally holistic, nonprogrammed approach to transfer is the way we learn as we go about our everyday business; it's the way children master, order, and transfer the complex and huge amount of information they structure into something called language. What is needed, then, is an instructional framework that is soundly informed by cognitive research findings but that isn't mired in, and modeled on, the details of that research.

Current standard instructional approaches that involve a very concrete, sequential, step-by-step type of instruction are similar to the programmed text approach to learning prevalent during the behaviorist-dominated 1960s and early 1970s, leaving little or nothing to be inferred by the learner. A detailed programming approach is more of a training than a learning approach. As such, like most training approaches, the emphasis—though not exclusively—is on instructional method and design rather than on the learner as the central cause of learning.

To break everything down into discrete tasks and procedures results in never-ending lists, as the programmed learning texts movement of a few years ago demonstrated. Moreover, even when programmed texts are successful, it's difficult to move us beyond them. And when we do move beyond them, we don't move very far.

I should note at this point that a general theory of transfer doesn't preclude the more traditional detailed and programmed instruction approach to learning in some situations and subject matters. A programming type of approach is basically relevant to lower-level, more concrete and detailed tasks. Jobs, or knowledge bases, that involve detail and that are technical are often best taught with this approach, at least initially.

A further downside of adopting an artificial intelligence–type model of learning is that if curricula were designed on the basis of these otherwise useful and excellent programming methods, it would increase the time required to learn any given subject at least tenfold, because unlike computers, we are not rapid calculators that can consciously recall long strings of rules and integrate them. David Lohman, chair of the Psychological and Quantitative Foundations department in the College of Education of the University of Iowa, similarly recognizes that applying computational findings to educational practice is often problematic. He says, "Although this work is theoretically encouraging, it's unlikely that it will have a significant impact on practical efforts to assess transfer."[27] Why? First, a detailed task analysis requires an incredible amount of work. Thus, such an approach would not generally be educationally feasible. Breaking learning down into minute components very quickly reaches a point of diminishing returns. While in theory breaking learning down into its elemental parts often looks reasonable, in practice, it's often not.

Again, with the exception of material that's inherently technical, like learning mathematics, accounting, and other similar material, a more holistic, nonconscious approach is often more effective. Even in these fields, however, on a higher level—after the basics have been practiced repetitively—many innovators function holistically. It's clear from reading the accounts of great innovators that they were able to come up with their discoveries by immersing themselves in a knowledge base. After such discoveries are made, however, they may then need to be back-translated into more manageable sequential, analytical, and technical terms. From a transfer perspective, adding up little bits of information will not lead to a big piece of knowledge, just as adding up little bits of knowledge will not lead to innovation and discovery.

NOTES

1. P. M. Senge, *The Fifth Discipline: The Art and Practice of the Learning Organization* (New York: Doubleday, 1990), p. 363.

2. F. C. Pratzner, *Occupational Adaptability and Transferable Skills* (Information Series No. 129) (Columbus, OH: National Center for Research in Vocational Education 1978), p. 13.

3. D. Bridges, "Transferable Skills: A Philosophical Perspective," *Studies in Higher Education* 18(1) (1993), p. 50.

4. Peter Block, in "The Future of Workplace Learning and Performance," *Training and Development* (May 1994), p. 36.

5. B. Friedman, "Six Ways to Make It Work at Work," *Training and Development Journal* 44 (December 1990), p. 17. Italics added.

6. Senge, *The Fifth Discipline*, pp. 5–11.

7. See Denis R. Towill, "Common Foundations between Control Engineering and Manufacturing Management," *European Journal of Engineering Education* 13 (1989), pp. 415–430. See also J. W. Forrester, *Industrial Dynamics* (Cambridge, MA: MIT Press, 1961).

8. D. L. Georgenson, "The Problem of Transfer Calls for Partnership," *Training and Development Journal* 36 (October 1982), p. 75.

9. Thomas Steward, "Brainpower," *Fortune* (June 3, 1991), p. 44.

10. Linda Tetzlaff, *Transfer of Learning: Beyond Common Elements* (Research Report RC 12596) (Yorktown Heights, NY: IBM Thomas J. Watson Research Center, 1987), p. 1.

11. I would like to thank David Allie, of Phoenix Systems, for these examples from his introductory material on transfer of learning in teaching computer competencies.

12. Simon Collinson, "Managing Product Innovation at Sony: The Development of the Data Discman," *Technology Analysis & Strategy Management* 5 (1993), pp. 285–306.

13. Walter Kiechel, "The Organization That Learns," *Fortune* (March 12, 1990), p. 133.

14. W. J. Heisler and P. O. Benham, "The Challenge of Management Development in North America in the 1990s," *Journal of Management Development* 11 (1992), pp. 16–31.

15. Ibid., p. 23.

16. See P. J. Marsh, "On-the-Job Learning," *Technical & Skills Training* (August–September 1994), p. 7.

17. Training and Development, "The Future of Workplace Learning and Performance," *Training and Development* (May 1994), p. 36.

18. J. C. Georges, "Transfer of Training," *Training* 26 (November 1989), p. 72.

19. A small group of educational researchers, largely outside of mainstream educational theory, have recognized the importance of the context in which instruction takes place as well as the need of social support systems for transfer. Most of this research is coming from research on informal learning situations (see Chapter 7).

20. T. T. Baldwin and J. K. Ford, "Transfer of Training: A Review and Directions for Future Research," *Personnel Psychology* 41 (1988), pp. 61–105.

21. T. Oates, "Core Skills and Transfer: Aiming High," *Education, Training and Technology International* 29 (1992), p. 227.

22. P. Hallinger and R. Greenblatt, "Designing Professional Development for Transfer of Learning," *Planning and Changing* 21 (1990), p. 195.

23. R. Zemke and J. Gunkler, "Techniques of Transforming Training into Performance," *Training* (April 1985), p. 48.

24. Hallinger and Greenblatt, "Designing Professional Development for Transfer of Learning," p. 195.

25. L. J. Cronbach, E. R. Hilgard, and W. B. Spalding, "Intellectual Development as Transfer of Learning," in L. J. Cronbach, E. R. Hilgard, and W. B. Spalding (eds.), *Educational Psychology* (New York: Harcourt, Brace and World, 1963), p. 338.

26. P. H. Phenix, "The Architectonics of Knowledge," in *Education and the Structure of Knowledge*, Phi Delta Kappa Symposium on Educational Research, University of Illinois (Chicago: Rand McNally, 1964), p. 44.

27. David Lohman, "Learning and the Nature of Educational Measurement," *National Association of Secondary School Principles* 77 (1993), p. 42.

4

Intellectual Capital: Learning Organizations and the Transfer of Knowledge

---

The essential point about learning in the workplace is that the corporation is going to become a university that can add more value than its competitors around the world. If it doesn't, we will watch our standard of living deteriorate significantly.

Tom Peters[1]

Currently what are called learning organizations are all the rage in the business world. I don't think they're a fad, however. In some form, they are here to stay. So, what's a learning organization? There's no simple or single answer to this question. In fact, there exists no such ideal organization. The concept of a learning organization is just that: a concept, an idea. It's at once a new idea and an old one. Organizations that learn have always existed, since all organizations must learn simply in order to function. But the current idea of a learning organization is not just new wine in an old bottle. It is, however, an aged concept, as the following 1962 quote by Warren Bennis illustrates. He noted that "the organization of tomorrow, heavily influenced by the growth of science and technology and manned by an increasing number of professionals, appears to have the necessary requirements for constructing organizations based on inquiry."[2] An organization based on inquiry, not one based on training, *is* a learning organization. In an information age, the choice facing chief executive officers (CEOs) and managers is not whether or not to be a learning organization but to what degree learning is to be built into the very structure of the organization. Whatever the eventual definition of a learning organization turns out to be, transfer of learning will be central to it.

In this book, I will not attempt to outline the requirements of a learning organization; many others are currently engaged in this task; neither will I be reiterating the principles of learning; many others have already done that, as well. Rather, I will be addressing the necessary *cognitive foundations* of any learning organization, however the concept may be eventually defined. That foundation is transfer. In a recent article in the *Training and Development* journal, entitled "Grasping the Learning Organization," the authors list a number of requirements for what constitutes a learning organization. The items were the result of a series of focus group meetings. One requirement that all members agreed upon was that "[l]earning organizations learn to use learning to reach their goals."[3] Although this may at first glance appear to be an obvious requirement, the implications are perhaps not so obvious.

For the learning organization, learning is integrally built into its very organizational structure and infrasystems, including job descriptions, reward system, management roles, team building, and so on; for the learning organization, innovation is constant. Learning organizations are based on constant change and can perhaps best be summed up by saying: If it's *not* broke—fix it.

In learning organizations, then, adapting to innovation and change in one's job and being able to adapt to others' jobs in simple or cross-functional teamwork require adaptability. Again, as Frank Pratzner has concluded from his research on occupational adaptability and transferable skills, occupational adaptability is based on individuals "who can generalize, transfer, or form associations so that the skills, attitudes, knowledge, and personal characteristics that have been learned or developed in one context can be used readily in a different context."[4] Thus, transfer relates directly both to opportunities in career development and to opportunities for job transfers.

Underlying all adaptations is transfer of learning. Accordingly, in this chapter, I will be focusing on the learning organization from a specific perspective: that of the transfer of learning. I will not be outlining a series of techniques but a broad model of how transfer provides the foundation for learning organizations. As Tom Peters, has lamented about most discussions of learning organizations: They typically deteriorate into "discussions of techniques and devices we already know. I think we need much bolder models for what organizations are all about."[5] Transfer is such a bold model. In a companion volume, I will provide more detailed techniques based on research findings on the transfer of learning.

So what's the learning organization all about from a transfer perspective? The short answer to this question is what this chapter is about; and again, the long answer is what this book is about. Organizational transfer is about creating and sustaining a competitive edge. Ray Stata, chairman of Analog Devices, maintains, "The rate at which individuals and organizations learn may become the only sustainable competitive advantage, especially for knowledge intensive industries"[6]—and, I might add, for organizations that function in a highly complex and globally competitive market. This means that those in organizations, especially executives and managers, will have an added role. In the words of longtime organizational and management sage Peter Drucker, "Managers will have to learn to manage knowledge for productivity."[7] In managing knowledge, transfer is fundamental. Moreover, managing knowledge "spawns whole new disciplines," says Ted Smith, director of knowledge-based systems at Baby Bell, U.S. West.[8] This book is about one of those—not so new—disciplines, the transfer of learning. And transfer requires intellectual capital.

INTELLECTUAL CAPITAL

At first glance, the phrase *intellectual capital* may sound like a contradiction in terms or, worse yet, an ironic phrase conjured up by some esoteric postmodern Marxist humanities professor. But it isn't. It's a phrase being used increasingly by hardheaded, bottom-line business executives. So what's meant by the phrase? Peter Drucker presaged the answer in 1989. He saw the emergence of what he called "the post-business society, with a work force dominated by knowledge workers."[9] More and more, business is both based on and producing knowledge. The design, creation, utilization, and transfer of complex technology require employees with knowledge (see Chapters 6 and 8). Corporations in the business of software, databases for computers, and research in technology, genetics, communications, and just about all areas including multi-million-dollar research consulting firms, publishing, and advertising require constant acquisition and use of knowledge—and its transfer.

The term *intellectual capital* is defined by Larry Prusak, of Ernst & Young's Center for Business Innovation in Boston, as "intellectual material that has been formalized, captured, and leveraged to produce a higher-valued asset."[10] As technology and information products increase, says Hedley Donovan, former editor of *Fortune* magazine and *Time*, "more and more people in business are genuine intellectuals."[11] Donovan calls the people he managed in the journalism and publishing trades intellectuals. He defined an intellectual as a person who deals mainly with knowledge and ideas, not things. While some of my colleagues in academia would cringe at combining the term *intellectual* with business and finance (depending on how the term is defined), the fact remains that more and more "jobs" in business require professionals with an extensive systematic knowledge base who are able to retrieve, generate, analyze, evaluate, and otherwise process data and ideas. In short, to think.

The term *intellectual capital* is increasingly being recognized as not just a nice metaphor for monetary capital; it *is* capital. Recently, in *Fortune* magazine a feature cover story title read: "Your Company's Most Valuable Asset: Intellectual Capital."[12] For some reason, some of my academic colleagues believe that to be an intellectual, one has to think about profound, philosophical, social, or political ideas—and to do so in a state of existential angst. Equally mistaken are many business executives and managers who also cringe at the very term *intellectual*, believing the term describes either politically radical or ivory-tower types.

In an interesting book entitled *The Last Intellectuals*, Russell Jacobi laments what he sees as the loss of intellectuals in the U.S.-born, post–World War II generation.[13] As Jacobi uses the term, it refers to someone who writes for the public on social, political, philosophical, and economic ideas. Consequently, academics are not intellectuals. Why? Because by Jacobi's definition, they do not write for the public. Along with other reasons, according to Jacobi, with the mass expansion of the college and university system in the early 1960s, those who would be intellectuals became professors. Thus, says Jacobi, the university systems have siphoned off the public's intellectuals. Jacobi makes no mention, however, of potential or incipient intellectuals being siphoned off by business, by the knowledge industries. The fact is, it's happening. In 1991, Skandia Assurance & Financial Services appointed Leif Edvinsson the corporate world's first director of intellectual capital. And in 1993, Dow Chemical created a similar position with the title director of intellectual asset management.

Intellectual capital is corporate America's most valuable asset and competitive edge. As Tom Peters has put it in *The Future of Workplace Performance*, "[v]alue added through brains is, simply put, the only strategy— whether you are a broom maker in Illinois competing with the Mexicans, or a software designer for Lotus in Massachusetts."[14] In business, intellectuals are found in brokerage firms, IBM, Bell Labs, and the *Washington Post* as well as in the small firm. Brainpower has never been so important for business.

It's not widely recognized, but according to a survey, about 30 percent of the CEOs of the Fortune 500 industrial companies and Service 500 companies have M.B.A degrees, and some 5 percent hold doctoral degrees.[15] While few would seriously maintain that one needs a Ph.D. in order to have brainpower, the fact remains that as the need for processing information and knowledge increases, so does the need for higher-level experience and instruction in methods for using that information and knowledge.

There have always been arguments both pro and con about higher-level training and advanced degrees in business. Some maintain that such training enables a person to manage and analyze data, to focus in on essential elements of a problem, while others maintain that it creates a person of narrow focus. Another argument is that in the hectic world of business, decisions need to be made on the spur of the moment—that the executive needs to play hunches, to use his or her intuition, instead of waiting for the data to be assessed. But, as I will suggest later, the intuition and unconscious hunches are the result of having a large intellectual capital account (i.e., knowledge base) and having acquired expertise in an area.

Leif Edvinsson points out that the value of intellectual assets vastly exceeds the value of assets that typically appear on a company's balance sheet; after all, intellectual capital is the basic material from which financial results are made. He says that managers must distinguish between two kinds of intellectual capital: human and structural. This is an important distinction. Human capital is the source of innovation and renewal, whether it issues from knowledge base, brainstorming, laboratory findings, or leads that a sales representative has acquired. Putting this capital to work, however, requires structural intellectual assets. These include information systems, actual market channels, and other management structures. To engage in a little transfer, we might view individual intellectual capital as the software and the structural capital as the hardware to implement it. As one writer observes, "In a trend not easily measurable now in monetary terms, the concept of the 'organizational memory' has become real. Companies are capturing the knowledge of the expert skills important to them and using it. An entirely new industry is now in place to serve and enhance this economic development."[16] One company exemplifying the valuing and reaping of profits from intellectual capital is Merck pharmaceuticals.

Since 1981, Merck has introduced ten major drugs, with each one creating at least $100 million in annual sales. Apparently responsible for this success was Roy Vagelos, an M.D. and biochemist. Merck has accomplished this by sinking enormous amounts of dollars not only into research and development (R&D) but also into intellectual capital, the people it hires to conduct the research and come up with new discoveries and ideas. In 1989, Merck's R&D expenditure was $755 million, or about 11 percent of sales; in 1990, Merck sank $854 million into R&D; in 1991, it planned to invest $1 billion in R&D. Moreover, unlike most other companies who treat R&D as an expense, Merck classifies it as capital and thus as an asset.

More important, Merck values intellectual capital, knowing that it pays off. It has wooed academic researchers away from Harvard and Yale. "Merck has some people of higher quality than you can find at the best academic institutions," says John Powell, Merck's vice president for clinical research. International headhunters know that you just don't send Merck good people. "There are plenty of good people around, but I wouldn't send them to Merck," says Virgil Baldi, vice president of the Korn/Ferry International executive recruiting firm. "I send Merck only people with world-class reputations."[17] The value of intellectual capital: The knowledge that people have will increase in worth in our complex world.

"Intellectual capital—the knowledge necessary to make a product that produces wealth—has always existed," says Walter Wriston, retired chairman of Citicorp, "but in the future, the ratio of intellectual capital to materiel is going to continue to tip in favor of intellectual capital."[18] This is so because research clearly shows that what is required for creative and productive transfer is intellectual capital and that those with intellectual capital are the ones who are more likely to engage in productive transfer. Intellectual capital seen in this light gives new pragmatic meaning to the old phrase "Knowledge is power." Learning organizations and intellectual capital, along with transfer, are joined at the hip.

Intellectual capital is not just any knowledge. In the HRD context, it is productive knowledge, knowledge that leads (at some point) to financial gain. It's the difference between having the knowledge to win at the game Trivia and systematic and tutored information. In addition to just plain knowledge of or about something, intellectual capital is knowledge that can be usefully employed. Inert knowledge is not intellectual capital. Over and above just having intellectual capital, however, is intellectual capital that can be transferred to other areas. This kind of intellectual capital draws compounded dividends.

True learning in an organization, says one researcher, is the "business's ability to generate new ideas *multiplied by its adeptness at generalizing* them throughout the company"[19] (italics added). The very meaning of generalization is, of course, transfer. Skandia's new director of intellectual capital, Leif Edvinsson, working with technologists and actuaries, cut about half the time and costs involved in opening an office in a new country by identifying techniques and technology that could be *transplanted* to almost any context. To do this required that they abstract out the commonalities, the generic structure of a Skandia office.

In short, to accomplish this, Edvinsson and the others involved applied transfer principles. The kind of thinking they engaged in was a lowercase form of what Alfred Sloan did when he revolutionized the structure of management organization by transferring ideas from Adam Smith's notion of division of labor to management practices, creating smaller, decentralized managerial units, each with a specialized bureaucratic function (see Chapter 2).

While few executives would let their cash be idle or leave their factory space idle, when CEOs are asked how much of the knowledge in their companies is used, they typically reply, "About 20 percent" One way to get this intellectual capital working is by learning to transfer. Transfer knowledge is intellectual capital that's twice and three times used; it's thus intensely *leveraged* knowledge. It's like having your money earn dividends for you in multiple places at the same time.

MANAGING INTELLECTUAL CAPITAL AND THOSE WHO CREATE IT

Intellectual capital needs to be managed carefully. Investing in intellectual capital is very much like investing dollars: You can use them now or invest them in the anticipation of greater value at some later point. Like some stock investments, some intellectual capital investment may pay off immediately, some in the near future, and some may not begin to pay dividends for years. Like stock investments, there are no guarantees of profitable returns. Like some investments, some intellectual capital may seem like a bad investment, appearing that there never will be dividends, that perhaps it was a bad investment and will have to be written off as useless knowledge. But like the monetary market, you never know what the invisible hand of the intellectual market will do. What may appear to be a bad investment may turn out to be a gold mine. This seems to be especially true for intellectual investments.

An example from the Du Pont Corporation demonstrates the rewards of patience when investing in intellectual capital. Nathaniel C. Wyeth, grandson of famous artist N. C. Wyeth, brother of Andrew, and uncle to Jamie, well known for their paintings, took a road less traveled by his famous family: He became an engineer for Du Pont. In the mid-1970s he had been experimenting for a considerable time, trying to engineer a plastic soda bottle that would hold carbonated soda without expanding and blowing apart. Soda bottles were made out of glass at the time. Meeting with repeated failure, Wyeth continued to show his distorted and misshapen plastic "bottles" to the director of the laboratory. His boss expressed serious concern about investing further corporate money in such "terrible looking bottles." Wyeth recalls, "I'd bring over this terrible looking sample and call it a bottle. He'd look at it and say, 'Is this all you've done for $50,000? . . .' 'Yeah,' I said, 'but it's oriented, and it's hollow. . . .' 'But what a terrible-looking bottle,' he said. 'It looks like something dug up out of the ruins of Carthage.' "[20] But the director of the lab maintained confidence in Weyth's work and kept investing in it. Wyeth, of course, finally succeeded in creating a safe soda bottle—and raising, I might add, Du Pont's profit level.

What "apparently useless knowledge" means for the learning organization is that, unlike in the past (at least for many), corporations must measure intellectual capital in long-run terms, not in the bottom-line monthly, quarterly, or even annual report. Unlike training, which almost by definition pays immediate dividends, intellectual capital is based on learning, which almost by definition may not pay immediate dividends. The same is true for transfer. The learning organization must learn to delay gratification. Indeed, some intellectual capital is like stock market speculation. But corporations cannot live by futures alone; there is always a pragmatic trade-off of immediate needs with future benefits.

Because of varying extended time lines for intellectual capital investments to pay off, the learning organization needs planning and evaluation formulas. These need to be agreed upon not just by middle-level managers with the CEO but between the CEO and the board of directors. Finally, managing those who create intellectual capital needs to be managed differently from traditional management practice.

Having worked with people who create intellectual capital and having been a department chair in a university for a number of years, I know what it means to work and to manage people whose job it is to create intellectual capital. Most are a special breed. Of course, there are various kinds of people who work in the knowledge industry with ideas, just as there are in any profession. At the high end of the scale, there are people like those described earlier who work for Merck and similar corporations, who function with high levels of information, ideas, and transfer. Then there are those who perform at the lower end of the knowledge scale. Although there are differences between these two types, in the learning organization, it's important to recognize that everyone possesses and creates intellectual capital to one degree or another. Because of my background and experience, however, I will mainly be talking about those at the middle to higher end of the intellectual capital scale.

Given the historical differences and interaction between the corporate and academic worlds, the interactions often bordering on antagonism, it's somewhat of an irony that the corporation and the university are now each taking on some of the important characteristics of the other. These characteristics are important for both the university and for the learning organization for transfer. Since this book is about transfer and the learning organization, however, I will confine myself to the transfer of university characteristics to the learning organization.

While thinking about the similarities of knowledge workers and intellectual capitalists—as it were—between the university and the corporate world, I ran across the 1989 article in *Fortune* magazine by Hedley Donovan entitled "Managing Your Intellectuals." It was gratifying to learn that many of my perceptions about these similarities were born out by Donovan. He starts out by saying that "managing these brainy, often quirky individualists can be quite a challenge."[21] I only too well understood what he was talking about when he described working with intellectuals. After all, I not only have worked with and managed these people: For better or for worse, I am one.

People who create intellectual capital—be they in business or in academia—by definition, think in some depth, exhibit originality of thought, see relationships, and have a broad context of information to interpret data. These people often have a need to share their thinking with anyone around who will listen to them or read their writings. They typically hate meetings more than most, and when not engaged in their speciality, they become bored very quickly. I think what Mark Fuller, managing director of the Monitor consulting firm in Cambridge, said about the new breed of M.B.A.s applies or transfers to many intellectuals. Fuller says, "These are people who crave intellectual stimulation the way other people crave drugs."[22] Many of them either are—or think they are—star performers; they tend to be impatient with others. They are never totally for hire, and often their loyalty is not as much to the organization as it is to their ideas or their profession. So they're not without costs. But the good ones are worth it.

With corporations flattening their hierarchy, delegating authority, functioning in teams, and creating consensus decisions, the academic work environment model is an appropriate transfer model for understanding the learning organization. Historically, the university has (at least ideally) functioned as a flattened hierarchy, with the various faculties being work teams that set the standards, internal structure, and product of the institution. Although there is a hierarchy and an authority structure beginning with teaching faculty, department chairs, and deans and ending with the president, all are typically considered to be faculty and peers. Then, of course, like many corporations, there is the board of trustees or board of directors. Technically speaking, although a teaching faculty is "outranked" by a department chair or a dean, faculty are still seen as peers.

With the flattened hierarchy and fuzzy line of authority between the faculties and administration, the situation tends to be somewhat anarchic, with decisions sometimes "just happening." Even when the line of authority is relatively clear, the department chair, the dean, and the president all are quite careful to consult with the teaching faculty before rendering a decision and are quite careful to maintain the appearance that their decision is just the "will of the faculty" being carried out. The reason for this is that presumably it's the faculty who have the knowledge pertinent to the decisions. The department chair role is that of decision maker and of evaluating faculty performance. Traditionally, the chair, like the academic dean, has been considered the leader of the faculty, a kind of first-among-peers management philosophy. The point is that as corporations approach the ideal of a learning organization, the more they are likely to resemble and to function like a university. Certainly, corporations like Merck do not order their world-class researchers and knowledge workers around; neither does management see them and treat them as subordinates. The transition to a universitylike learning corporation is a difficult one for many business managers and CEOs, although many are already doing it.

I recall a few years back that the newly hired chair of the business department came into my office after a department chair meeting. He had been at the university for about a month. He had come from a rather traditionally structured, hierarchical chain-of-command large corporation. Entering my office shaking his head, he said, "Rob, how does anything get accomplished around here?" I replied, "Jim—very slowly." It's reported that General Dwight Eisenhower, when he became U.S. president, complained to one of his aides that unlike when he was general of the army, as president he would issue an order and nothing would happen. Transfer is tricky business. For example, after the U.S. Desert Storm Operation, it was suggested that General Norman Schwartzkopf be a candidate for the chancellorship of at least one large state university, ostensibly because of his intelligence, organizational abilities, and leadership experience. The assumption seemed to be that despite differences in a military organization and a university, with its faculty activism, student activism, a lack of a military chain of command, and so on, his leadership qualities would transfer. I find this prospect quite unlikely. The university is a cumbersome organization. In fact, it's almost a nonorganization, with its flattened (at least informally) operating hierarchy, creating a kind of inertia. Learning organizations need to find ways of preventing this kind of inertia.

THE FUTURE OF TRANSFER

I have thus far been transferring a university model to the learning organization. But as with all models and comparative analyses, there are differences that may be just as important—perhaps more so—than the similarities. Certainly, learning organizations can benefit from understanding the more or less democratic structure and function of the university— the virtual prototype of the learning organization. The model must be adapted, however, not taken whole cloth. As much as I admire the university and, indeed, think it should operate in no other way, let me be clear about one thing: If a learning corporation functioned exactly like a university, it would go bankrupt in short order. As a former business department chair once said to me, democracy is a political system, not a management philosophy. At least a pure democracy will not work. It's too slow, political, cumbersome, and does not function on a rational basis. Some modifications are required.

Quite frankly—and it hurts to say this—I don't see academia adapting to the HRD support systems model of transfer that I outline in Chapters 7 and 8 any time soon. It's in the corporate university that the promise of transfer will likely be fulfilled, at least on an applied level. Why do I say this? First, I say this because unlike the teachers and learners in the corporate university, most faculty and students in academia don't function under the bottom-line constraints that those in the corporate university do. Second, most educational institutions don't have the motivation required for reengineering or redesigning programs for transfer. There are, after all, two crucial preconditions for embracing change. The first is motivation; the second—is motivation.

It's the corporate university that is thus more likely to take what it needs from the academic model and adapt it. Business is already finding in the prototype of the learning organization, academia, that business schools are not keeping pace with the changes in the corporate environment. In a recent article entitled "What's Killing the Business School Deans of America?" the author describes cases of deans being ousted because of trying to make curricular changes. In that article, Ross Webber, chair of the management department at the University of Pennsylvania's Wharton School, laments that academic B-schools are not changing to keep pace with business. He says, "The business world is ahead of the university in promoting teams, cross-functionality, and project groups that bring together disparate elements."[23] In general, he's probably right.

Managing knowledge workers in a learning organization requires different skills from traditional management strategies. And managing change—which is one of the things that the learning organization is all about—requires additional skill and experience. Managing requires that the manager have transfer skills in order to understand the various mental models used by the diversity of people now being managed (see Chapter 5).

In addition to interpersonal and leadership skills in small-group/team functioning, the optimal learning organization manager must have other skills as well. He or she should have both a general and a specific knowledge base in the area he or she is managing. If there is one thing the transfer research shows, it's that there is no substitute for knowledge of an area and being able to transfer this knowledge in a noncookbook fashion. Knowledge of leadership and problem-solving strategies need to be evaluated carefully. While the game of chess is supposed to be a general model of war strategy, the typical strategy of controlling the center of the board may not always be successfully transferred—indeed, as General Custer found out too late. Controlling the center of the conflict is a context-specific strategy.

As I have already pointed out, one of the primary conditions of transfer is a large knowledge base. In managing groups and teams of people who create intellectual capital, knowledge base becomes more important. In learning organizations, the manager is a designer of learning and a teacher. Groups and teams being managed, almost by definition, constitute a system and require that managers of these systems have a working knowledge of the system and its subsystems in order for them to be optimally effective. The principle of requisite variety, developed by well-known systems theorist Ross Ashby,[24] can be viewed as demonstrating the need for managers to have an extensive knowledge base of the systems they are managing. The principle of requisite variety states: For one system to control (in our terms, manage) another system, it must be more complex than the system it is controlling.

NOTES

1. Tom Peters, in "The Future of Workplace Learning and Performance," *Training and Development* (May 1994), p. 43.

2. Warren Bennis, "Towards a 'Truly' Scientific Management: The Concept of

Organization Health," in L. V. Bertalanffy and A. Rapoport (eds.), *General Systems: Year Book of the Society for General Systems Theory*, Vol. 7 (Ann Arbor, MI: Society for General Systems Research, 1962), p. 279.

3. G. Calvert, S. Morley, and L. Marshall, "Grasping the Learning Organization," *Training and Development* (1994), p. 41.

4. F. C. Pratzner, *Occupational Adaptability and Transferable Skills* (Information Series No. 129) (Columbus, OH: National Center for Research in Vocational Education, 1978); cited in I. L. Goldstein, *Training in Organizations: Needs Assessments, Development, and Evaluation* (1986), p. 13.

5. Peters, in "The Future of Workplace Learning and Performance," p. 43.

6. R. Stata, "Organizational Learning: The Key to Management Innovation," *Sloan Management Review* 30 (1989), p. 63.

7. Quoted in "Stars of the 1980's Cast Their Light" [interviews], *Fortune* (July 3, 1989), p. 66.

8. In T. Stewart, "Brainpower," *Fortune* (June 3, 1991), p. 45.

9. See "Stars of the 1980's Cast Their Light," p. 66.

10. In T. A. Stewart, "Your Company's Most Valuable Asset: Intellectual Capital," *Fortune* (October 3, 1994), p. 68.

11. H. Donovan, "Managing Your Intellectuals," *Fortune* (October 23, 1989), p. 177.

12. Stewart, "Your Company's Most Valuable Asset: Intellectual Capital."

13. R. Jacobi, *The Last Intellectuals* (New York: Farrar, Strauss and Giroux, 1987).

14. Peters, in "The Future of Workplace Learning and Performance," p. 36.

15. R. Tetzeli, "Ph.D.s: Another Way to the Top," *Fortune* (June 17, 1991), p. 8.

16. E. A. Feigenbaum, "What Hath Simon Wrought?" in D. Klahr and K. Kotovsky (eds.), *Complex Information Processing: The Impact of Herbert A. Simon* (Hillsdale, NJ: Lawrence Erlbaum Associates, 1989), pp. 177–178.

17. "Leaders of the Most Admired," *Fortune* (January 29, 1990), p. 40; see also Stewart, "Brainpower," p. 54.

18. "Today's Leaders Look to Tomorrow," *Fortune* (March 26, 1990), p. 67.

19. In Stewart, "Your Company's Most Valuable Asset: Intellectual Capital," p. 72. Italics added.

20. Kenneth Brown, *Inventors at Work: Interviews with 16 Notable American Inventors*, Tempus Books (Redmond, WA: Microsoft Press, 1988), p. 370.

21. Donovan, "Managing Your Intellectuals," p. 177.

22. Quoted in A. Fisher, "The Ever-Bigger Boom in Consulting," *Fortune* (April 24, 1989), p. 130.

23. Brian O'Reilly, "What's Killing the Business School Deans of America?" *Fortune* (August 8, 1994), p. 64.

24. W. R. Ashby, "Variety, Constraint, and the Law of Requisite Variety," in W. Buckley and A. Rapoport (eds.), *Modern Systems Research for the Behavioral Scientist* (Chicago: Aldine Publishing, 1968), pp. 129–136.

5

Teaming with Corporate Transfer: Personal Development and The Small Group as Team and Microworld

Mastering team learning will be a critical step in building learning organizations.

Peter Senge, *The Fifth Discipline*[1]

Few areas on the human side of the corporate training equation have spawned so much attention as learning how to function in small groups and teams. As I noted in Chapter 1, the use of team functioning is becoming so prevalent that this practice is perhaps more aptly described not merely as a practice but as a new principle of corporate organization. Because most people do not know how to work in small groups effectively, the team mode of organizational functioning has virtually spawned a separate training industry within the HRD training profession. Even if not formally a team, most work environments are team oriented.

Learning how to function cooperatively and corporately is a need in all organizations. Certainly it's a crucial need in today's global business environment. Groups and teams are especially important in the learning organization, with its reengineering involving the increasing use of work groups and cross-functional teams. In 1991, when the Polaroid Corporation managed to develop and put on the market a new medical imaging system in record time, CEO MacAllister Booth attributed the success to working in a team. He says, "Our researchers are not any smarter, but by working together they get the value of each other's intelligence almost instantaneously."[2] MacAllister is pointing out the value of group and team interaction for high-performance organizations.

A team is a special kind of group. There are multiple worlds of research on small groups and teams coming from the corporate, educational, and academic literatures, and there is certainly no shortage of popular books and training programs. Most of this literature explains team processes and dynamics and provides instructional programs for learning how to work in groups and teams. I will not repeat this literature here; instead, I will confine myself to what is essentially missing in this literature: transfer of learning for understanding and working in teams.

Few people enjoy working in groups. It's difficult and frustrating. Indeed, functioning in groups has been the brunt of many jokes that border on folklore. Is there anyone not familiar with the joke that a camel is really a horse that was designed by a committee? Why do we have such jokes? That groups are frustrating to be a part of, constantly having to coordinate with others, is a tempting answer. But the meaning of such jokes goes much deeper than that. Our culture is largely to blame. Not only does our culture fail to socialize us about how to function in a group, but it negatively socializes us for being a group member. We are taught from very early on to be an individual and to march to our own drummer, to be master of our ship and captain of our soul. This is why groups are often counterproductive. We live in a high-tech, space-age culture with a frontier value of rugged individualism. Not a good prescription for effective group performance.

Certainly individualism is a good value—if not carried to an extreme. We have, however, carried it to an extreme. So much so that we do not know how to function well in groups and to be a productive member of a team. But the problem is not just seeing ourselves as group members. The problem is knowing how to function as a group member. We may see ourselves *as* a group member but not know how to *be* a team member. Even knowing how to function *in* a group is not the same as knowing how to function *as* a group. Functioning as a group means *team*. The reason we must understand both individual and group processes is that if we don't, then we inadvertently sabotage the effectiveness of our goals.

All too often we exclusively concentrate on the task of the group and ignore what are called its *maintenance* needs. Maintenance refers to becoming aware of and working through the individual and group problems and issues that affect the task or goal of the group. Utilizing transfer of learning methods is a crucial aspect of group maintenance. I have been conducting small-group, experiential courses and training sessions for many years where participants learn how to work in a group by actually functioning as a group. In doing so, I have been especially occupied with transfer of learning in teaching people how to function in, and to be, a group and how to learn from the group itself as a transfer medium. As a logical outgrowth of this concern with transfer of learning, over the years I've developed transfer of learning methods for teaching group skills. These methods, however, are not so much cookbook-type techniques as they are ways of "seeing," of understanding groups using transfer thinking. While this book is not the place to present my transfer exercises as a workbook might do, I will nevertheless draw on these exercises.

PERSONAL DEVELOPMENT AND SELF-MASTERY: THE PROBLEM OF OTHER MINDS

Perhaps the single most essential problem of living and working with others is understanding what each other is thinking and feeling. Since I can't get inside your mind or your feelings, I can't know exactly what you're feeling, and you can't know exactly what I am experiencing. So how is it that we can understand each other at all? This is not an academic question. And it's central to personal development and self-mastery.

Has the lack of understanding one another not been responsible for many of the eternal issues between females and males? In modern times, beginning with the suffragette movement of the early 1900s through the women's liberation movement in the 1960s to the current feminist movement, women have made it clear that males tend not to understand the female experience. Likewise, women tend not to understand the male experience. Hence, the eternal conflict between man and woman—and most of it due to lack of transfer—in this case, the transfer of experience.

The problem of understanding each other is an increasingly important one as our society and our workplaces become ethnically diverse. On top of gender, we now have different cultural "minds" and experiences to understand. Many ethnic minorities have maintained that white people can never know what it's like, for example, to be a black person. The assertion implies that whites have nothing in their experience that enables them to understand what it means to be black. Similarly, a male can never know what it's like to be female. If we are to survive, however, we must understand others' experiences. But how do we do this?

The "master" (read: generic) blueprint of understanding others can be found in philosophy. I have always held the belief that within philosophy are to be found the master blueprints of most human issues. Philosophy is a kind of generic language, as it were, that can be transferred to many areas. After all, it's from philosophy that all the modern sciences derived. Being the original science, through the years philosophy has worked out the logic of the problem of understanding the other person more extensively and systematically than have other disciplines like psychology. This blueprint is known as *the problem of other minds*.

Without explaining the details of this blueprint, the essential solution to the problem of understanding others is what philosophers have called *analogies of experience*. Analogies of experience are simply this: I have certain *similar* experiences to yours. Thus, I can understand you by analogy or similarity of experience. When you prick your finger with a pin or experience some other kind of pain, since I am not you, how do I know what you are experiencing? Simple. I have pricked my finger at some time in my life and have experienced pain. I can thus know what you are experiencing—or at least this is the closest I will get to understanding your experience.

Similarly, while I am a white person and have not experienced the oppression that a minority has, I have nevertheless experienced oppression in my life. At least to the degree of my experience, to the degree of my sensitivity, to the degree that I can use my imagination to transfer my experience of oppression, I can understand what it means to be a minority—ethnic or gender. What else do we have but analogies of experience to understand others? It should be clear that the process I am describing here is the transfer of learning. To the extent that we have in common certain cultural, social, group, or family experiences is the extent to which we can understand each other; to the extent that we are sensitive, and have the capacity to transfer, is the extent to which we can understand each other. Sociopathic personalities do not have this transfer capacity to put themselves in another's world. This is why they have no conscience. Sociopaths lack the ability to *generalize* themselves, to transfer or generate analogies of experience.

There is, however, a dangerous downside to analogies of experience—negative transfer. Negative transfer is inappropriately transferring *likenesses* that should not be transferred because they are not in fact the *same*. It's the flip side of positive transfer. No one is *exactly* the same as you. Negative transfer of analogies of experience can lead to serious misunderstanding. My closest, most enduring, and dearest friend is a "black man." We have been friends for over 20 years. While his early childhood experience was that of growing up in a black ghetto, he now holds two doctoral degrees—one in education and one in psychology. In our early professional lives, Aaron and I taught together. We immediately liked each other. We both were interested in psychology, sociology, and philosophy. Since I grew up in a lower socioeconomic white "ghetto," many of our early experiences were also similar.

Having never considered myself prejudiced, and in my inexperience, as well as being the good "liberal," I saw Aaron just as a "human being," not as a black man. Indeed, I saw no "Jews," "Hispanics," or "Asians," only human beings. My mental model was that of a universal humanity—which meant that we are all *the same*. Of course, on one level this is true: We are all human beings. In point of fact, I saw Aaron as a human being *just like* me, with the only *difference* being that he "just happened" to have dark skin. In overtransferring this universal analogy of experience, I was denying Aaron's differences. He is not simply a human being, that is, a "white" human being with dark skin; he is a human being with a different cultural heritage and experience.

Until I understood this difference, I was not only doing Aaron an injustice, but I really didn't understand him. Indeed, each person is a kind of subculture of one. Diversity isn't just something we visually see; it's something that makes us—uniquely—who we are. In all that we do and think, we need to be acutely aware of negative transfer.

TRANSFER METHODS OF "TEAMING WITH TRANSFER"

An analogic team transfer method uses analogies of experience to reveal recurring patterns—archetypes and generic structures—of relationships among group events and interpersonal interactions among its members. There has been considerable research on analogical reasoning showing that when people predict the behavior of other people or the outcome of a social situation, they often use an analogy to a previous experience with individuals or situations.[3] The advantages of adopting what I refer to as an *analogic* transfer method of group learning are considerable.

- It fosters an awareness of the particular group experience as a microcosm of larger groups and as a macrocosm of smaller ones.
- It facilitates the transfer of knowledge learned in a particular situation to other individual and group situations.
- It creates a general attitude of searching for similarities among events and verbal categories.
- By using comparisons, it reduces the psychological distance among seemingly disparate situations and individuals.
- It creates familiarity among events.
- It contributes to the growth of a common bond among members.
- It creates an atmosphere of immediacy and hence relevance when discussing events that have their focus outside the group.
- It helps members see how they are related to each other.

An analogic transfer method is not an entirely new way of doing business. We use implicit (unconscious) comparisons all the time. For example, many of the expectations (often erroneous, or negative transfer) we hold about groups come from "seeing" the group simply *as* a collection of individuals instead of *as* a sovereign unit that is relatively independent of the individuals that make up the group. Being implicit, these unconscious metaphors determine our behavior in the group.

THE TEAM AS MICROCOSM AND MICROWORLD

One of the transfer methods I have developed is viewing the group—and the interaction within it—as a microcosm of the world outside it. The contemporary corporate training term for microcosm is *microworld*. A microworld is a simulation of a real work situation, with the goal being the transfer of what is learned in the microworld to on-the-job performance. In this sense, a microworld is an analogue of the workplace. Taught as a microcosm, the small group becomes a mirror of the larger world that it's a part of and a virtual world of the work group or on-the-job team. Within this microworld, there are a near infinite number of generic and archetypal themes that are similar to the generic and archetypal themes in the larger world outside;[4] in fact, they are the microversions of them, the cognitive equivalents of even more general or generic and archetypal themes (see Chapter 10).

In order to effect transfer from one group situation to another—whether it be a training group or just another similar group situation—we must make transfer linkages between these worlds. In short, making such linkages is what transfer is all about in the world of groups and teams—of seeing the *group as* by using metaphors, parables, and analogies.

Learning about groups must be personally experienced. This is what is meant by experiential learning. Can you imagine learning how to drive a car by simply listening to a lecture or by simply reading about driving a car? Of course not. With experiential learning, you connect past experience with the current situation. You make linkages. Now, much of experiential learning takes place unconsciously, by unconscious comparisons from experiences in memory (see Chapter 11). In so doing, we emotionally and intellectually *resonate* to our past group experiences; that is, we make deep-learning connections to our past experiences and transfer them to the present. These connections are what I term *analogic transfer.*[5]

THE TEAM AS A SOVEREIGN UNIT

Largely because of a rugged individualist view of ourselves, we tend to see groups as just a collection of individuals. Most American psychologists—being socialized into the rugged individualist view—also see the group as simply a bunch of individuals. Most European psychologists and sociologists understand that a group is a unit in and of itself. Until we understand this, we will not function well in groups. A typical response to this "group as sovereign unit" view is: How can a group be more than the individuals in it? The answer can be explained as follows. In the natural world, there is the individual element hydrogen (H) and the individual element oxygen (O). When we put them together, we have water—H_2O—something that resembles neither hydrogen nor oxygen. Similarly, our bodies are made up of individual cells, but what we call a human being is more than a collection or heap of cells that simply get added up into a person. In both cases, it's the *organization* of the separate elements that creates a new level of reality. The same is true for groups: H_3O (H = humans, 3 =

people, + O = organization, = group). As body, we are not just a bunch of cells; we are cells that have been organized in a particular way.

As a sovereign unit, we must now understand that groups have developmental stages. To use an analogy of an "individual" human, groups have a childhood, an adolescence, an adulthood, and an old age, and they die. Unfortunately, we all too often see a newly formed group as an adult when organizationally it is a child. It seems to make sense to us because, after all, everyone in the group is an adult. But our implicit metaphors are incorrect. We have incorrectly transferred our knowledge to the group; we have engaged in negative transfer.

What makes a group? Issuing from our rugged individualist view, American psychologists—and most everyone else—answer, "Two or more people." From a true group perspective, however, the answer is "Three people." Why three? The answer is that only when we have three people do we then have the possibility of a coalition. Two people are simply two people, a pair, a couple, a dyad. On some level, we have always understood this. That is why individuals relating with another have always known that "three's a crowd." If we are to be successful as a group—either a small one/team or a big one/corporation—we must understand the sovereign nature of groups.

THE FAMILY ARCHETYPE AND THE CORPORATE TEAM

It is often useful for understanding a group to use a mental model of a family and ask the transfer question: How is a group like a family? In applying or transferring what we know about family behavior to a small group or to a corporation, we will find recurring group patterns, generic structures, and archetypes. This should not be a surprise. The family is, after all, the original or protogroup, the primal matrix out of which we initially acquire our mental models about others.

It's nearly cliché for corporate leaders to characterize the organization with the metaphor of a family; to say, "We are like a family here, so we must stick together." The assumption behind the metaphor, of course, is of a "good" family. But is it? There are differing family communication styles and interaction patterns, with some healthy and some not. These differing metaphors of the family might be examined. For instance, some families give members who behave inappropriately the "silent" treatment; it might be explored if members are relating to specific individuals in the group as they relate to members of their family. In addition, a group member may be reacting to other group members in terms of rivalry, say, a sibling or parental rivalry.

It might also be explored if members have feelings toward the group as a whole that are *similar* to feelings toward their family, such as feelings that the group demands too much of them, imposes too many rules, is overprotective, has to "prove" himself or herself, or simply places too many demands on one's time. Using Freudian terminology, the mental structures called superego, ego, and id can be applied to a group or to an entire corporation. In Freudian terms, a group's or a corporation's superego is its conscience, that is, its value system; its ego is its conscious sense of self, that is, its resources and its style of doing business; its id is its primitive unconscious impulses, that is, its implicit assumptions, folklore, and unrecognized feelings that unconsciously influence conscious or formal organizational behavior.

Using this family model, romantic affairs in the workplace are equivalent to family incest, with all of the ensuing problems and behaviors including denial of the problems. It's in the family that we learn our first—and often lasting—social lessons about authority, power, jealousy, rivalry, and peer relationships that we bring with us to corporate life. Using a family model, corporate acquisitions are *like* marriages, and corporate mergers *are like* modern two-family (re)marriages where the "kids" from both families must learn to become one new family. What we know about each of these two parts of the family analogy can help us understand the other. There is knowledge of the merged family that can be applied to the corporation and knowledge of the corporate merger that can be useful in understanding the merged family.

Family life and the myriad of classic archetypes seem to be eternal generic structures of social life. Archetypes of eternal family behaviors are to be found in the classic Greek myths and in the Christian Bible. Most people in Western culture are familiar with the Greek story of Oedipus, who killed his father and married his mother, or with the biblical stories of Cain and Abel. In more modern vernacular, the (overused) term *dysfunctional* family has become a kind of archetype or mental model for seeing contemporary families and has been repeatedly applied (none too rigorously) not only to describe corporate life but to describe our entire society. The family model applied to corporate life may explain why different personalities are attracted to or repelled by different companies' management styles: They *remind* them of (are like) their early family styles.

Using the family as a model of organizational life is not a mere analogy. In General Systems terminology (see Chapter 10), they are isomorphic structures—general "laws" that are a part of certain kinds of systems, whether they are family systems, small groups and teams, or organizational systems. Thinking in these terms reduces the load on one's memory by creating patterns and categories that are all related in some way. It is leveraged learning. But most of all, perhaps, thinking in these terms leads to understanding and to insights into, between, and among small-group, team, and corporate events.

Like others before me, in conducting groups for years, it has become clear that members of a group fall into generic patterns of behaviors that constitute archetypal roles. Each time I conduct a group, though I may never have had any of the members in a group before, I soon recognize the archetypal role each will be playing and can often predict each member's behavior. Certainly, each member brings a certain uniqueness to the archetype, but it remains an archetype, nevertheless. There are heroes and heroines, mediators, instigators, the silent member, the stud, the sex kitten, the good child, and the scapegoat. Ah, yes! Always a scapegoat, always. The scapegoat is one of the most enduring archetypes in human behavior, from the prototypical family group to the modern corporation. Observing such archetypes and group dynamics has become like watching a continuous "rerun" of a movie, over and over, with different actors bringing their unique personalities to the archetypal role.

A COMMON GROUP TRAGEDY

An archetype that Peter Senge describes and one that I have used in my social psychology classes for years is the tragedy of the commons.[6] Garrett Hardin, a biologist, explained the extinction of many old English pasturelands used by herdsmen for grazing their livestock. Herdsmen could use the commons for all their livestock. It was called a commons because the land was not owned by any individual. As the population of herdsmen and their livestock increased, the commons became overgrazed and turned arid. It became overgrazed because there were no group rules for its use. The herdsmen would not create rules; they saw it as their inalienable right to make use of the commons as they saw fit. Because each individual used the commons for short-run gain, they lost collectively. We all lose in the commons scenario.

This is not just a story specifically about an old English commons grazing land; it's a generic story, an archetype, a transfer story, a powerful model of small-group functioning. This archetype has been played out—has recurred again and again—all over the world. By transfer thinking, we can see the *same* dynamics occurring with other "commons" like air, water, oil, forestation, and other natural resources. The plot remains the same; only the characters change.

The archetypal dilemma exemplified by the tragedy of the commons is the individual versus the group, and the solution to such dilemmas is often counterintuitive. Because our Western mental model of individualism tends to see the causes of events as residing in autonomous individual action, we seek individual solutions to social problems like the commons. In the commons, or in individual units of a corporation, it will do little good to appeal to the moral integrity of the individual not to graze so many livestock, or not to be so concerned with the department or division unit's monthly bottom line, when the reward structure reinforces individualistic and short-run behavior. People generally act in their self-interest. The simple solution, then, is to change the reward structure to reinforce long-term and group interests. If we think we are in environmental trouble now, think what our situation would be like if we had not passed environmental "commons laws."

Corporations have their commons, too. They are finances, intellectual capital, customers, and morale. In fact, each corporation is itself a commons. "Individual" may also mean the individual unit of a corporation, where each unit operates on the basis of its short-run interest at the expense of the entire corporation. The essential moral of this archetypal or transfer story is an individual, administrative department, or an entire corporation "doing their own thing" for short-run profit at the eventual expense of the long-run benefit of the group, team, or stockholders.

SPECIFICALLY APPLYING TRANSFER OF EXPERIENCE

In teaching and conducting small group, analogies of experience have occasionally been used as a technique. For instance, if members are receiving negative reactions from the group regarding their style of interaction, it's frequently pointed out to them that possibly their behavior outside the group is similar and causes similar reactions by others in their everyday lives. This transfer approach to learning about groups and teams has not been raised to the level of a general method.

Before the goal of teaching with analogies of experience is implemented, however, a systematic method should be formulated, a methodology that provides a clear plan for the consistent use of the parallels. Unless analogies of experience are used systematically and consistently, along with being clearly and explicitly formulated as a method of transfer, I doubt if a significant amount of transfer will occur. More important, a significant amount of negative transfer may occur. Caution should be exercised when using such analogies of experience, however. Transfer always involves interpretation, and certain parallels in certain conditions may not be appropriate. For example, although we may find it useful to view a corporation as a family, corporations should not perhaps be expected to operate as a family, just as the military should not function as a democracy.

Interindividual transfers of experience. Interindividual analogies of experience are parallels that can be drawn between or among members of the group or persons whom members know outside of the group. Within the group, for example, John may react to the authority figure in the group in the same manner as Jill. In terms of similarities to persons outside the group, Marilyn may explore how her behavior in the group may be similar to persons outside the group with whom she has difficulties interacting. Or, again, within the group, John may be seen as evidencing similar defensive behaviors as Jill when a certain value or an analogous set of values is threatened. Interindividual analogies are used to facilitate members seeing the nature of their relationships to others. Frequently, members cannot see their own selves clearly until their characteristics are pointed out in others.

Intraindividual transfers of experience. Intraindividual analogies of experience compare an individual's behavior in a specific instance with other similar instances, thus discovering patterns of behavior that manifest themselves in analogous situations. For example, it may be pointed out to a member that he or she responds similarly to different instances of feedback regarding his or her behavior. Members may frequently rationalize their behavior instead of seriously considering the possibility that the perceptions of others may be correct. Perhaps members react analogously to persons of high status in the group in the same manner as they react to authority figures in general. Through intraindividual analogies, then, members come to see specific instances of their behavior as related to other instances.

Intergroup transfers of experience. Intergroup analogies of experience are similarities that can be drawn between the specific group and other (outside) groups. For instance, analogies might be pointed out between the dynamics of the small group and a family, a nation, a committee, or a work group in another department of the company. One such dynamic might be the situation of a new member entering the group who threateningly questions the value of the group. It can be pointed out that the response of the group when it reacts in concert to the new member in order to defend itself is similar to the response of other groups, say, a family, when it's threatened by an outsider. Transfers of experience facilitate discovering patterns of behavior that manifest themselves in analogous situations.

MENTAL MODELS, SMALL-GROUP TRANSFER DYNAMICS, AND ORGANIZATIONAL CHANGE

As organizations flatten their hierarchies, as they become more learning oriented, as they increasingly work in groups and cross-functional teams made up of members from different parts of the organization, transfer and mental models become more important as a tool for understanding and communicating with others. This is also true with increasing electronic communication via computer networks and e-mail, both within and external to the organization. Such communication requires us to understand in a more diverse manner. To understand a person's mental model is to be able to map (i.e., transfer) one's own mental model onto the mental models of others. Briefly, a *mental model* is a kind of road map that we have in our heads about how something works, the world, a person, a task (see Chapter 9).

If we work by ourselves, we don't need to understand the mental models that others have in their heads. But working in groups and teams requires more variety in our mental models. A few years ago, I was involved in organizational change. I was appointed the head of an academic department that had stagnated and was in need of development. I will briefly describe my transfer of mental models in bringing about change in the department (I have described this process in more detail elsewhere).[7]

The department was a ten-member multidisciplinary academic department. Such a department can be considered a small group, and the chairperson, the group leader. The group was primarily composed of counseling psychology, social psychology, child psychology, and sociology. Being a multidisciplinary department, I viewed the department as composed of multiple mental models, with each discipline being a model of reality that shaped people's behavior. Departments within organizations, academic or otherwise, are institutionalized mental models. For example, an accounting department's mental model of an organization is quite different from a research and development department's mental model.

The basic mental model of human behavior of American psychology is that of individualism. For most psychologists, only individuals are "real," with groups and teams simply being an abstraction. For the clinical or counseling psychologist, the typical mental model of the human organism involves a humanistic free will philosophy. For sociology (à la Émile Durkheim and/or Herbert Spencer), groups are as real as are individuals. For sociology, groups shape individual behavior. The department was dominated by the psychological/counseling model. In part, I saw my task as reframing and linking the various mental models to bring about change.

Being primarily a social psychologist, my mental model was closer in certain respects to the sociologist's than the counseling psychologists'. What I wanted to do was forge a merger between the psychological and sociological models and create a new curriculum reflecting both models. Typically, people's mental models are superimposed on their span of influence. For example, the psychological, individualistic model was extended beyond the individual to the departmental structure. The department as a unit of analysis separate from the individual did not in effect exist for most department members: Only department members were "real"; hence, the department business was conducted on the premise that it was simply a bunch of individuals. Administratively and procedurally the department hardly existed.

In addition to using an interpersonal relations model, I used a macro-model (organizational level) to analyze the department as a small group. This included analyzing and being aware of

1. the history of the department,

2. department norms and values,

3. roles and status,

4. department reward and procedural systems,

5. the department as an integral subsystem within a larger institutional system,

6. the need to establish an "authority" structure,

7. the fact that authority was not merely invested in the individual who was chair but had to be socially and structurally transferred to the position, and

8. the group as a unit.

It may be difficult for nonacademics to understand, but the preferred communication model of most academics is a written-word model, not face-to-face interaction. The printed word seems to communicate much more to an academic than verbal communication.

In keeping with this model, rather than institute a group discussion around the changes I wanted to make, I first sent book chapters and journal articles to the faculty. This strategy also averted a status problem, that of confronting a peer as their supervisor, and thus served as a face-saving strategy. I selected journal articles and chapters from books that were of three types, with each type exemplifying the three operating models: (1) articles from psychology journals analyzing the traditional individualism model in psychology; (2) articles from psychology journals and book chapters linking the individualistic counseling model to social psychology findings; and (3) articles from sociological journals that reflected the macro/sociological model.

Because of my social psychology background, the first linkage I made in the department was to the sociologist. I initiated informal discussions with him. For years, he had been the only sociologist in a predominantly psychological department. As a consequence, he had come to adopt this more individualistic psychological model. Fairly quickly he began to make the transition back to his professional macrosociological model. Having both a B.A. and an M.A. in an interdisciplinary major between psychology and sociology, and having taught sociology years before, I was able to speak the sociologist's language.

I initiated a second linkage by informal talks with one of the newest psychologists who taught human development. In the course of these discussions, I learned he favored the Urie Bronfenbrenner ecological model of human development instead of the more traditional individualism model. This model includes a more systems and social model view of human development. Eventually, the sociologist and this faculty member became clear, yet cautious, allies.

During subsequent meetings with the faculty, I reframed and mapped objections to the new curriculum model onto the psychological model. For example, I pointed out that individualistic/humanistic values were in fact shown to be better served by the new model. In response to an objection that the commitment to student counseling skills was being violated by the sociological model, I suggested that the individual model trained students simply to repair the damage done to individuals by the social conditions and that individualistic counseling skills did nothing preventative in terms of future psychological harm to individuals.

The psychologists maintained that in the interests of individual integrity and free will, the students should be free to choose their curricula. I reframed this objection into the new model by suggesting that since the students had been socialized in an individualistic pop-psychology-oriented society, it was in fact largely society that was making the choice of becoming counselors, and that the new model would increase their free (willed) choice. Gradually, the department cautiously adopted—in principle—the merging of the psychological and sociological curricula.

There was then a move to construct the new curriculum before the two new faculty that had been allocated for the new model were hired. I indicated that this was not appropriate as we did not have the expertise. They disagreed. I suggested that not yet having the two new faculty on board with the expertise and appropriate information base to construct the new curriculum model was *like* males constructing a curriculum for women's studies. Since most of the male and female faculty were pro women's studies, this reframing into a gender model seemed to make sense to them.

The actual change process was, of course, much more complicated than this brief account, but the point is the use of mental models in thinking, their use in organizations and in organizational change, and the importance of a broad knowledge base providing the necessary requisite variety and mental models for managing interpersonal and organizational systems.

POSTSCRIPT: A CAUTIONARY TRANSFER TALE

With all of the current focus on teams, it's generally taken for granted that performance of groups and teams is superior to individual performance and learning. I am reminded here of the joke that says a group could probably have come up with Einstein's famous relativity theory—but Einstein would have to have been *a member* of the group. It's also widely assumed that whatever is learned in the group transfers to situations outside the group. Does it?

This is a simple enough question, but its answer is complex. As early as 1965, Henry Ellis, in his classic book *The Transfer of Learning*, pointed out that the automatic assumption that "skills acquired in group activity will necessarily transfer to the individual situation is unwarranted."[8] He cited research showing that often what individuals learn *in a group* and what is learned *as a group* may not be transferred by individuals outside the confines of the group. Later research suggests that learning in a group may be beneficial but not significantly so.[9] Still later research again suggested that group learning may not always be better than individual learning.[10] More recently, another study found that group learning may not transfer to individual learning.[11]

While a number of reasons may be involved in the failure to transfer a group or team learning experience, the point is that we need to pay much more attention to group and team transfer, especially when current findings are suggesting diminishing returns on many group and cross-functional teamwork situations owing to the increased organization, coordination, and communication costs of working as a team.[12]

The moral of this cautionary tale is that we need to be careful not to think that teams are the quick answer to organizational problems. The human resource literature with its many anecdotal tales of the wisdom of teams is nearly legendary. Very little of it, however, is based on solid evidence (see Chapter 1).

NOTES

1. P. M. Senge, *The Fifth Discipline: The Art and Practice of the Learning Organization* (New York: Doubleday, 1990), p. 238.

2. In T. Stewart, "Brainpower," *Fortune* (June 3, 1991), p. 44.

3. S. J. Read, "Analogical Reasoning in Social Judgement: The Importance of Causal Theories," *Journal of Personality and Social Psychology* 46 (1984), pp. 14–25; S. J. Read, "Once Is Enough: Causal Reasoning from a Single Instance," *Journal of Personality and Social Psychology* 45 (1983), pp. 323–334.

4. See, for example, P. Slater, *Microcosm: Structural, Psychological and Religious Evolution in Groups* (New York: John Wiley, 1966).

5. R. E. Haskell, "An Analogical Methodology for the Analysis and Validation of Anomalous Cognitive and Linguistic Operations in Small Group (Fantasy Theme) Reports," *Small Group Research, an International Journal of Theory, Investigation and Application* 22 (1991), pp. 443–474.

6. G. Hardin, "The Tragedy of the Commons," *Science* 162 (1968), pp. 1243–1248.

7. See R. E. Haskell, "Small Group Dynamics, Mental Models and Chairing the Academic Department" (*proceedings of the Seventh Annual Conference on Academic Chairpersons*, Kansas State University, National Issues in Higher Education, 1990), pp. 169–178.

8. H. C. Ellis, *The Transfer of Learning* (New York: Macmillan, 1965), p. 68.

9. L. M. Huckabay, P. G. Cooper, and M. C. Neal, "Effect of Specific Teaching Techniques on Cognitive Learning, Transfer of Learning, and Affective Behavior of Nurses in an In-service Education Setting," *Nursing Research* 26 (1977), pp. 380–385.

10. B. A. McDonald, C. O. Larson, and D. F., Dansereau, "Cooperative Dyads: Impact on Text Learning and Transfer," *Contemporary Educational Psychology* 10 (1985), pp. 369–377.

11. J. G. Lambiotte, D. F. Dansereau, T. R. Rocklin, B. Fletcher, V. I. Hy-

thecker, C. O. Larson, and A. M. O'Donnell, "Cooperative Learning and Task Taking: Transfer of Skills," *Contemporary Educational Psychology* 12 (1987), pp. 52–61.

12. B. Dumaine, "The Trouble with Teams," *Fortune* (September 5, 1994).

6

Product Development, Technological, and Defense Conversion: Illustrating the Economics of Analogical Transfer

The thing that hath been, it is that which shall be; and that which is done is that which shall be done; and there is no new thing under the sun.

Ecclesiastes 1:9

If it's true that American business has a declining rate of innovation in many areas, then as Ray Stata, CEO of Analog Devices, says, "The challenge lies in better understanding innovation and in determining how to do more of it."[1] The general product of intellectual capital is innovation. More specifically, it *is* the basis of product development, technological and defense conversion, and invention, all of which mean increased productivity and profits. Transfer is about how to do more of all of these. The bottom line of transfer is the bottom line.

The psychology of invention or innovation, then, is of crucial concern for today's business and industrial organizations. In this chapter, I'll illustrate the use and economic importance of the ability to engage in transfer thinking with examples from product development, invention, technological, and defense conversion. The thinking involved in all of them is essentially the same. Where one draws the line between them is largely arbitrary. Engaging in transfer thinking himself, Donald Schon of the Massachusetts Institute of Technology, a pioneer in industrial consulting, recognized that the process of product development and invention are the *same* process "as they occur in industry; that the two kinds of development can be seen as embodiments of a single underlying process, which I call the displacement of concepts."[2] The displacement of concepts is transfer thinking. Again,

different terms are used to describe the same—or at least very similar—
processes. Whatever the name, from product development, invention, technological, and defense conversion, the game is the same: It's called transfer
thinking.

Historian George Basalla in his book *The Evolution of Technology* contends, "Any new thing that appears in the made world is based on some
object already in existence."[3] Despite the crucial significance of transfer
thinking in product development, invention, technological, and defense
conversion, it has not received a great deal of attention. Moreover, in reading accounts of these processes, little attempt is made to examine the actual
thinking processes of the person who developed the product or created the
invention. Historically, part of the reason for this neglect is that the creative
or discovery process was thought to be mysterious and complex and
therefore unexplainable. Another reason is that the discovery process has
been seen as the consequence of organizational or cultural factors (see below). Whatever the ultimate answer to the apparent mystery of creativity,
I'll demonstrate that transfer thinking is central to it. It's thus important
for learners to see transfer thinking in action, for as I've noted, one of the
best ways to instruct people about transfer thinking is to read examples of
transfer. Throughout this book, I've given examples of transfer thinking.
This chapter, however, will highlight transfer thinking in its various forms
by using analogies.

DEFENSE AND ECONOMIC CONVERSION

With the closing of many commercial and military defense industries,
there's a need to transform or reengineer them into civilian uses. Further,
with the increasing competitive globalization of business, along with the
trend toward corporate downsizing, comes an increased need to innovate
and convert individual job skills, specific technologies, and entire organizations to *new* uses. Technological, economic, and defense conversion refers to finding new "applications" for these businesses and industries;
conversion refers to transferring the knowledge and skills that these organizations have to new applications and economic markets. Conversion
means finding new but *similar* applications for industries.

A conceptually trivial example of defense conversion (transfer) is con-
verting military shipbuilding into commercial shipbuilding. This involves
analyzing what shipbuilding skills can be converted to the production of
other industrial products. Conversion, then, requires the psychological skill
of extending knowledge beyond its original use. While this is a trivial example from the perspective of transfer thinking because there are more
obvious similarities than differences, it's not financially trivial.

Technology transfer, then, is more than the simple exporting of knowledge from one physical place to another, as from one country to another,

or from academia to business; rather, technology transfer opens new uses for skills and techniques in organizations. The need for economic, industrial, or defense conversion is not a new problem. It occurred on a smaller scale during the 1970s when the aerospace industry declined and many highly skilled personnel had to find new "related" occupations. Conversions have been ongoing in many industries. NASA, for example, has continued to find civilian applications for its innovative space technologies.

There are four facets to this challenge: (1) to understand what conversion is; (2) to understand what psychological processes make conversion possible; (3) to recognize the need to acquire and develop conversion skills; and (4) to institute the management of innovation, that is, creating organizational procedures, policies, and support systems that foster innovation.

Government funding contributed an initial $500+ million in a Technology Reinvestment Project (TRP) to support the first year of conversion research. No small matter. The question is, What does it take to accomplish these activities successfully? The answer, as you may have surmised by now, is transfer of learning.

Transferring weapons into plowshares. Through transfer thinking, weapons are being beaten into plowshares. A farming products company was looking for a method to plant seeds at precisely the same distance apart.[4] How did the company solve this problem? Here's a hint: The solution has to do with a machine gun. Have you solved it yet? (If not, see note 5.)[5] But there remained another problem. The problem was what to do with the material the seeds were planted in after they had germinated. How was this problem solved? (See note 6.)[6]

Ballistic X-rays. On a more heavenly plane, what do mammography and a digital imaging technology developed for ballistic missile systems have in common? The answer is: Digital imaging technology developed for detecting imperfections in bombs and missiles is being applied (transferred) to mammography. The Lawrence Livermore Laboratory nuclear research facility is working with Fisher Imaging to develop a digital mammography device that will produce pictures of women's breasts that are clearer and that use less radiation than standard procedures.[7]

Ballistic missiles and eyeballs. What does a ballistic missile defense system have to do with removing a tumor from a person's eye or correcting the shape of the cornea of the eye? For the millions of us who must wear eyeglasses, laser surgery may soon be able to correct our vision by changing the shape of the cornea. But there is a problem that precludes this laser operation: The eye will not remain stationary. No matter how hard we try, our eyes are constantly making small, rapid, almost imperceptible jumping movements that fixate from point to point. This is called saccadic movement. Without the ability to compensate for this involuntary motion, a laser is not able to perform the delicate operation to change the shape of the cornea.

Consider what a ballistic missile defense system does. First, the system must detect a missile in a cluttered background of clouds, earth, and numerous decoy missiles; then the system must track the missile, direct an interceptor at the target, and destroy it. Now consider what a doctor must do to remove a tumor or change the shape of a cornea. First, the doctor must detect the tumor in a background of healthy tissue, then precisely detect the location and size of the tumor and remove it without harming the surrounding healthy tissue. In the case of the cornea, the surgeon must aim precisely at a specific location of an irregularly moving eye. The two processes are very similar.

In responding to this medical need, Autonomous Technologies Corporation of Orlando, Florida, is adapting object detection and ranging technology originally used in missile targeting and in space docking systems to track saccadic eye movements so that tumor and corneal operations can be accomplished. Thus, destroying a ballistic missile and operating on the eye require similar technologies. A surgeon engages in a search-and-destroy mission just as a national defense system does.[8] Sound like science fiction? Or, with hindsight, does this similarity sound obvious?

Such transfer thinking not only benefits individual people who have medical problems; it creates jobs. Not all transfers are as psychologically dramatic as this one. I say dramatic, as I consider this example to be a case of far transfer. Other cases, while closer to near transfer, are, nevertheless, as dramatic in financial and other effects.

Outersight. What do satellite-based remote sensing techniques based on scanners that record the visible and near-infrared light developed by NASA have to do with growing grapes? Answer: NASA-developed remote sensing scanners are being transferred (applied) to the early detection of grapevine "stress." Wine growers in California were experiencing a serious crisis of grapevine infestation by the phylloxera aphid, a root louse that kills grapevines by sucking the juice from the plants' roots. It takes two to three years before the above-ground part begins to show visible signs of sickness. By that time the infestation may have spread too far. Pesticides are ineffective because they penetrate only three to five feet below the surface, and phylloxera aphids live ten to twelve feet underground.

The only way to remedy is to replant with phylloxera-resistant roots. Replanting costs about $20,000 an acre—but the overall cost can be reduced substantially if remote sensing can detect infestation early. A program called "Grapes" is employing a multisensory, multiscale approach to measure several early indicators of plant disease. Scanners record the visible and near-infrared light from grapevine leaves to detect early nutrient deficiencies that would not be apparent by visual inspection until it was too late. Thermal scanners also record minute differences in grapevine temperatures. These differences are indicators of plant health. Stressed plants are warmer because they cannot pass water through their membranes effectively.

Satellite and aircraft-based imagery, used in combination with a computerized database, will provide an overview of the how, the where, and the why phylloxera spreads. This overview will lead to development of "risk maps" enabling wine growers to better manage the replanting process. The cost of the "Grapes" program is $350,000 a year. It's being shared by NASA's Office of Advanced Concepts and Technology and Robert Mondavi Winery. Mondavi, which plans continued use of the technology, will make the results of the study available to other wine growers.[9]

Outer space suits for earthly matters. What does a spacesuit undergarment developed for cooling astronauts on the surface of the moon or during extravehicular forays outside a spacecraft or space station have in common with multiple sclerosis, helicopter pilot helmets, and hypohidrotic ectodermal dysplasia? Multiple sclerosis (MS) is a chronic, progressively disabling disease of the central nervous system; it is a wasting of the nerves, caused by loss of a substance known as myelin. MS can affect vision, manual dexterity, balance and sensation, and thought processes. Myelin forms a coating around nerves like insulation around a wire. The myelin insulation allows signals to be conducted throughout the nervous system; conversely, its absence inhibits the efficient functioning of the nervous system.

Over 30 years ago it was discovered that body cooling can produce improvement in MS symptoms. Studies have shown that nerve conduction can be restored temporarily to demyelinated nerves by cooling the body's core temperature only one degree Fahrenheit. Physicians have for some time used cold showers, pools, and air conditioning to lower the body temperatures of MS patients. The treatment is sometimes useful, but it has many drawbacks. So the answer to this question is that MS patients are now benefiting from a "cool suit" originally developed for space travel. It's not a cure, nor does it help all MS patients.

The suit is more formally known as the Mark VTI Micro Climate Medical Personal Cooling System. It's made by Life Support Systems, Inc. (LSSI), Mountain View, California, a NASA spin-off company. The suit is being used to treat symptoms of MS and other illnesses where temperature regulation can be helpful, such as in hypohidrotic ectodermal dysplasia. People with this condition are born without sweat glands and cannot maintain a constant body temperature. The transfer of this space technology has been used to develop a liquid-cooled helmet liner for helicopter pilots and for a self-contained cooling system for mine rescue work.[10]

INTERNAL VERSUS EXTERNAL CONVERSION

As Eric Pages has argued persuasively, there are two basic approaches to conversion within the $500+ million initial Technology Reinvestment Project support program: internal and external conversion.[11] Internal conversion involves utilizing existing defense technologies and converting or finding civilian uses for them. According to Pages, this is the classic "dual-use" strategy. It is the most common approach; it is also apparently the only strategy directly supported by federal conversion programs like the current TRP program. External conversion involves the promotion of technological innovation and entrepreneurship, for example, creating new start-up companies and the support for new firms that spin off from larger defense firms by commercializing defense-related research. While Pages clearly comes down on the side of external conversion, I would suggest that on a more fundamental level, internal and external conversion are not in opposition but conjoined, by transfer-of-knowledge skills. While transfer of knowledge is perhaps more clearly evident in internal conversion, it also undergirds external conversion. Internal conversion must occur before entire companies can be created.

CORPORATE AND TECHNOLOGICAL CONVERSION

A solution was the solution. Consider the problem encountered in the days before solid fuels for space travel were developed: How do you get liquid fuel to feed into a spacecraft engine under conditions of weightlessness? Here is a hint (see note 12).[12] Can you solve the problem now? If not, here is another hint (see note 13).[13] Do you have it now?[14]

The transfer-based solution has since been further generalized to other fluids, now called ferrofluids. These ferrofluids are responsible for rotary feedthrough seals for the semiconductor industry and other sealing systems for contamination-sensitive applications, such as computer disc drives, halogen lamps, and medical X-ray equipment. Still other products include hydrodynamic bearings, a high-performance alternative to mechanical bearings, and inertial dampers for such applications as plotters, printers, optical scanners, machine tools, medical equipment, fully automated crystal growing systems, and fluids for home and automotive loudspeakers.

Ferrofluidics Corporation of Nashua, New Hampshire, a NASA spin-off company, has taken an obscure idea originally developed for use in space and made itself the world's leader in ferrofluid technology. It has grown from a tiny firm that had $65,000 in sales during its first year into a $30 million a year company with subsidiaries in Europe, Japan, and Taiwan. Constantly developing new applications, Ferrofluidics is now ranked among *International Business Magazine*'s list of the 100 fastest-growing U.S. firms. Analysts believe that sales will top the $100 million level before the end of the decade. It's thought that the ferrofluid environmental seal alone can generate $100 million a year in sales within the next five years. The Ferrofluidics story is one of the top classics in the history of aerospace technology transfer. But this is not the final "moral" of this transfer story.

The final moral of this transfer story has to do with the importance or usefulness of useless knowledge that I spoke of in Chapter 8. It seems that just when the NASA scientist solved the problem of how to get liquid fuel into a rocket engine under weightless conditions by inventing ferrofuel, solid rocket fuel was invented, rendering this ingenious piece of transfer thinking "useless." The idea laid around for a few years until it was picked up again at Avco Space Systems Division as a possible solution to controlling the temperature in an orbiting spacecraft.

Again, however, it was shelved in favor of another solution, once more rendering it a piece of useless knowledge. Later, two Avco scientists, Dr. Ronald Moskowitz and Dr. Ronald Rosensweig, recognized great potential in ferrofluids. They formed Ferrofluidics Corporation in 1968. The rest is history.[15]

Bold bolts. Erie Bolt Corporation was about to go bankrupt when a new CEO was hired who thought in terms of generic structures. Rather than asking how Erie Bolt could make better bolts, he asked a more generic question: What business was Erie Bolt in? His answer was that the company was not simply one that made bolts but one that (1) forged metal, (2) heat-treated metal, (3) did the machining of metal, and (4) performed other metalworking functions. When Erie Bolt was *seen as* not just a manufacturer of bolts, it could then reengineer and reinvent itself by transferring its new-found knowledge into new products (see Chapter 10).[16]

Mapping expertise. Yet another simple example of transferring existing company knowledge that I illustrated in Chapter 2 that's similar to the Erie Bolt example was of a company that had the know-how to drill minute holes in ultrathin plastic rings for fiber-optic connectors. While the company was successful, they wanted to grow in a market that was only so large. So what was it to do? The company brought in a consultant with expertise in "mapping" the company's assets. Mapping is a skill that's part of transfer of knowledge and involves comparing two things systematically. In this case, it was the comparing of microdrilling skills in the fiber-optic industry with possible microdrilling needs in other industries.

In mapping the company's skills the consultant "saw" that its microdrilling expertise in fiber-optic connectors could be transferred to drilling connectors for fine copper wiring systems. This transfer required a person who had the knowledge base and the transfer ability to be able to make this mental connection. Although I consider this transfer to be only a minor case, its payoff was nevertheless of major financial benefit to the company.[17]

With hindsight, of course, such simple examples may seem obvious. Once a transfer is recognized, it often appears simple, even childlike. This is the deceptive nature of transfer of knowledge. The fact is, however, that most people become mentally stuck in the details, stuck in the concrete content area of their knowledge, and are not able to see different applications for the same knowledge or to see in a different way. Psychologists call this "functional fixedness."

The color of energy. Another example is the development of tetraethyl lead. Speculating on why kerosene made engines knock worse than gasoline, it was reasoned that it might be because kerosene did not vaporize as easily as gasoline. It was recalled that the wild flower trailing arbutus, with its red-backed leaves, blooms early in spring, even when it's under the snow. It was then reasoned that if kerosene were dyed red, it might—like the leaves of the trailing arbutus—absorb heat faster and thus vaporize quickly enough to burn in an engine like gasoline.[18] It worked. No small financial matter.

Many transfer connections are possible for any given invention. Two of the ingredients that were obviously required to transfer the trailing arbutus were knowledge of the flower and knowledge that darker colors absorb radiant heat more than lighter colors. Who would have this kind of knowledge? Although I have some knowledge of color and the absorption of heat, my knowledge base does not contain the trailing arbutus. So someone like myself would not have been capable of making this exact transfer. However, unlike the knowledge about heat absorption and color, knowledge of the trailing arbutus is not necessary to solve the kerosene problem. There are many other transfer connections or analogies that could have made possible the connection with color. Thus, while knowledge of the relationship between heat absorption and color comes from an "everyday" knowledge base that most people possess and is most likely necessary to this analogical connection, the knowledge of the trailing arbutus is not part of most people's repertoire. Perhaps the person who made this connection grew flowers as a hobby, or perhaps he or she just had this piece of information in his or her "useless knowledge" file (see Chapter 8).

Potato leaves. Now consider the following problem of potato chip manufacture: Bags of potato chips take up considerable space on store shelves when they are packed loosely, and they crumble when they are packed in smaller packages. One manufacturer found a solution to this problem by using transfer thinking. Ask yourself, What object in nature is like a potato chip? What about dried leaves as an answer? Dried leaves crumble very easily and are bulky. Now what about pressed leaves? They're flat. Could potato chips somehow be shipped flat, or nearly flat, the manufacturer asked? The problem of crumbling remained, however. Then the manufacturer realized that pressed leaves are not pressed while they are dry but rather while they are still damp. It was then determined that if potato chips were shipped in a stack, and were moist enough not to crumble yet sufficiently dry to be flat, or nearly flat, the problem was solved. It was. You guessed it: The result was Pringle's potato chips.[19]

Of football passes and satellite orbits. Did you ever wonder why football quarterbacks spiral their passes and navy guns spin their shells? In 1964, Harold Rosen, an electrical engineer, did. And his curiosity resulted in the invention of the geosynchronous satellite that today provides communication links for everything from television to lifesaving medical information being globally transmitted instantaneously. The key to satellite communications is a satellite that can remain in a fixed, nondeviating orbit relative to the earth. This was the problem. The geosynchronous satellite is a satellite whose orbit around the earth is synchronized with the earth's rotation. While the development of the first geosynchronous satellite required a team of people, the invention of a stabilized satellite came from the mind of Harold A. Rosen, who later served as a vice president of engineering for the Space and Communications Group of Hughes Aircraft.

Around 1957, after Russia launched Sputnik—and the United States realized we were technologically behind the Russians—Rosen and his colleagues began thinking about communications satellites. Others had been thinking about satellites, and the idea of a geosynchronous satellite was not new. As early as 1945, the well-known science fiction writer Arthur C. Clark outlined the benefits of a geosynchronous communications satellite. In hindsight, Rosen's solution for the geosynchronous satellite was quite simple: to have the satellite spin constantly to maintain a nondeviating orbit.

Rosen recalls the origins of his solution. In a physics class at the California Institute of Technology, he had Nobel Prize–winning professor Carl Anderson, who had discovered the positron. When studying dynamics, he asked Anderson if he could explain in simple language the effectiveness of the spin in the stabilization of objects such as footballs in a spiral pass and the trajectory curve of shells coming out of a big gun with rifling in it. He did. And Rosen later transferred the dynamics of the quarterback's spiral pass and the spin of large artillery shells in inventing the solution to the geosynchronous satellite. The orbit of a spinning satellite tends not to degrade.

Brain neurons and semiconductors. Now consider: What do amorphous metals and brain neurons have in common? Stanford Ovshinsky, a self-taught machinist, discovered the answer in 1968 when he published his ideas in the prestigious *Physical Review Letters*. In the mid-1950s and early 1960s, scientists and engineers were developing solid-state electronics using the natural structure and order of crystals of silicon. Ovshinsky, however, began to study amorphous metal materials, (i.e., without crystalline structure). He did not consider a crystalline structure necessary for making semiconductors. No other scientist or engineer thought amorphous metal could be used to design semiconductors or computer memory.

He created two types of electronic "switches" out of the inherent properties of amorphous metal. The first switch was made from a thin film of an amorphous metal, typically on the order of a micron in thickness. In its "off" state, the switch acts like a nonconductor, keeping current from flowing, but when a small amount of voltage is applied above a certain threshold, the switch becomes a conductor and conducts electricity; once the voltage drops below a certain level, it becomes nonconductive again. The amorphous material in the switch is stable and undergoes no structural change.

So, how did Ovshinsky come to invent his semiconductors? He describes this process:

I started developing my theories about amorphous materials by thinking about the relationships between the surfaces of neurons in the brain and the storage and encoding of information. I was also interested in the relationship between information and the energy transformations that occur in the brain. It was obvious to me that what was going on did not involve crystalinity.

He wanted to find a way of duplicating the neuron's storage of information, that is, memory. He realized that he was working on a problem not explained by conventional memory systems or by the mainstream thinking of a crystalline approach to solid-state physics. With this transfer thinking, he says, "I was able to prove that by using thin films of noncrystalline material, it's possible to build analogs or devices realistic in size and function that could resemble neuronal action in the brain. And as I pursued this, it seemed to me that I was onto something very important."[20] Ovshinsky's molecular "memory" switches are now standard on many personal computers.

Music in the heart. Wilson Greatbatch, an electrical engineer, invented the implantable artificial pacemaker for the heart. He quit his job and started building them in a barn behind his house. Today, more than 300,000 pacemakers are implanted worldwide each year. A pacemaker stimulates an area of the heart called the sinus node. The healthy heart has an adequate pacemaker of its own that generates a minute electrochemical impulse that gives the heart a small shock every second or so, causing it to beat rhythmically. The sinus node functions like an electronic metronome. Interestingly, the circuitry in his artificial pacemaker physically looked *like* a metronome. At the time, then, these talks and the information that came from them were useless knowledge. But they remained in his knowledge base until needed.

Greatbatch was also led to acquired immunodeficiency syndrome (AIDS)–related research by his propensity for transfer thinking. He and some colleagues were working on trying to synthesize a gene from a fish called the Arctic flounder, found in the freezing water of the Arctic Ocean. The flounder doesn't freeze because it has peculiar peptides in its blood that act like a natural antifreeze. One morning, says Greatbatch, he was reading about AIDS research in the newspaper. He suddenly realized, "My god, some of the things they're trying to do in their research are exactly what we're doing."[21]

Bugs in the system. While some engineers are trying to remove "bugs" from complicated systems, some are trying to put bugs into the systems.

Atlas Copco Roc Tec, a mining equipment company, used an analogy to develop an earth-moving machine that would both dig ore and load it onto a conveyor belt. One of the members of the problem-solving team was an entomologist; he suggested the praying mantis as an analogy. As the praying mantis eats, it clutches its food between its forelegs and shoves it into its mouth. The result of this analogy was the ROC 302, a huge tractor with shovels on each side (like the mantis's forelegs) that load the ore onto a conveyer belt running through the middle of the tractor.[22]

Once a fertile transfer connection has been made, it often then becomes a systematic means of discovery. Researchers at the Oregon State University have begun to examine spiders and other such insects as analogies or models to improve the stability and movement of robots. Researcher Eugene Fichter says that insects are "magnificent models for walking machines." Insects are carefully filmed and their motions analyzed by computers to see if their architecture can be transferred to the design of heavy robots. In like manner, researchers in England developed a new optical storage disc by using the unusual eye structures of moths as an analogy. A host of products is expected to evolve from the new designs, such as medical diagnostic kits, map projection systems for automobiles, and nonglare instruments and computer screens.[23]

Each of these transfer illustrations was developed by using analogical transfer, using analogies as mental models to see what others did not see. These technological conversions are writ large examples of using a fingernail file for a screwdriver.

TWO MODELS OF INNOVATION AND INVENTION: INDIVIDUAL VERSUS CULTURAL

All of the above examples of transfer thinking, and a host of others, were out there in "reality" to be discovered or invented. Most people, however, did not see the transfer. Some people make the appropriate transfer connections; most don't. Why? Part of the answer lay in two different theories or explanations for the discovery process. One explanation is the "great inventive genius" model of discovery. In his *The Evolution of Technology*, Basalla notes that the explanation often given for these great inventions (read: transfer thinking) is the inherent creative genius of some individual's mind. The other is that the discovery is "in the air" at the time—that the cultural conditions are ripe for the discovery. These two explanations of discovery stem from two opposing views of human behavior: an individualistic explanation versus a group or social view.

The analog of the great inventive genius model of invention in the field of history is what is called "the great man" theory of history. According to this theory, it's the great individual who changes history. The contrary view is that historical conditions create the "great man." The sociocultural model of invention includes such factors as economics, opportunity, and support systems for promoting transfer. While I do not propose to resolve this split, it's nevertheless important to comment on it briefly.

As I noted in the opening of this chapter, the significance of transfer thinking in technological innovation and invention has not received a great deal of attention. What attention it has received has been from the perspective of organizational conditions and support systems. Little attempt has been made to examine the thought processes of the great innovator. As in the history of science, the field of invention has focused largely on the sociocultural conditions that are believed to generate great innovations.

There is little doubt that historical conditions are often responsible for great innovations, but not always. One has only to examine the ideas of Leonardo da Vinci (1452–1519), for example, his inventing the helicopter, to see that "the times" often have little to do with creative genius. But often they probably do. But even when sociocultural or historical conditions are necessary, they are not sufficient.

There is an extensive literature on the sociocultural conditions for innovation. There isn't on the individual's mental models for generating innovation. Historically, business has been almost exclusively concerned with the management of innovation by creating organizational procedures, policies, and support systems that foster innovation. The sociocultural model of invention is a higher-order example of the business and industrial support systems approach to transfer. The social conditions include economics, opportunity, and sociocultural factors like support systems for promoting transfer. Business and industry provide many of these preconditions. There's an extensive business literature on organizational support systems for innovation. There isn't on the individual's mental models for generating innovation. For my purposes here, I'm interested in the individual psychology of innovation.

As important as management systems for transfer are, they are not sufficient. Many have had the support systems that the above accounts of invention required, yet they did not make the transfer. Why? Stanford Ovshinsky adopts the great man model of invention. He says, "[I]deas don't come out of a collective process. People who say an invention is in the air or is a product of the times simply can't understand the process." As Jacob Rabinow points out, "[I]nvention . . . is not a logical process, and one invents by putting things together that normally don't go together."[24] Stanford Ovshinsky describes his view of invention this way: "For the most part," he says, "my inventions come from seemingly unrelated information. Therefore, I can only imagine that my brain works that way and that I make paths and connections where other people do not. There are a lot of people who may be smarter than I—so what is it that makes me a successful inventor? It's got to be that I process my information differently and draw

Figure 6.1
The Transfer of Knowledge in Business and Industry

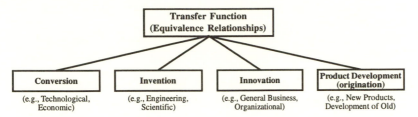

upon my store, my environment, differently."[25] Indeed, he does. And the difference is transfer.

All the support systems in the world will not create significant transfer thinking (unless by serendipity—which in fact may occur more often than we would like to believe) if the individual preconditions described in this book are not present. The invention of a new representation seems to involve a basic insight into the nature of the problem to be solved. It may well be that the inventing of such representations is the highest of human intellectual achievement.

CONVERSION ENGINEERS

Each of these illustrations of conversion requires someone who is good at transfer thinking (see Figure 6.1). For lack of a better word, we need what might be termed *transfer* or *conversion engineers*. A conversion engineer is anyone with the skills and the intellectual capital to transfer knowledge in the service of technological, industrial, and defense conversion, creating new products and economic markets. Conversion engineers may be found almost anywhere. Like inventors, they need not be formally educated. In fact, sometimes formally acquired expertise may be a liability.

An engineer friend of mine only has a high school education. But he worked his way up to a high-level engineering and supervisory position in the local industry. Doug accomplished this by educating himself—by constantly reading and increasing his knowledge base. You wouldn't call him an inventor with a capital *I*, but he is an inventor. Accordingly, neither would you call him creative with an uppercase *C*, but he is creative. In fact, he has told me that he sees himself as not being a creative person. Nor at first glance would you see him engaging in transfer thinking. The facts show otherwise, however.

Over the years, we have had many discussions. Most of them have not been about engineering but about psychology and various other topics. With the exception of quality science fiction, Doug is not an especially avid reader outside his field. Consequently, in our discussions, he has always amazed me with his innate acumen and analysis of the topic we are discussing. In looking at some of our discussions, it's clear that he is using a finely tuned, perhaps hardwired, transfer thinking. His ability at transfer thinking is to be seen most clearly in his engineering feats. An example is the magnificent house that he engineered. I purposefully do not use the word *built*; the house was engineered, with its steel girders, miles of electrical wiring, heating pipes embedded in concrete, with its highly ordered control room of shiny copper and brass pipes and fittings, not to mention its towering 30-foot peak that rivals many church steeples.

I watched him design and physically construct it. I even helped him a little—mostly as a gopher. I observed many of the problems he needed to solve and the apparatuses and "rigs" that he had to invent to build his house. From the previous chapters, it should be evident that Doug mostly engages in near transfer. It should also be evident, however, from the other examples of near transfer that I have cited that near transfer does not mean insignificant transfer, psychologically or financially. Doug is hardwired. I know he has saved his employer millions of dollars. With a little coaching in transfer thinking, a person like Doug can develop creativity with a capital *C* and invent with a capital *I*. Organizations need to seek out and reward these kind of people. They're worth their weight in gold.

Over the years, I have observed that some people need a large knowledge base to do a little, whereas some need only a little knowledge base to accomplish a lot. To function in this latter way requires expertise in transfer thinking. Expertise at transferring knowledge, at conversion, is a powerful leveraging skill for any business, industry, or economy.

CAUTIONARY POSTSCRIPT

In business training the use of analogical and metaphorical reasoning to solve problems and to enhance creativity is not new. For years, Edward de Bono in his *Lateral Thinking for Management* stressed the use of analogy and metaphor, as did William Gordon's *Synectics: The Development of the Creative Capacity* and others more recently.[26] While these techniques and programs to enhance thinking and creativity can be useful, without a thorough understanding of the psychological basis of transfer, coupled with an extensive knowledge base, they end up as little more than cookbook strategies. As I have explained throughout this book, for techniques and strategies to be optimally effective requires an extensive intellectual capital or knowledge base and the appropriate background to be able to access the pertinent data in that knowledge base. To use analogy and metaphor as simply a "training game" strategy for increasing one's creativity is like NASA using an abacus or Picasso having painting by numbers.

Whether they are "recognized spontaneously" or are the result of the use of "creativity exercises," brainstorming with analogies or metaphors, or designed by *Lateral Thinking* or *Synectics* or similar type programs, transfers, in most cases, are accomplished by people who do not make them by sheer force of technique; those who invent creatively are people who already possess what the theory presented in this book describes. Finally, used as disconnected strategies and techniques, analogy and metaphor end up—more often than not—simply creating larger or differently shaped candles, not inventing the light bulb.

The history of science and engineering reveals that innovative practitioners possess an extensive content and historical knowledge base in their areas of research; they also have the spirit of transfer and naturally engage in transfer thinking.

NOTES

1. R. Stata, "Organizational Learning: The Key to Management Innovation," *Sloan Management Review* 30 (1989), p. 63.

2. D. Schon, *Displacement of Concepts* (London: Tavistock Publications, 1963), p. ix.

3. G. Basalla, *The Evolution of Technology* (New York: Cambridge University Press, 1988), p. 45.

4. O. Magaly, "Get Crazy! How to Have a Breakthrough Idea," *Working Woman* (September 1990), p. 148.

5. Using transfer thinking, they transferred a machine gun bullet–belt design as a solution. They thought of a long, tape*like* bullet belt, where the bullets in the belt are seeds, then they layered the bullet belt-seeded tape in furrows.

6. The company created a biodegradable bullet-belt-seeded tape.

7. N. Perry, "Star Wars Mammography," *Fortune* (March 7, 1994), p. 20.

8. Ballistic Missile Defense Organization, *Technology Applications Report* (Alexandria, VA: National Technology Transfer Center, 1993).

9. NASA, *Spin Off* (Washington, DC: Office of Advanced Concepts and Technology Commercial Development and Technology Transfer Division, 1993).

10. Ibid.

11. E. R. Pages, "Next Steps in Business Conversion: Supporting Innovation and Entrepreneurship," *Maine Policy Review* 3(2) (September 1994), pp. 13–22.

12. The solution would be easy if the fuel was a metal you were trying to feed into a chamber. You would just "attract" it into the fuel chamber with a magnet. Unfortunately, the fuel is not metal.

13. What if you "see" or think of liquid fuel as *like* metal? What would this mean? The answer lies in skill at transfer thinking.

14. A scientist working on this problem transferred the idea of magnetic attraction to liquid fuel and invented what was called a ferrofuel. Ferrofuel is a fuel in which microscopic metal particles have been suspended, allowing the liquid fuel to be drawn into the spacecraft engine by a magnetic force. A quite ingenious piece of transfer.

15. NASA, *Spin Off.*

16. Cited in J. Lipnack and J. Stamps, *The Teamnet Factor: Bringing the Power of Boundary Crossing into the Heart of Your Business* (Essex Junction, VT: Oliver Wight Publications, 1993).

17. T. Steward, "Brainpower," *Fortune* (June 3, 1991), p. 44.

18. W. Gordon, *Synectics: The Development of Creative Capacity* (New York: Harper & Row, 1961).

19. R. Berkeley, "Imagination to Go," *Psychology Today* (May 1984), p. 48.

20. Kenneth Brown, *Inventors at Work: Interviews with 16 Notable American Inventors*, Tempus Books (Redmond, WA: Microsoft Press, 1988), pp. 151, 152.

21. Ibid., p. 40.

22. Magaly, "Get Crazy!" pp. 145–148.

23. G. B. Latamore, "Moth's Eyes Inspire Advances in Optical Changes," *High Technology* (April 1987), p. 67.

24. Ibid., p. 208.

25. Ibid., p. 163.

26. E. de Bono, *Lateral Thinking for Management* (New York: Penguin Books, 1971); Gordon, *Synectics*, The development of creative capacity. James Higgins, *101 Creative Problem Solving Techniques* (Winter Park, FL: New Management, 1994).

7

The Transfer Spirit: Contexts and Cultures of Transfer of Learning

To insure transfer, therefore, the attitude in question must be raised to the plane of an ideal and given an emotional tone.

J. J. Ryan[1]

With few exceptions, there has been almost no discussion in either the academic or the HRD training literature—beyond giving it lip service—of what, for lack of a better term, might be called the transfer spirit (or the spirit of just plain learning, for that matter). One exception is Rita Richey in her book *Designing Instruction for the Adult Learner*. She notes, "While it is usually assumed that knowledge acquisition and retention is prerequisite to transfer of training, the question of the role of learner attitudes in this regard is rarely addressed in the literature."[2] Virtually all discussion is about techniques, strategies, skills, and methods of instruction. There has been very little discussion on the spirit to learn and to transfer learning. Spirit is a trainee attribute, a state of being of a learner, not just an educational product or an instructional technology. Although *spirit* may seem at first glance to be a very soft term, in fact it is a very hard-nosed concept. So what is the transfer spirit? The short answer is that the transfer spirit is a psychological, emotional, and motivational orientation toward learning and transfer.

There are four basic ingredients necessary for fostering transfer, all of which have been largely neglected: The first is knowledge base, which I outline in Chapter 8; the second is the transfer spirit; the third is creating cultures of transfer; and the fourth consists of strategies. The question is, How are these areas to be integrated? I have suggested that knowledge base is the primary ingredient in transfer. I suggest this because without knowledge base the other types of knowledge cannot exist. Next in importance is the spirit of transfer, followed by cultures of transfer. Lastly are strategies and techniques. The full implication of knowledge base is long run, with the mechanisms involved constituting a kind of general theory of transfer. Strategies and techniques are short run, with the mechanisms constituting what I consider to be a kind of special theory of transfer. Transfer spirit and cultures of transfer are more global conditions of transfer.

The current emphasis in training programs on strategies and techniques appears to be a no-nonsense method. While instructional technologies are important, from my years of experience in teaching and from my review of the significant transfer research, I have come to believe that without the transfer spirit there is precious little transfer. I self-consciously use the word *precious*, as transfer, generated by technique, strategy, and method (when it does occur), is typically near transfer and is extremely costly; its cost-benefit ratio is typically way out of proportion to its significance.

Given the primacy of knowledge base and the messy or buggy nature—to use the computerese language of the artificial intelligence field—of the everyday and business worlds, the instructional implications are clear: As one educational researcher has aptly noted, "The knowledge potentially required for the ill-structured problems that may arise in real life is so broad that it is unteachable except in the sense of providing broad experience and a general education."[3] This is certainly contrary to the current vocational zeitgeist, but it appears to be good advice, given findings suggesting that the average person changes vocations (not merely job locations) five or six times in the span of his or her life.

THE SPIRIT OF TRANSFER

The transfer spirit is not quite the same as motivation to transfer; it's more than that. In contrast to spirit, motivation is often task specific and short run; spirit is a drive and a mental set to transfer, to see, to approach knowledge in a certain way. The transfer spirit is self-generating. Its embodiment includes an extensive knowledge base, with an emotional disposition and a mental set to integrate that knowledge base. Unlike psychological motivation, the transfer spirit originates from a natural and primitive *need to know*. The history of science and invention clearly shows that the great innovators were deeply moved, some by religion, some by fame, some by money. For some, their motivation bordered on obsession.

Isaac Newton and Johannes Kepler, for example, were motivated out of deep religious convictions to discover the perfect law and form of God's design; Johannes Gutenberg was motivated to invent the printing press by his desire to mass-produce the Christian Bible. I am not suggesting that we all should become obsessed. I am simply pointing out the deep spirit that *possessed* those who were good at transfer. More attention needs to be focused on the transfer spirit.

Some educational theorists have recognized the necessity of a more fundamental motivation for learning and transfer, calling it by different names. Jerome Bruner points to a spirit of transfer, calling it the "abstract attitude." An abstract attitude, says Bruner, "is one in which the individual can not only tear himself away from the given but actually may not deal with the given, save as an exemplar of a more generic category."[4] A similar idea of the need for a deep-seated *disposition* to transfer is found in the cottage consulting industry of teaching critical thinking. In a minority report, of an otherwise majority, maintaining an orientation to teaching critical thinking as techniques and strategies, the author C. D. Brell contends:

A concept of critical thinking as transfer . . . calls attention to the fact that teaching for transfer is less a matter of transmitting knowledge, skills, strategies, and principles of thinking (though it is that, too) than it is of fostering in students from the start an inquiring disposition, by which I mean a readiness to consider the bearing of apparently discrete frames of reference on one another and toward the construction of a more integrated world view.[5]

In an optimal sense, the transfer spirit envelops the whole person.

Wilbert McKeachie, who is well known in education research, recognizes the significance of motivation in the transfer of learning. He specifically refers to achievement motivation. If we can develop achievement and other aspects of motivation for learning, he says, "we might be facilitating the development of important transferable human characteristics that would, in turn, increase the likelihood of transfer of cognitive skills."[6] Laura Resnick, also a well-known psychological researcher, holds a similar view. She says, "There is good reason to believe that a central aspect of developing higher order cognitive abilities in students is a matter of shaping this kind of disposition to critical thought."[7]

A general disposition toward transfer is not a new idea in educational psychology. In 1951, J. J. Ryan noted, "Generalization itself will not tell the whole story. To insure transfer, therefore, the attitude in question must be raised to the plane of an ideal and give an emotional tone."[8] The idea here is that the more meaning knowledge has for an individual, the richer his or her conceptualization, and the deeper the understanding. This in turn leads to increased transfer possibilities.

More recently, Peter Gamlin has stressed that "the learner must acquire a general strategic orientation to acquiring knowledge, developing a sense of the general nature of the problem, the big picture, so as to determine what counts as relevant information in problematic or unfamiliar situations. I argue that this is the key to transfer."[9] What the spirit of transfer does is to infuse information with meaning, and when information is meaningful, it becomes knowledge by acting as a kind of gigantic mental model. In short, meaning transforms *information* into *knowledge*. Information transferred is near transfer; knowledge transferred is far transfer. Information belongs to training; knowledge belongs more to learning.

The necessity of a spirit of transfer has been known for over 2,000 years, at least since Plato. It persists today with a minority of researchers—known by many names—yet it's basically ignored in instructional settings. Why? Part of the answer lies in our culture demanding instant and easy success. Yet at no time in history have we been required to process the amount of information that we do today. But the mind doesn't generally work that way. The brain is an old and wise organ that has its own evolutionary reasons for functioning the way it does. There is an evolutionary lag between the development of our brain and our current need to process information. There exist no known instant learning methods that have been proven effective by rigorous evaluation research to learn or to transfer information. Knowledge of transfer is a way to shorten this lag.

A typical research finding on training for strategy use is that when strategies do seem to work, they often work very quickly, often with little more than simple instructions to use some strategy. The problem is that people who are induced to use a strategy may apply it immediately but often fail to apply the same strategy on later occasions. In short, learning strategies often do not transfer any more than any other kind of learning. The same discouraging results have been generally found for teaching critical thinking.[10]

One reason strategies often do not transfer is that such strategies in fact require an appropriate knowledge base. The use of terms like *problem-solving skills, management skills*, or *interpersonal skills* is deceiving because they rest on considerable sophisticated knowledge, whereas the term *skill* actually implies something relatively routinizable that is low in cognitive content and something typically learned through rehearsal or repetitive practice. According to Peter Senge, one of the ideal goals of learning organizations is personal mastery, the development of the whole person. In an interesting article published in the *Oxford Review of Education*, author W. A. Hart says that education, "whatever else is involved in it, is about the individual person and his development; and . . . only that which is more than simply a skill can contribute to that development, the continual forming and reforming of the person."[11] Transfer and the transfer spirit can be a mechanism to personal mastery, especially since it's transfer that creates integrative connections among events and situations.

Again, I would like to make it clear that strategies and skills are useful, but they are not sufficient for the shift from training to learning. Skills versus a deeper kind of thinking based on broad knowledge is a continuing discussion extending back in time over 2,000 years of Western history—

and most likely in non-Western history as well. In ancient Greece, teachers of rhetoric known as Sophists were famous for their ingenuity in argumentation and cookbook approaches to wisdom; they were known for their adroit thinking, not for the soundness of their reasoning. During that time, there was great debate over what were called cookbooks on rhetorical strategies. Modern approaches to thinking skills and strategies are very much like the ancient Sophists' cookbooks, and there hasn't been much new added to this ancient discussion by modern educators. The present discussion on knowledge base versus strategies and skills is a continuing part of that historical debate.

Just as the Greeks thought that instruction in mathematics and geometry taught people to think, and just as the nineteenth-century classical curriculum was constructed on the belief that learning Latin would teach people to think, in like manner, twentieth-century psychology has invested its stock in a computer programming model of the brain and learning, where information is broken down into its ever-decreasing and isolated components. But as the newer cognitive theories are suggesting, the brain is not simply a wet computer.

Without the transfer spirit—and the knowledge base connected to it—learning is not sustained; it dies. Without deep-seated spirit of transfer, previous knowledge is not reincarnated into new forms. In Bruner's terms, attitude—or what I am calling spirit—determines the way learning is encoded into usable forms that can be brought to bear (transferred) to new situations. A common finding is that even if transfer takes place in the learning situation—be it classroom, laboratory, or on the job—it seldom transfers beyond it. The lack of a deep-seated disposition or spirit seems to effect a necessary deeper coding of information so that it can be used at a later time and in other contexts.

Research clearly shows that how information is encoded determines how it is retrieved. If knowledge is encoded as isolated bits of information, then this is the way it will most likely be retrieved; if it is encoded for a test or exam, this is the way it will be retrieved; if it is encoded for connections to other information, then this, too, is how it will be retrieved. If it is encoded for transfer, it will be retrieved for transfer. Somehow feelings deeply affect the way we encode information and somehow facilitates transfer by tagging information as either relevant or nonrelevant to new situations to which it could be retrieved and applied. In short, so as a person encodeth, so shall a person retrieveth.

Pertinent here are the findings of John Hayes on the years of preparation required by successful composers and fine art painters. Hayes points out that time requirements are an important piece of information that should be made clear to students. Given our cultural expectations of instant success, many people become inappropriately discouraged by early setbacks and the amount of preparation because they believe that if they do not attain immediate mastery of a field, it means a lack of talent, or intelligence, rather than lack of knowledge.

Jerome Bruner notes that instruction for transfer of learning requires extensive preparation. He says, "If we really intend to study the conditions of generic learning by the use of the transfer-of-training paradigm . . . then we shall have to keep our organisms far longer and teach them original tasks of greater diversity than we now do."[12] In addition, there are those who believe that they are destined to perform great acts of creativity with little or no effort on their part by sheer force of intellect. Some even avoid acquiring knowledge, believing that it may spoil the purity of their individual creations. This is nonsense. The overwhelming majority of us mortals, however, do not function on the basis of a disembodied intellect.

TRANSFER-ABILITY AND THE SPIRIT OF TRANSFER

I have suggested elsewhere that the transfer mechanism is the basis of metaphorical and analogical reasoning.[13] In recent years, cognitive psychologists have recognized that the metaphorical capacity is not just a literary device; it's a cognitive ability. Psychologist Howard Gardner, in analyzing the skilled use of metaphor, asks, "Is there an adult form of metaphoric capacity . . . which some individuals have developed to a high degree, so that they can bring it to bear upon particular intellectual domains?"[14] From Gardner's perspective, the mind is composed of relatively separate modules. He concludes that the metaphorical (read: transfer) capacity is probably not a general one—that even people who are good at transfer are probably good at it only from their given domain of expertise or mental module.[15]

Thus, says Gardner, a person highly skilled in transfer, like the scientific essayist Lewis Thomas, will be able to discern and exploit resemblances in the areas of music or dance; but his chief mode of operation will still be in logical-mathematical areas. Similarly, the redoubtable poet W. H. Auden, another insightful (and inveterate) metaphorizer, will comb the world through his poems, but his principal metaphoric point of departure will remain the linguistic realm. Metaphor may spread to many localities, in other words, but it retains a favored "home intelligence" all the same.[16] Gardner does not hypothesize a transfer intelligence or module.

First, although I respect Gardner's insights and integrative mind, my experience and reading of the literature lead me to disagree with him. I believe that there exists in the brain—if not a mental module—at least a transfer function that underlies all mental activity, modular or not. And it's the transfer spirit—in conjunction with knowledge base—that essentially activates it to varying degrees of power and breadth or scope. I disagree with Gardner because there are too many exceptions to his rule of limited transfer. In my judgment, general systems theorists are exceptions. Indeed, Gardner himself is such an exception. One can but read his books to see that he exhibits a high degree of general transfer ability. I also disagree because he does not seem to place sufficient importance on knowledge base.

Is there a relationship between transfer ability and wisdom? And can transfer be transferred? In what has now become a kind of classic article in the business literature, "Because Wisdom Can't Be Told," published in the *Harvard Alumni Bulletin* by Charles Gragg, cites Balzac: "So he had grown rich at last, and thought to transmit to his only son all the cut-and-dried experience which he himself had purchased at the price of his lost illusions; a noble last illusion of age."[17] What Balzac is lamenting is that transfer cannot be passed on to the next generation. But the prior question is whether transfer is related to wisdom. To answer this we need to have an understanding about what wisdom is.

According to Gardner, wisdom may involve a considerable amount of common sense and originality in one or more areas, conjoined with a seasoned metaphorizing or analogizing capacity. The wise individual, says Gardner, can draw upon these abilities appropriately and make wise evaluations of situations. This is what we expect, he says, from older individuals who have a wide range of experiences in their earlier lives and can now apply them in the current circumstances. Implicitly embedded in Gardner's view of wisdom is the ability to transfer past experience appropriately to present circumstances.

I would add to Gardner's account of wisdom that high levels of wisdom require a broad knowledge base, at least in a given domain, plus the ability to transfer from one's experience. Like Balzac, Freud understood this, too. One of Freud's favorite quotes was from Goethe's *Faust*, where Mephistopheles says, "After all, the best of what you know may not be told to boys."[18] Lacking the knowledge base, wisdom based on cookbooks is doomed to failure. Cookbook and strategy approaches to transfer are like trying to pass on wisdom to the next generation, and attempts to do so themselves reflect a lack of wisdom.

CONTEXT AND TRANSFER

As I have noted previously, a consistent finding in the transfer literature is that learning tends to be welded to the context in which it is learned. The encapsulation of learning within a learning context is the paradigm case of cultures of transfer. Each specific learning context is in fact a culture in lowercase; each is a world unto its own, and each shapes transfer. Thus, to understand cultures of transfer it will be useful to understand how context affects transfer.

It's recognized that the context of learning mathematics in school and the context of everyday applications of the mathematics are quite different. Everyday contexts of activity are organized according to the social, per-

sonal, and physical social resources available as well as the cues of interacting with a familiar environment. School contexts tend to organize
information according to concepts and principles of the academic discipline
with the goal of providing the learner with a logically coherent conceptual
structure. School mathematics, for example, tends to relate multiplication
of fractions to multiplication of whole numbers and to the concept of fractions and contrasts multiplication with addition of fractions. These abstract
mathematical relationships are often not salient in the workplace and do
not cue the relevant needed information. Transfer does not take place.

There is long-standing research in psychology that we can transfer in
order to understand the encapsulating of learning in a particular context.
In psychology, we have known for some time that learning is cued by the
place or environment in which the learning occurred. Appropriately
enough, this is called *place learning*. In place learning, cues from the learning environment facilitate the recall of the learning. A poignant example of
place learning from therapy with children will illustrate the power of context. Children undergoing therapy for speech conditions were required to
monitor their speech (a learning strategy) under two conditions. The first
condition was in the clinic setting only; the second in conditions outside
the clinic. Learning acquired by the children within the clinic setting
showed no transfer outside the clinic. The learning was encapsulated or
welded to the clinic context. However, children required to monitor their
speech outside the clinic setting showed transfer in a variety of situations.
The similarity here for learning in different work settings is clear.[19] Context
not only influences psychological orientations; it also shapes responses to
the physical workplace activities. For example, context affects the physical
fidelity (similarity) of industrial simulators and other mock work situations
like training restaurants, hairdressing salons, and car maintenance facilities.
Simulations are designed to duplicate as closely as possible real physical
work environments. Despite their close similarity to real work situations,
the attempts are substitutes at best in terms of the cues provided by the
real social and cultural context of the workplace.

Evidence is mounting that challenges the traditional view of transfer applied to high-fidelity industrial simulators. Ever since 1901 when Edward
Thorndike put forth his identical elements view of transfer, it has been
thought that transfer is best facilitated by creating simulators that resemble
as closely as possible the real situation that they were constructed to train
for. From a situated learning perspective, however, it's not the close physical fidelity of simulators per se that contributes to high positive transfer
but the presence of retrieval information. Thus, simulators low in fidelity
should be effective in facilitating transfer as long as they provide the trainee
with essential cuing relationships.[20]

Research on context learning has led psychologists to understand learning and cognition as *situated*. More specifically, what situated learning re-

fers to are the features of the context in which learning occurs. "Knowledge—perhaps better called knowing—is not an invariant property of an individual, something that he or she has in any situation. Instead, knowing is a property that is relative to situations, an ability to interact with things and other people in various ways."[21] Research on how experts solve problems shows that they rely on a variety of cues provided by the environment in finding solutions.

Laura Resnick, a well-known instructional researcher, notes, "The process of learning is aided when there are many opportunities to observe others engaging in such thinking activities. Finally, such dispositions require sustained long term cultivation and do not emerge from short term quick-fix interventions."[22] We still do not know all the relevant factors that influence context and transfer. Learning a computer program in one context may not influence its use in a different context. In fact, it probably doesn't. On the other hand, social and interpersonal skills are highly context dependent and variable. Because we do not have all the evidence on these matters, however, does not mean we cannot act on the knowledge we do have about the importance of context and transfer.

CULTURES OF TRANSFER

The transfer spirit is shaped by social and group systems that house it. Cultures of transfer are important for learning organizations, especially with the increased use of learning groups and team functioning. Organizations need to restructure the work environment into learning cultures. Some are currently doing just this. As Peter Senge and colleagues point out, "Without innovations in infrastructure, inspiring ideas and powerful tools lack credibility because people have neither the opportunity nor resources to pursue their visions or apply the tools."[23] The research on the social and environmental context of learning, however, is not well developed. I can only outline the importance of and the processes by which the social environment shapes individual learning.

We might begin, however, by noting that Western society in general, and psychologists in particular, have a long tradition of seeing the individual as separate and distinct from the collective (anthropological), societal (sociological), and group (team) contexts of their lives. The same abstracted view of the individual has unfortunately been transferred to the understanding of learning and transfer. We need, however, to understand transfer as a group, team, and social process (I have discussed transfer and the collective nature of small groups and teams in Chapter 5). From understanding the historical development of an idea, to acquiring motivation, receiving reinforcement or positive feedback, as well as balancing feedback from others, to building on others' ideas, learning is a collective process.

One does not have to interact physically, however, to feel the benefit of a culture of support. A group or culture is not necessarily defined by the close physical proximity of its members. Many scientists and scholars, for example, are solitary animals, but they have an abstracted culture of support. They communicate and feel the support in the privacy of their own minds while reading professional journals, newsletters, and books; they also receive support by participating in teleconferences, by bulletin boards on the Internet, and with fax machines. The point is, the phrase *cultures of support* can take on many forms and facilitate transfer in many ways. I am defining culture of transfer in a general sense, to include all social and group influences on transfer.

By a culture of transfer, I mean not only a system of support for the individual to apply or transfer knowledge but a learning system as well. As I briefly noted in Chapter 2, in most academic settings, students have no social context of support to facilitate transfer. By and large, on most campuses social life is often counterproductive to transfer; at best it's neutral. Even most academic classrooms are not structured for optimum transfer. Likewise, most nontraditional or adult learners, though they live off campus, do not have a culture of transfer. Our society does not generally value deep learning. Students know this and bring this value to campus. With the exception of vocational courses, most students are just spending time to obtain credit toward a degree.

In contrast, learners in corporate environments have a built-in context of transfer application and support: their job. Even by default, the very structure of the workplace is a support system, a culture of transfer to some degree. It is a support system because learning is a valued goal (the job), it is meaningfully evaluated (job performance), it is rewarded (paycheck), it is based in activities (applied), and it involves social interaction with other workers around work activities.

In terms of the transfer spirit, the structure of the workplace and its social norms can encourage or discourage motivation to learn and to transfer. Classic in organizational and industrial psychology is the rate-buster phenomenon. Rate busting refers to a person in a work situation who is much more productive than his or her fellow workers. Because the high rate of productivity makes the other workers look inferior, they bring measures to bear on the person to reduce his or her productivity. In group dynamics, we refer to these measures as group pressure. Like many who teach, I have observed this industrial rate-busting phenomenon in the classroom for years. Since I emphasize transfer of learning in my classroom, it's not uncommon in my experience to see students bring measures to bear on anyone who repeatedly offers examples of transfer in class discussions. It occurs in the office as well.

People and organizations often develop myths about themselves that are perpetuated by the group culture. For example, research has shown that despite American children scoring far lower in mathematics than children in China and Japan, American children and their parents tend to regard themselves as above average or superior in mathematics, while the superior Asian students don't regard themselves as highly. The same research found that American students denigrate the importance of hard work in achieving a skill. When asked what they considered most important for doing well in mathematics, over 60 percent of the Chinese and Japanese students responded by saying studying hard, whereas less than 25 percent of the American students said studying hard is important.[24]

Social and work situations, then, shape a person's sense of achievement, competence, self-image, and sense of standards. If we can learn how to develop these individual characteristics through social activities, says Wilbert McKeachie, "we might be facilitating the development of important transferable human characteristics that would, in turn, increase the likelihood of transfer of cognitive skills."[25] Once we see that individuals' behaviors, their thought processes, and their mental models are profoundly shaped by social situations, it follows logically that transfer of learning must be understood as a sociocultural process.

In part, a work culture consists of the procedural knowledge and skills necessary for the carrying out of relevant knowledge. These procedural skills are constantly performed in production, communication, and other social areas of activity. Most of these skills are learned by new members through direct observation and verbal transmission. There may also be separate skills for subculture groups in a single organization.

Transfer has been viewed from four different models of the mind—the rationalist, the empiricist, the sociohistorical, and the ecological—with each relating to transfer. The rationalist model of mind views transfer as being inherent in the brain/mind. The empiricist model views transfer (e.g., similarity) as being inherent in phenomena. The social and historical view of the mind assumes that transfer processes reside not so much in an individual mind but in the social world. As such, the focus is on transfer structures constructed within social activities. Accordingly, for most people, transfer depends largely on participating in a social (or work) activity where the very structures that form, facilitate, and cue transfer are found. Thus, transfer is primarily socially defined.

The ecological model of transfer assumes that transfer is inherent in the external world; it does not have to be constructed by internal mental processes. Like the sociohistorical model, the ecological model focuses its attention on structures in the physical world. Equivalencies and invariants result from direct perception rather than being mediated by mental representations; invariance is not constructed or deduced, it's out there to be discovered. Both the sociohistorical and the ecological models direct their attention to what in effect is a learning culture, more specifically, a culture of transfer.

If we adopt the view that learning is situated, that transfer is social in a fundamental way, then we understand also that learning occurs in the context of people engaging in social activities—in our case, work activities. Moreover, the meaning and significance of these activities derive from the roles defined by the work activities. The goals of the activities, too, are defined socially and determine what elements of the work situation are important to attend to and which ones are not. In addition, conversations with others in the work activity influence attention and cue learning. In short, the social work situation creates a universe of meaning for the participant that shapes learning, memory, and transfer possibilities. Indeed, memory is largely a collective process. Its locus is the interpersonal interaction among people engaging in activities and in recollections. In fact, some memory, like reminiscing, often only takes place within social interaction. We frequently only remember personal things when they are socially meaningful. As an example, it's well known that most people recall exactly where they were and what they were doing on November 22, 1963: the date President John F. Kennedy was assassinated.

With an increasingly diverse workforce, it's important to begin to understand the influence of culture on learning and transfer. It's useful to see each gender and ethnic group as *like* a separate culture with its unique evolutionary characteristics, cultural norms, and different ways of knowing that affect transfer. Culture powerfully shapes cognition and thus transfer. Howard Gardner points out that, given consistent differences found on intelligence tests, females score somewhat lower on spatial ability, it's reasonable to assume that Eskimo males might perform better on spatial tasks than Eskimo females. In fact, skilled performances on spatial tasks are found among Eskimo females as well, demonstrating either that the sex differences in spatial abilities reported regularly in our Western culture can be overcome in certain environments or that biases in our own environments are producing apparent spatial deficits in females.

Different ethnic cultures, like different work cultures, influence learning. Again demonstrating the affects of culture, Gardner notes that at least 60 percent of Eskimo children score as high on tests of spatial ability as the top 10 percent of Caucasian children. Moreover, this increased ability generalizes not only to tests of conceptual ability but to tests measuring visual details.[26]

Understanding how people from different cultures classify things in the world around them is important for transfer because transfer is often dependent on how we classify our environment. In turn, our classification systems determine how we make inferences and thus how we transfer. When we say something is typical, what we mean is that it's a kind of prototype of what we are talking about, that it shares many similar features of whatever is being discussed. But different cultures classify things differently. For example, when talking about birds, a robin is more typical than a swan to North Americans, but a swan is more typical than a robin to the average Chinese citizen. When classifying sources of meat, a Westerner's core concept includes cows. This would obviously not be true for East Indians. Instead, since cows are sacred, for them "cow" belongs to the concept of religion. Each context may change our classification system. For example, a raccoon and a snake are much less similar when judged in a general or biological context than when judged within the context of pets.

Research on cultures of diversity, whether it's on different work contexts, gender, or ethnicity, would greatly improve our understanding and implementation of transfer. As D. Bridges recognizes, "We need to ask . . . what would make one social context different from another to the extent that it might constitute a challenge to the transfer of skills?"[27] What we need is more understanding about cultures of transfer, especially for the workplace.

NOTES

1. J. J. Ryan, "Transfer of Training: Subject Matter," in R. Pintner, J. Ryan, P. West, A. Aleck, L. Crow, and S. Smith (eds.), *Educational Psychology* (New York: Barnes and Noble, 1951), p. 89.

2. R. Richey, *Designing Instruction for the Adult Learner: Systemic Training, Theory and Practice* (New York: Kogan Page, 1992), p. 163.

3. N. Frederiksen, "Implications of Cognitive Theory for Instruction in Problem Solving," *Review of Educational Research* 54 (1984), p. 380.

4. J. S. Bruner, "Going Beyond the Information Given," in J. Anglin (ed.), *Beyond the Information Given: Studies in the Psychology of Knowing* (New York: W. W. Norton, 1973), p. 227.

5. C. D. Brell, Jr., "Critical Thinking as Transfer: The Reconstructive Integration of Otherwise Discrete Interpretations of Experience," *Educational Theory* 40 (1990), p. 54.

6. W. J. McKeachie, "Cognitive Skills and Their Transfer: Discussion," *International Journal of Educational Research* 11 (1987), p. 710.

7. L. B. Resnick, "Instruction and the Cultivation of Thinking," in E. De Corte, H. Lodewijks, R. Parmentier, and P. Span (eds.), *Learning and Instruction*, Vol. 1 (Oxford: Pergamon Press, 1987), p. 433.

8. Ryan, "Transfer of Training," p. 89.

9. P. J. Gamlin, "Strategy Instruction: Issues for the Transfer of Knowledge," *Canadian Journal of Special Education* 6(2) (1996), p. 145.

10. C. Furedy and J. J. Furedy, "Critical Thinking: Toward Research and Dialogue," in J. G. Donald and A. M. Sullivan (eds.), *Using Research to Improve Teaching: New Directions for Teaching and Learning* (San Francisco: Jossey-Bass, 1985), pp. 51–69.

11. W. A. Hart, "Against Skills," *Oxford Review of Education* 4 (1978), p. 213.

12. Bruner, "Going Beyond the Information Given," p. 232.

13. See Haskell, "Analogical Transforms: A Cognitive Theory of the Origin and Development of Transformation of Invariance, Part I, II," *Metaphor and Symbolic Activity* 4 (1989), pp. 247–277.

14. H. Gardner, *Frames of Mind: The Theory of Multiple Intelligences* (New York: Basic Books, 1983), p. 296.

15. In his book, Gardner puts forth a theory of intelligence based on a kind of modular view of the mind. For example, he says that what we in the West have measured intelligence by is only one given module: a logicomathematical module upon which many of the skills we value are based. Musical ability would be one ability that is based on a logicomathematical capacity.

16. Gardner, *Frames of Mind*, pp. 292–293.

17. C. Gragg, "Because Wisdom Can't Be Told," *Harvard Alumni Bulletin* (October 1940), p. 79.

18. S. Freud, *The Interpretation of Dreams* (trans. J. Strachey) (1900; London: George Allen & Unwin Ltd., 1954), p. 142.

19. See R. L. Koegel, L. K. Koegel, K. Van Voy, and J. Costello Ingham, "Within-Clinic versus Outside-of-Clinic Self-monitoring of Articulation to Promote Generalization," *Journal of Speech and Hearing Disorders* 53(4) (1988), p. 392.

20. See S. Billett, "Towards a Theory of Workplace Learning," *Studies in Continuing Education* 14(2) (1992), pp. 143–155; S. M. Cormier, "The Structural Processes Underlying Transfer of Training," in S. M. Cormier and J. D. Hagman (eds.), *Transfer of Learning: Contemporary Research and Application* (New York: Academic Press, 1987), pp. 151–181.

21. See J. G. Greeno, J. L. Moore, and D. R. Smith, "Transfer of Situated Learning," in D. K. Detterman and R. J. Sternberg (eds.), *Transfer on Trial: Intelligence, Cognition, and Instruction* (Norwood, NJ: Ablex, 1993), p. 99.

22. Resnick, "Instruction and the Cultivation of Thinking," pp. 433–434.

23. In P. Senge, C. Roberts, R. Ross, B. Smith, and A. Keiner, *The Fifth Discipline Fieldbook: Strategies and Tools for Building a Learning Organization* (New York: Doubleday, 1994), p. 46.

24. Cited in R. M. Dawes, *House of Cards: Psychology and Psychotherapy Built on Myth* (New York: Free Press, 1994).

25. McKeachie, "Cognitive Skills and Their Transfer," p. 170.

26. See Gardner, *Frames of Mind*.

27. D. Bridges, "Transferable Skills: A Philosophical Perspective," *Studies in Higher Education* 18(1) (1993), p. 49.

8

Knowledge, Expertise, Practice, and Transfer of Learning: The Usefulness of Useless Knowledge

Learning often cannot be translated into a generic form until there has been enough mastery of the specifics of the situation to permit the discovery of lower order regularities which can then be recombined into higher-order, more generic coding systems.

Jerome Bruner[1]

The past 95 years of research on transfer clearly show that general transfer of learning doesn't occur in most educational and work situations. This is largely because we have not paid sufficient attention to knowledge base. In descriptions of important trainee characteristics, Timothy Baldwin and Kevin Ford, as well as other trainers, seldom specifically mention knowledge base as a requirement for transfer. This is a striking and critical omission, an omission, however, that unfortunately flows logically from a training perspective as opposed to a learning framework.[2]

I consider knowledge base the absolute requirement for transfer of learning. Contrary to most current thinking, I believe the research shows that knowledge base is *the* essential ingredient for transfer. While this may seem obvious and commonsensical, in practice, knowledge base is often given only lip service. The trend in training has been to gain quick fixes with the use of what are thought to be general problem-solving strategies and thinking techniques (see Chapter 9). Transfer of learning, however, requires more than quick-fix strategies. This is important for learning organizations.

For transfer to occur, learning must be transformed into a generalized form, or what Peter Senge and others have called generic structures (see

Chapter 10); this requires knowledge base. Robert Glaser, a well-known instructional researcher, finds, "The evidence indicates that what humans actually do as they learn and acquire experience is to build up an extremely large store of structured knowledge."[3] And lots of it. It's the generic coding of information that leads to expertise. Contrary to popular notions, there is virtually no evidence suggesting that experts have access to general problem-solving techniques that novices do not have (see below). The essential difference between experts and novices is knowledge base—the quantity of knowledge one possesses—and how that knowledge base is organized.

In this chapter, I will present the general knowledge base conditions necessary for optimal transfer of learning to take place and explain its importance. Let me first say that I define knowledge base quite broadly. It's not acquired from formal education alone. It includes knowledge acquired by general reading, personal experience, careful listening, reading research, and astute observing. Knowledge base also includes thinking, for when you think, you add to your knowledge-base. From both my personal experience and from my review of research findings, it's clear that there is no substitute for a large knowledge base in promoting transfer, whether it's in quantum physics, in cost-benefit analysis, or in management decision making. Unfortunately, there are no shortcuts to transfer.

It's also clear, however, that knowledge is not enough. To achieve transfer, there are requirements that are incompatible with many current training and social values. These requirements include individual dispositional characteristics such as attitude, motivation (see Chapter 7), and the persistence to engage in a great deal of practice, plus the willingness to rote memorize material and master a certain amount of theoretical knowledge. The degree to which these requirements are met is the degree to which transfer will occur. This is as true in engineering as it is in fine art. It's as simple as that.

In reading about great innovators, this becomes clear (see Chapter 6). Stanford Ovshinsky, the inventor of the amorphous metal semiconductor, says, "You must have a knowledge of technical subjects, but that does not necessarily mean a formal education. After all, I worked in the field of medicine, was published in medical journals, and I had nothing but a high school and trade school education. However, I am continually learning and educating myself."[4] Jacob Rabinow, electrical engineer and renowned inventor and holder of many U.S. patents, contends:

An inventor has to be well trained. You're not going to combine ideas if you have none to start with. An amateur can invent very well, but he will invent old junk because he doesn't know what's new. That is one of the tragedies of these self-styled inventors who come to us at the Bureau of Standards with an idea. They're nice people, but they have no training. It's as if they want to write but have never read a book.[5]

It's crucial to understand why and in what way knowledge base is important for proficient performance in transfer.

THE IMPORTANCE OF KNOWLEDGE BASE FOR TRANSFER

With a shift from training to learning in organizations, and the new emphasis on intellectual capital, the quantity and quality of one's knowledge become increasingly important. This is true whether you are an engineer, a product development specialist, a cost accountant, or a file clerk; every job—no matter what the level—requires its own extensive knowledge base if it's to be done with efficiency and creativity. Unlike transfer of training, the transfer of learning requires more extensive knowledge in at least the specific area of performance. For general transfer beyond a specific area, still more knowledge is necessary.

Cognitive psychologists describe four basic kinds of knowledge: (1) declarative knowledge, (2) procedural knowledge, (3) strategic knowledge, and (4) conditional knowledge. I will add a fifth kind not typically mentioned, (5) theoretical knowledge. Declarative knowledge is what one knows; it's knowledge of or about something. A person either does or does not know what a Buick is. Procedural knowledge is how-to knowledge; while a person can identify a Buick, he or she may not know how to drive one.

Strategic knowledge is knowledge of one's mental processes, such as how one learns and remembers; it's the self-monitoring of one's progress in the use of learning strategies. Conditional knowledge is knowing when to apply knowledge in context-appropriate ways: One does not behave in the same way in all situations. Theoretical knowledge is understanding the deep-level relationship of cause and effect and other explanatory connections about phenomena. It's my view that knowledge base is defined by all five of these kinds of knowledge. People who possess—to varying degrees—all five kinds of knowledge are proficient at transfer of learning.

There are many books and training programs covering procedural and—to a lesser extent—conditional knowledge, so I will not repeat the material here. Instead, I will focus on declarative and theoretical knowledge. I'll review strategic knowledge in Chapter 9. Since most people think and reason with pragmatic reasoning schemas and mental processes that are based on knowledge of specific content, not with formal abstract rules, there can be no substitute for an adequate knowledge base. Research on expertise demonstrates how important knowledge base is. It is well known that expert chess players utilize an enormous amount of knowledge of chess patterns. To acquire this knowledge, chess players must spend thousands of hours in preparation—playing chess, reading books and magazines on chess, and studying chess positions carefully. For thinking and problem solving in most fields, there is no substitute for having an extensive knowledge base. An interesting study of successful composers and painters of fine art revealed that very few produced masterworks with less than ten years of reflective experience.[6] It's also well known that in the engineering field the knowledge base required is very large. I have known experts in many fields. The good ones have always had an extensive knowledge base.

Wilson Greatbatch, also an engineer and renowned inventor, says, "I firmly believe that a broad background is helpful when it comes to inventing. I give credit for much of what I've been able to do to Cornell University, where I did my undergraduate work, and to the breadth of course work they gave me in engineering. I had much more chemistry and physics and math than anyone would ever need in order to do just electrical engineering."[7] The need for comprehensive and valid knowledge is clear.

There are two kinds of expertise. One is routine expertise; the other is adaptive expertise. Each kind is based on the amount of knowledge acquired and how it's used. Routine expertise rests on a restricted knowledge base in a particular area; adaptive expertise, on the other hand, is based on a more extensive knowledge base. Adaptive experts utilize procedures flexibly, can modify them based on feedback demands, and can invent new ones to deal with novel problems and situations. To use an *analogy*, someone who implements a recipe quickly and accurately can be called a routine expert, whereas an adaptive expert would be able to substitute ingredients in the recipe if necessary and modify it for different requirements. In general, training leads to routine expertise, whereas learning leads to adaptive expertise. Accordingly, routine expertise leads to narrow transfer within an area, while adaptive expertise leads to broad transfer extending beyond a specific area or task. By comparison, a child is a kind of routine expert, and an adult is a kind of adaptive expert.

Although it's difficult in practice to separate the five kinds of knowledge, it's my view that declarative knowledge, knowledge of or about something, is the most crucial for transfer. I say this because

1. it's declarative knowledge that provides the preconditions necessary for the other four kinds of knowledge;
2. it often includes or generates the other four kinds of knowledge;
3. declarative knowledge frequently provides a general framework for assimilating more detailed new knowledge;
4. it often facilitates the elaboration of newly acquired knowledge, and
5. it frequently provides useful analogs to help in the understanding of new knowledge.

People high in knowledge base exhibit more superior memory and encoding procedures for retrieval and transfer than do those low in knowledge base.

At first glance, the intuitive explanation has been that those with good memory are able to amass and retain a large knowledge base. But this isn't considered to be the correct explanation. Somewhat counterintuitively, acquiring a large knowledge base is not the consequence of a superior memory; rather superior memory is the consequence of having a large knowledge base. The explanation is that a large knowledge base provides more frameworks and related connections for information to be maintained and retrieved, that is, remembered. Studies have shown that master chess players could not remember where the pieces were on a chess board that was randomly set up any better than chess players of lesser ability.

Other studies, too, indicate that cognitive processing is greatly enhanced by experience with new information. Cognitive psychologists Mark Singley and John Anderson, although known for their work on procedural knowledge, nevertheless assert, "Indeed, one could argue that the defining feature of declarative knowledge is that it serves as the basis for transfer to multiple tasks. . . . [D]clarative training does represent somewhat of an antidote to the encapsulation of knowledge."[8]

THEORETICAL KNOWLEDGE AND TRANSFER

The more complicated and high-tech our personal and corporate worlds become, the more we need a good (valid) theoretical knowledge base to compete and survive. As Peter Senge and his associates note, "Without theory, methods, and tools, people cannot develop the new skill and capabilities required for deeper learning."[9] Timothy Baldwin and Kevin Ford, in their classic review "Transfer of Training: A Review and Directions for Future Research," note that in the research on trainee characteristics there is a "lack of theoretical frameworks to guide research. . . . [and] . . . the lack of a systematic approach to this area has resulted in minimal improvements in our understanding of the transfer process."[10] For many of the same reasons that I consider declarative knowledge the most important of the five kinds of knowledge, I consider theoretical knowledge to be second in importance. People typically want only weak forms of declarative and procedural knowledge; they want just the facts and how-to (procedural) knowledge. Theory is thought to be abstract and speculative. Having just the facts and how-to knowledge are helpful, but they are not enough. If, as the research findings indicate, theoretical knowledge is understood and applied by children in order to learn and transfer, it can certainly be used by anyone.

Contrary to popular conception, theory is not anymore abstract than is much of our everyday thinking. It's not ivory-tower, philosophical speculation. Theory is as natural as everyday thinking itself. Simply put, a theory is merely a logical and ordered explanation of a phenomenon based on tested evidence (facts). Certainly most of our knowledge is not as extensive or as precisely tested as scientists', but we are theoreticians, nevertheless. In fact, our everyday understanding of people is almost entirely theoretical. As I outlined in Chapter 5), since we cannot get inside people's feelings and thoughts, we can understand them only by inferring from their behaviors, *comparing* them to ourselves, and weaving plausible connections (theory) between the everyday evidence we have of them. The choice, then, is not between having theoretical knowledge or not having theoretical knowledge. The choice is between (1) being aware of our theories so that we can use them and (2) not being aware of them so that they use us. Most of our theoretical knowledge is implicit; we are not aware of it. Our theoretical knowledge is often inaccessible. It often takes the form of unconscious mental models (see Chapter 11).

Learners bring their own everyday theories to learning. Instruction then fosters an evolution from these untutored theories to more sophisticated theories and conceptualizations. It may perhaps come as a surprise that even for young children theoretical knowledge is crucial for transfer. It's theoretical knowledge, not simple surface perception, that tells not only children but us that a whale is not a fish: We have knowledge of evolutionary theory about what constitutes a genus or a species. Science advances by the use of theoretical knowledge. In the evolution of chemistry out of alchemy, it was only when theoretical laws and principles were developed that chemical knowledge advanced rapidly.

Theoretical knowledge provides us, simultaneously, with (1) a rule to guide our transfer, and (2) a framework to constrain runaway transfer. Theory instructs us (consciously or unconsciously) as to why we should look in this place and not in that place. Theory thus acts as an efficiency manager. Each time we recognize a similarity, or transfer a piece of knowledge, we get *reinforcing feedback* to seek more. Since there are similarities among all phenomena, if we noted similarities among all events, we would very quickly be overwhelmed. As a consequence, we need balancing feedback. It's theoretical knowledge that creates the constraints, or *balancing feedback*; it's our hedge against a runaway system of thinking, our hedge against random access to reality.

In a trivial but common way, children provide a model for understanding the importance of theoretical constraints. Before they acquire theoretical knowledge, children are famous for runaway transfer or overgeneralization. For example, until they absorb theoretical knowledge, all four-legged animals are kitties or doggies (depending on what pet they first have experience with). Ann Brown concludes from her work with young children that they fail to transfer only when they lack theoretical knowledge.[11] Theoretical knowledge, then, is a necessity for creating coherence out of a bunch of novel or otherwise disconnected experiences. It's theoretical knowledge that's more likely to be transferred to new situations.

THE USEFULNESS OF USELESS KNOWLEDGE FOR TRANSFER

As a freshman in college, I remember reading in an edited book a chapter entitled "On the Usefulness of Useless Knowledge," written by Abraham Flexner, a physician, well-known educator, and onetime director of the Institute for Advanced Studies at Princeton.[12] In this chapter, Flexner cited examples of knowledge that appeared to have absolutely no use but that years later someone saw as something other than what it appeared to be and was able to transfer it to another area that then turned out to have major applied importance. The mathematical theories of James Clerk Maxwell, the Scottish physicist who formulated the relationship between magnetism and electricity, were thought to be useless at the time he formulated them. The detection of Maxwell's theoretical electromagnetic waves came only much later by German physicist Heinrich Hertz.

The work of both Maxwell and Hertz was thought to be relatively useless until Guglielmo Marconi, the Italian physicist, applied this useless knowledge and invented wireless telegraphy. The same can be said of English physicist Michael Faraday's discovery of induced electric current from magnets. Without this useless knowledge, I would not be writing these words—as I am now doing—on my word processor at night. Moreover, this chapter on useless knowledge has been tucked away in the back of my mind for years. I have never used this chapter in my teaching or writings; until using it here as an example of the usefulness of useless knowledge for promoting transfer, it was a useless piece of information.

Mathematics is perhaps the field that historically exemplifies the usefulness of useless knowledge. Non-Euclidian geometry, invented by Karl Friedrich Gauss, German mathematician and astronomer, was originally considered useless. In fact, Einstein's general theory of relativity could not have been formulated without it. Likewise, group theory in mathematics was considered useless but is now the basis of the quantum theory of spectroscopy. Such examples of seemingly useless knowledge are not rare. More recently in mathematics, knot theory was a system for describing and classifying knots. It was thought to be a quite useless kind of mathematical game; it remained so until someone transferred this knowledge to another field of knowledge. Knot theory is currently important in the biochemical analysis of explaining how jumbled strands of DNA in the nuclei of living cells divide without becoming entangled. In short, someone saw knots as *like* jumbled strands of DNA.

When early in his career Abraham Pais, a theoretical physicist, discovered the K-meson particle, it was thought to have no useful application. Today, however, meson particles are used to treat cancer because they can be beamed at cancerous cells without burning the tissue around them. Pais points out that what at first looks like useless knowledge has turned out in the past to have practical applications. Electronics, transistors, television, radio—all are based on discoveries made by people who are just interested in conceptual questions.[13] All started out as intellectual capital investments. Stanford Ovshinsky, the renowned inventor, says. "For the most part, my inventions come from seemingly unrelated information."[14]

On the lighter side of transfer thinking is an example from renowned inventor Jacob Rabinow, whose inventions include the first optical character recognition or reading machine, still used today by many banks to scan bank checks and credit card slips, the magnetic-particle clutch, the self-regulating clock, and the automated sorting machines used by the United States Post Office. He tells the story of how he invented what was perhaps the first telephone answering machine, a device that would let a person know when he or she returned home if a telephone answering service had called, indicating that someone had phoned. What did his mind do to invent this device?

It seems that when Rabinow was eleven years old, he worked in his uncle's store. He recalls a toy that was a small cardboard box shaped like a doghouse. If you put a toy dog in the door in front of the doghouse, the dog stayed inside the house. In the back of the box were two wires that were part of a circuit controlling an electromagnet holding a plate against a spring. A thin piece of brass hung in the back of the doghouse, and as long as it touched the two wires connected to the electromagnet, the circuit stayed closed. However, if you made a loud noise or yelled "Rex!" (the dog's name), the back vibrated, shaking the brass plate. This broke the connection for an instant, the spring-loaded plate was released, and the dog came out of the doghouse. Now, what does this have to do with a telephone answering machine light?

Rabinow says, "I thought that same setup would work with the phone." He went home, took a cigar box, made a loose electrical contact underneath the lid so that the circuit wire barely touched the contact, wired it across a shunt, and connected a resistor in series with a neon light. Using a second resistor, he set them so that the neon light received 70 volts (which is not enough to light it). However, if the contact was broken for an instant, the shunt disconnected, resulting in an increase in voltage sufficient to fire the neon light. Even though the contact was broken for only an instant, the light would stay on because neon lights exhibit differential voltage; that is, once lighted at 90 volts, they will stay on even at 70 volts. "Look at the stunt that my brain did!" says Rabinow. "I knew how that toy worked in 1921, and I remembered it in detail in 1959."[15] He transferred this ostensibly useless and irrelevant information into an answering machine.

KNOWLEDGE OF THE PAST CREATES A VIABLE
CORPORATE TRANSFER FUTURE

Virtually overlooked in the HRD training field is knowledge of history. I'm not talking world history here; I'm talking *business* history. The history of an area is important for transfer, whether it be in the psychological laboratory or the workplace. Research on expertise shows that experts not only possess a large knowledge base but have knowledge of the history of their area. Those with a sense of the history of a problem or area are typically able to recognize key variables and to see quickly what the key issues are early in the problem-solving process. A sense of history of one's area provides valuable transfer knowledge, inoculates against fads and fashions, and guards against reinventing the wheel. Reinventing the wheel—assuming we even have what it takes to reinvent it—takes time, and time means dollars spent that could be spent elsewhere. Forward-looking learning *is* a form of scholarship, and scholarship is based on a history of knowing not only what has already been done, what has already been thought out, and what has already been solved but what has already been done, thought, or solved that may be *like* what needs to be done, thought, or solved now.

Knowledge of the history of business issues and problems is key for the learning organization; it's key to the competitive edge for corporate survival. As long as competitors did not effectively use historical information, or data, corporations could get away with doing likewise. But this does not appear to be the case in our new high-tech, knowledge-based business climate. As an area of study and investigation, business is essentially *like* any other area—or should be. Accordingly, it should be approached as an area of practical scholarship. Certainly the model of pure science or pure scholarship is not the model for business. There are dissimilarities between pure scientific investigation and the investigation needs of business, time pressures being the primary difference. Science can afford not to come to a conclusion until all the evidence is in; business can't. Herein lies the difference.

The investigative model for the learning organization is an applied one like engineering. The productive and inventive engineer, either informally or formally, functions as does a scholar, knowing the history of his or her area of application and knowing—either implicitly or explicitly—what has been useful and should be transferred and what has not been useful and thus is not appropriate to transfer from the engineering knowledge base (i.e., the history). Otherwise, he or she will end up either reinventing the wheel or, worse yet, reinventing an inferior wheel. In HRD training, there is considerable reinventing of wheels—and often inferior ones. In many of the books on teams and team building, for example, there is a lack of awareness of the years of pragmatic research on all aspects of small groups in psychology, sociology, education, communication, and other fields. Much of the literature on corporate teams is the small group reinvented—and often not reinvented very well.

PRACTICE, DRILL, AND TRANSFER

How is transferable knowledge base acquired? As unpopular as it may be, the answer is: over a long period of time, repetitive practice and drill. And lots of it. I should note that not just any kind of practice and drill is important. We're not talking just sheer old-time rote learning here, though this is necessary as well. I'm talking about reflective, deliberate practice, self-conscious practice, where practice isn't just repetition but learning. A simple illustration: Benjamin Franklin, American statesman and inventor, described in his autobiography how he learned to write in a clear and logical style. He said he would repeatedly read through a passage in a well-written book to understand it rather than memorize it and then practice reproducing its structure and content. He would then *compare* his writing with the original and identify the differences. By repeating this practice cycle of reading, reproducing, and comparing his writing with the well-structured original, Franklin maintained that he acquired his skill in organizing his thoughts.[16] Clearly a transfer process in itself.

Again, let me illustrate by using the Wyeth family. In recalling the training and upbringing in his famous artist family, Nat Wyeth, engineer and inventor, exemplifies the importance of extensive preparation and knowledge base for expertise. His father, N. C. Wyeth, told him, "Before you can do a really good job at anything, you've got to be well trained in the basics." Knowledge and practice bring understanding. If something is drawn with a sense of understanding, says Nat, you can feel it.

His artist brother Andrew was taught by his father. He told young Andrew, "[W]hat you do on your own time is all right with me. But when you're working for me as a student, you're first going to learn how to draw. You're going to learn the basics of drawing things as they are." For years, his father made Andrew draw very simple objects—cubes, spheres, pyramids—over and over again. This repetition drove the sensitive Andrew almost crazy. But that kind of training clearly shows in Andrew's paintings, in his beautiful sense of proportion. In the HRD training field, practice and drill is an overlooked instructional requirement.

Of his brother, Nat says, "He has an eye like an eagle. His pencil sketches of a rope or the limb of a tree are simply phenomenal. It didn't just come by saying he wanted to do it. He had to work at it." In the *same* way, says Nat, an engineer must have a very fundamental training and understanding of the laws of physics before he or she can use them. "This is particularly important," he says, "when you're using your skills in fields or areas where you're really exploring for the first time. We have enough problems without moving in false directions because we haven't learned the basics in engineering."[17]

At the extreme, years of practice are required for attaining expert proficiency. Again, the study by John Hayes of successful composers and painters of fine art revealed that very few produced masterworks with less than ten years of reflective experience. Hayes found that what composers need in order to write excellent musical scores is not maturing but rather musical preparation. The results make it dramatically clear that no one composes outstanding music without first having had about ten years of intensive musical preparation.[18] In short, ten years of reflective practice.

In analyzing how expertise is acquired, Hayes and others conclude, "The most obvious answer is practice, thousands of hours of practice. . . . There may be some as yet undiscovered basic abilities that underlie the attainment of truly exceptional performance . . . but for the most part practice and ability level are by far the best predictor of performance."[19] Other studies have found similar results.

All too often we tend to think that great expertise in an area is due largely to innate talent. There is no shortage of anecdotal biographical accounts that seem to confirm this belief. The evidence, however, is to the contrary. Expertise is largely due to practice, practice, and then more practice. K. Anders Ericsson and Neil Charness, in their seminal research-based paper, "Expert Performance: Its Structure and Acquisition,"[20] found in comprehensive reviews comparing the beginning ages and the amount of practice for international, national, and regional-level performers in many different areas of performance that those who attained higher levels of performance tended to start practicing from two to five years earlier than did the less accomplished performers. Moreover, those who attained higher levels of performance spent considerably more time on deliberate practice than did the less accomplished individuals—many more hours.

There is a direct and continuous correlation between the number of hours spent on practice and the degree of expertise. For example, it has been found that by age 20 top-level violinists have practiced an average of 10,000 hours. Think about this statistic: It means that by age 20 these violinists have practiced the equivalent of nearly 40 full hours a week for nearly five years, or nearly one quarter of their entire lifetime. By contrast, the next most accomplished violinists had practiced an average of 7,500 hours. The top-level violinists have practiced 5,000 more hours than the lowest level of expertise. This was true even when there was no difference in the total amount of time that both groups spent on related activities. In other words, you can still have a life.

These kinds of findings have implications for other than instruction; they have implications for student expectations as well. Findings such as these prompted John Hayes to suggest that since the mastery of a field requires many years, "it's an important item of metacognitive knowledge that we ought to teach to our students. Some students may be inappropriately discouraged by early setbacks because they believe that failure indicates lack of talent rather than lack of knowledge,"[21] and practice. On the other hand, contrary to Hayes's admonition, in our society such knowledge may discourage learners. It is well known that U.S. college students are avoiding majors that are perceived as requiring hard work, like science, math, and engineering. I wonder why it is that we take for granted that to acquire expertise in music and sports requires much practice and drill, but we tend not to expect the same for other everyday learning.

It's clear that proficiency at transfer requires a great deal of effort. The human brain is millions of years old and functions in its own fashion. Shortcuts and quick fixes to learning and transfer do not typically work very well. Herbert Simon and colleagues summarize their years of research on expertise:

We have no reason to suppose, however, that one day people will be able to become painlessly and instantly expert. The extent of the knowledge an expert must be able to call upon is demonstrably large, and everything we know today about human learning processes suggest that even at their most efficient, those processes must be long exercised. Although we have a reasonable basis for hope that we may find ways to make learning processes more efficient, we should not expect to produce the miracle of effortless learning.[22]

CONCLUSION

To reengineer corporate training, we need to change our expectations about acquiring knowledge, about understanding theory, and about the importance of plain old practice and drill. A manager at Ford poignantly captured the essence of our expectations about training by noting:

If calculus were invented today our organizations would not be able to learn it. We'd send everyone off to the three-day intensive program. We'd then tell everyone to try to apply what they'd learned. After three to six months we'd assess whether it was working. We'd undoubtedly then conclude that this "calculus stuff" wasn't all it was made out to be and go off and look for something else to improve results.[23]

What else is there to say? This quote says it all.

NOTES

1. J. S. Bruner, "Going Beyond the Information Given," in J. Anglin (ed.), *Beyond the Information Given: Studies in the Psychology of Knowing* (New York: W. W. Norton, 1973), p. 232.

2. T. T. Baldwin and J. K. Ford, "Transfer of Training: A Review and Directions for Future Research," *Personnel Psychology* 41 (1988), p. 82.

3. R. Glaser, "Learning Theory and Theories of Knowledge," in E. De Corte, H. Lodewijks, R. Parmentier, and P. Span (eds.), *Learning and Instruction*, Vol. 1 (Oxford: Pergamon Press, 1987), p. 400.

4. Kenneth Brown, *Inventors at Work: Interviews with 16 Notable American Inventors*, Tempus Books (Redmond, WA: Microsoft Press, 1988), p. 158.

5. Ibid., p. 208.

6. See J. R. Hayes, "Three Problems in Teaching General Skills," in S. F. Chipman, J. W. Segal, and R. Glaser (eds.), *Thinking and Learning Skills*, Vol. 2: *Research and Open Questions* (Hillsdale, NJ: Lawrence Erlbaum, 1985,) p. 395. also in K. A. Ericcson and N. Charness, "Expert Performance: Its Structure and Acquisition," *American Psychologist* 49(8) (1994), pp. 725–747.

7. Brown, *Inventors at Work*, p. 130.

8. M. K. Singley and J. R. Anderson, *The Transfer of Cognitive Skill* (Cambridge, MA: Harvard University Press, 1989), p. 220.

9. In P. Senge, C. Roberts, R. Ross, B. Smith, and A. Keiner, *The Fifth Discipline Fieldbook: Strategies and Tools for Building a Learning Organization* (New York: Doubleday, 1994), p. 36.

10. Baldwin and Ford, "Transfer of Training: A Review and Directions for Future Research," p. 82.

11. A. L. Brown, "Analogical Learning and Transfer: What Develops?" in S. Vosniadou and A. Ortony (eds.), *Similarity and Analogical Reasoning* (Hillsdale, NJ: Lawrence Erlbaum, pp. 369–412.

12. A. Flexner, "On the Usefulness of Useless Knowledge," in L. G. Locke, W. Gibson, and G. Arms (eds.), *Toward Liberal Education* (New York: Holt, Rinehart and Winston, 1961), pp. 443–452.

13. Interview, "Today's Leaders Look to Tomorrow," *Fortune* (March 26, 1990), p. 78.

14. Brown, *Inventors at Work*, p. 163.

15. Ibid., p. 205.

16. In Ericcson and Charness, "Expert Performance."

17. Brown, *Inventors at Work*, pp. 373–375.

18. Hayes, "Three Problems in Teaching General Skills," p. 397.

19. N. Frederiksen, "Implications of Cognitive Theory for Instruction in Problem Solving," *Review of Educational Research* 54 (1984), p. 370.

20. Ericcson and Charness, "Expert Performance."

21. Hayes, "Three Problems in Teaching General Skills," p. 397.

22. J. Larkin, J. McDermott, D. Simon, and H. A. Simon, "Expert and Novice Performance in Solving Physics Problems," *Science* 208 (1980), p. 1342.

23. In Senge et al., *The Fifth Discipline Fieldbook*, p. 45.

9

Mental Models: Transfer Thinking and Leveraged Learning

We're not going to have to outscale our competitors, we have to out-
think them.

Steve Jobs[1]

Edward de Bono, the well-known business consultant who has been teaching thinking skills to business and industry for years, and author of *Lateral
Thinking*, puts forth the provocative notion: God cannot think. The reason
God cannot think, says de Bono, is because "[c]omplete information makes
thinking unnecessary and impossible, because thinking is moving from a
state of imperfect information to a state of more useful information."[2]
Thinking, then—for most of us mortals—is for getting us somewhere we
are not. And this requires transfer.

For the learning organization, there can be no more central issues than
thinking and reasoning. Unlike training, thinking and reasoning are more
intricate and long-term processes. The short of it is that thinking and reasoning are largely—if not almost completely—dependent on transfer. In
this chapter, as in the previous chapter, I will not be covering ground that
others have already covered; rather, I'll be explaining mental models as
they directly pertain to thinking and reasoning and showing that mental
models, thinking, and reasoning are based in transfer (see also the next
chapter). Before I do, however, it's necessary to examine what are called
learning strategies.

KNOWLEDGE BASE AND LEARNING STRATEGIES

There are many who believe that instruction in isolated learning and thinking strategies, that is, techniques that require little knowledge base, are the most effective way to create transfer thinking. In the move to organizations that learn, it is increasingly important to understand the role of transfer in thinking. Even some of those who teach thinking strategies sometimes recognize the importance of transfer. Edward de Bono recognizes that effective thinking depends on transfer. In fact, he says, "The problem of transfer is the most important problem facing any program that sets out to teach thinking skills."[3] The teaching of abstract strategies and skills, in my judgment, has been done at the expense of declarative and theoretical knowledge base and therefore has not yielded much benefit. We need to understand the role of strategies in thinking and learning.

The strategy view of thinking is that people reason using abstract rules that are relatively independent of a specific knowledge base and experience. In fact, some psychologists and many laypersons have a tendency to view thinking as somehow innate—that there is a hardwired power of the mind to reason and that some people innately have more of this power than others. While there is a kernel of truth to this belief, it's an oversimplification. For years, there have been many programs not only in the schools but in business training that purport to teach general, abstract, and critical thinking skills. These programs claim to produce positive results. Most evaluation research on these programs, however, suggests otherwise.

One group of researchers who investigated six of the most widely known programs flatly states that "there is no convincing evidence that any of the six approaches to strategy instruction . . . produce generally competent strategy users."[4] After reviewing numerous learning strategy programs, another researcher concludes that "research on all of these programs does not support the use of highroad mechanisms to foster transfer of higher order thinking."[5] The author goes on to say that while these programs have increased performance levels on exercises very closely similar to the ones used in the original instruction, the impact of the instruction on practical everyday performance outside of the learning situation have been either absent or inconsistent.

Wilbert McKeachie, while only somewhat more optimistic, suggests that teaching learning strategy skills produces only a moderate degree of effectiveness and transfer outcomes. In being moderately optimistic, however, he suggests that such programs require many hours of instruction. Quite unflatteringly, he says that "there does not seem to be much support for the relatively short-term programs widely promoted for gullible business managers."[6] To the degree that they do work, high-level cognitive skills require programs of no less than 40 to 60 hours of instruction. Again, there are no quick fixes to learning, let alone transfer.

In teaching contentless strategies, one must be quite cautious and extremely skeptical. First, there are so many possible strategies to teach. Second, we do not know which ones work at all or work the best. Third, a strategy approach may all too easily lead to a cookbook approach, and cookbook approaches to learning are all too easily misinterpreted by learners. In training and in classroom situations, problems are generally well defined, and the knowledge required to solve them is typically present.

It's important to understand that unlike in training or classroom instruction, most thinking, reasoning, and problem-solving situations in everyday life are messy or ill-structured. This creates extremely problematic conditions for transfer of learning. Again, an extensive knowledge base is what is required for coping with ill-structured problems. Accordingly, a broad knowledge base is a requirement for the shift to the learning organization; it is also what is required for broad transfer of learning and reasoning.

Just as the shift from training to learning does not mean that training is outmoded, so, too, the shift to instilling an extensive knowledge base does not mean that abstracted learning strategies are outmoded. Quite the contrary. Both are needed. Such strategies may occasionally useful for people who are confronted with problems in areas in which they do not have much knowledge. In short, knowledge-independent thinking strategies are sometimes useful when we do not know very much. Nevertheless, findings indicate that the people who are good at thinking and who use problem-solving strategies the most successfully also know a great deal about the world in general; they have an extensive knowledge base as well.

What this means is that people who are good at thinking with strategies are not good at thinking because of the nature of the strategies themselves; they are good at thinking with strategies because of their general knowledge base. For most of us, in order to think well, we have to think about something, and the more we know about that *something*, the better we think. Not only does Nature abhor a vacuum, so does the human mind.

As I outlined in the previous chapter, knowledge base affects strategic implementation in a number of ways. It often contains information that makes use of a strategy unnecessary, and often, material that is learned by relying on the knowledge base stimulates the use of strategies for material that is not congruent with prior knowledge. That is, strategy use, selection, and implementation are often knowledge driven. Further, many strategies can only be profitably executed by people who possess a lot of knowledge. Strategies are only weak thinking structures, unlike the strong generic structures that I'll detail in Chapter 10.

While teaching specific strategies is a viable approach for some situations, there are just too many of them and we do not know when or to what extent or under what conditions they work. Second, to break everything down into discrete tasks and procedures results in never-ending lists, as the programmed learning texts movement of a few years ago demonstrated.

Even when programmed texts are successful, it's difficult to move people beyond them. Like specific learning strategies, however, they are useful for some very technical tasks or perhaps for learning everyday math. It's doubtful if such methods would create even a middle-level mathematician. Conversely, isolated rules, or concrete strategies learned in particular situations, are less likely to be transferred. Applying strategies to areas where one has little or no knowledge *is like* applying a scientific methodology in a formula fashion outside one's area of expertise.

Without a large and valid knowledge base, the use of isolated transfer strategies (= training) is not likely to lead to transfer or to be transferred to situations outside the instructional context. This is largely the case, because without an extensive knowledge base, there is nothing to connect isolated strategies to. Applying general learning strategies and techniques to areas where one has little or no knowledge is like painting pictures by filling in numbered slots.

MENTAL MODELS, THINKING, AND TRANSFER

Not only is learning in fact transfer; mental models are transfer based as well. As Gray and Orasanu recognize in "Transfer of Cognitive Skills," "Teaching a problem solver a mental model is a type of learning-as-transfer." Why this is the case, they say, is because "[m]ental models contain declarative knowledge about the states and combinations of methods required to solve problems in the task problem space."[7] It almost follows logically from this that thinking is dependent on transfer—which it is.

Mental model is a term that has come dangerously close to being omni meaningful, with each profession that uses it having its own definition. Mental models can be as simple as generalizations or as complex as a scientific theory. On a concrete level, aeronautical engineers build scale models of the aircraft they are designing. Experiments are models for the everyday phenomena we wish to find out about. For example, aeronautical engineers simulate the effect of wind on their aircraft by building wind tunnel models. Social psychologists design experiments that model life situations. When we image some situation, we have a mental model of it.

For many people, thinking is mentally going through a sequence of operations with imaginary events and situations, that is, modeling. In this view, thinking is a kind of imaginary experiment carried out in the mind's eye, or what is called a *gedankenexperiment* or thought experiment. Even our unexamined view of the everyday world is technically a model of it, for we cannot really know it.

In industrial training, the term *model* sometimes refers to the understanding one has about a piece of machinery. David Kieras and Susan Bovair suggest that "by 'mental model' is meant some kind of understanding of how the device works in terms of its internal structure and processes. In the remainder of this paper, this type of mental model will be termed a device model, to distinguish it from the many other senses of the term mental model."[8] They continue:

The results of these three experiments not only show that device model information can have definite and strong facilitative effects, but also show how it does, and what kind of information is critical for an effective device model for this type of device. The earlier attempts to demonstrate effects may have been inconclusive because the wrong choice of task or model information would produce no effects. Furthermore, the explanation that the task becomes more "meaningful" as a result of having a device model can be replaced with a more specific explanation, that the device model helps because it makes possible specific inferences about what the operating procedures must be.[9]

In the course of our learning, we develop what cognitive psychologists and philosophers call *mental representations* of tasks. These representations are in fact mental models or schemas, and it is these models that guide our performance at a task. A machinist develops a mental model of his or her machine. In engineering, such a mental model is sometimes referred to as device knowledge. Industrial researchers find that "device knowledge organized as mental models provides an inference-base that enables procedures to be inferred when exact procedural steps are either not accessible . . . not previously known, or forgotten."[10] Experiments with engineering students learning electrical control devices have demonstrated that students presented with a model of the device prior to training learned faster, had better memory retention, and were better at transfer than students not presented with a model prior to training.[11] Models of a device or task facilitate thinking.

On one level, mental models mediate the transfer between a problem and its solution, providing information about how to solve the problem based on the similarity between the original problem and the model. In fact, teaching someone to problem-solve using mental models is a form of learning as transfer. Once again, the knowledge base that we possess about a task affects the quality of our models and thus the quality of our reasoning performance.

Peter Senge has written extensively on the effects of mental models in management theory.[12] As he points out, in organizations the mental models people have in their heads influence the way they think, act, and describe what they see, both in terms of interacting with others and in terms of the organization. He, too, has a distinct view of what a mental model is. According to Senge, working with mental models involves working with the direct data of experience, not mental abstractions derived from data. While I don't believe that the distinction between the direct data of our experience, on the one hand, and the abstractions from the data, on the other, can be made, it's nevertheless perhaps a useful distinction.

From a cognitive psychological perspective, even our experience is an abstraction from data.[13] I should also note that thinking, reasoning, and mental models cannot be explained adequately without at some point explaining the use of archetypes, generic thinking structures, and analogical reasoning. Reasoning by what is commonly called analogy has been a long-term interest of mine. In recent years, there has also been a great deal of research on analogical reasoning by psychologists who study thought processes. Senge has also insightfully applied the concepts of archetypes and generic structures to learning organizations and has demonstrated their everyday importance. Because archetypal and generic reasoning are so important, I will explain their cognitive and transfer basis, along with analogical reasoning, in Chapter 10. However mental model is defined, its use is crucial for building learning organizations because they involve thinking and transfer learning.

So, what are mental models composed of? As I noted earlier, cognitive research suggests that most of our everyday reasoning and thinking do not involve formal or abstract reasoning. Rather, they involve the manipulation of concrete mental models. At the very foundation of our perceiving the world are mental models. We acquire these models by identifying what Jerome Bruner and colleagues have called "the recurrent regularities in our environment." They go on to explain that the "task in identifying everyday recurrent regularity . . . requires either the construction of a model of this regularity or the employment of a model that has previously been constructed by the person."[14] Recurrent regularities are transfer-generated stabilizations of our constantly changing everyday environment. This is how we develop pattern recognition in the flux of apparent chaos. From these regularities, we create knowledge structures that enable us to think and reason and transfer.

THINKING, REASONING, AND TRANSFER

As I pointed out in Chapter 3, the shift from training to learning requires a shift in perspective on how we approach instruction. Likewise, the move to seeing organizations as learning organizations requires that we look at the role of thinking and reasoning in more depth than has traditionally been the case in organizational training—indeed, in the very everyday functioning of organizations.

Reasoning has generally been based on the assumption that people reason with abstract rules and that some are better at it than others. Thinking with abstract rules can be illustrated by the following:

1. *If A causes B, and C is like A in essential characteristics, then C will*

cause B. It seems reasonable to assume from this view that if someone understands (1), they will be able to engage in reasoning as follows:

2. *If W causes X, and Y is like W in essential characteristics, then Y will cause X.* It has been thought that if someone understands (1), they will be able to understand (2) because although they are different on the surface, they have the same generic or formal structure. Most don't.

For example, many students in grade school who learn how to multiply, add, and subtract numbers in school are unable to multiply, add, and subtract real items in their everyday lives. The converse is also true. Studies show that street children who do complex mathematical calculations in their street business are unable to do the same math problems when presented with them formally in a classroom situation.

Miriam Bassok examined the application of analogical reasoning by students who received instruction on solving physics problems involving constant change in speed. After finishing the physics training, the students were asked to solve either a population problem or an attendance problem as follows:

Population: "The rate of population growth in a certain country has increased steadily during the past 12 years from 3,000 people/year to 15,000 people/year. How many people total were added to the population during the 12-year period?"

Attendance: "An annual art fair is held on November 1 every year. The attendance rate at the annual fair has increased steadily during the past 12 years from 3,000 people/year to 15,000 people/year. How many people total attended the fair during the 12-year period?"[15]

These two population and attendance problems are similar to the physics distance problem since they use the same quantities (e.g., people per year) and the same phrasing (e.g., increased steadily). However, in a transfer study, 71 percent of college students used the distance equation to solve the population problem, but only 27 percent of them used the distance equation to solve attendance problems. Nearly all the research on analogical reasoning shows similar results.

In contrast to this view, the knowledge base view is that thinking and reasoning are dependent on content-specific knowledge of an area. In terms of the above examples where (1) if A causes B, and C is like A in essential characteristics, then C will cause B, and (2) if W causes X, and Y is like W in essential characteristics, then Y will cause X, a person would have to have specific knowledge of both A and W to make the transfer.

People who are good at transfer don't need knowledge of both A and W. Most people, however, do require specific knowledge of both A and W. They need specific content to reason with. Literally, it's *as if* someone can reason that: 1 + 1 = 2 but can't reason that one gaggle of geese and another gaggle of geese equal two gaggle of geese.

PRACTICAL REASONING SCHEMAS

Psychologists have proposed a number of mechanisms as the basic unit of human thinking. These mechanisms have been called *prototypes, exemplars, frames, scripts*, and *mental models*. The most widely—perhaps overly—used term is *schema*. A schema is a mental structure by which our knowledge is organized and processed. A model can be distinguished from a schema in that a schema is a generic knowledge structure existing in long-term memory and contains *generic slots* into which we place kinds of things (i.e., things that have the same structure), whereas a mental model is a more specific understanding of a task and its demands. A mental model also includes information for specifying what goes in the generic slots of mental schemas.

New information is thought to be assimilated, learned, and interpreted in terms of our relevant preexisting schemas. Translated into transfer of learning terms, this means that we understand newly learned material by transferring or mapping it onto older schemas. As such, much of the research on mental schemas is in fact transfer research, but without articulating the precise structures responsible for the transfer. J. F. Voss, for example, insightfully notes, "[W]hen the schema notion becomes sufficiently unpacked, we may find that we have highly specific transfer which is found frequently with high-knowledge individuals because of their varied experiences."[16] Typically, a schema can be seen as a nonconscious structure, and a model is an image that is conscious. In any event, however defined, understanding mental models is important in understanding thinking. And transfer of learning figures prominently in the creation and use of schemas and mental models.

The preponderance of current research suggests that most people reason with what is termed *pragmatic reasoning schemas*. These schemas are in fact everyday mental models and are dependent on the specific knowledge bases attached to them, not on abstractions or generic rules of logic. This type of knowledge base is made up of specific information about specific events or situations, of concrete instances of experience. Even many experts who reason abstractly or generically in their own domain do not apply formal logical reasoning outside—or at least very far outside—their domain of expertise, despite the fact that the reasoning may be quite *similar* or applicable.

Thus, we can better understand the logical reasoning of humans not by attributing to them any formal logical calculus but by attending instead to their pragmatic reasoning schemas and by direct implication to their specific experience and knowledge base. So knowledge base is important in two senses. First, it's important in the specific sense of reasoning concretely, or within a specific domain. Second, and contrary to much of the current thinking on this issue, knowledge base is important in a more generic sense for creating the conditions for general transfer-*ability*.

Howard Gardner notes that these pragmatic reasoning schemas are important. He says, "Just how one learns to construct such mental models, to integrate them with 'real world' knowledge, and to deploy them appropriately in the proper circumstances are fertile questions for developmental and educational psychology."[17] There are exceptions to reasoning with pragmatic reasoning schemas, as we will see in the next chapter on generic and general systems thinking.

On a basic level, transfer of learning is central to how we classify things. Classification makes it possible to categorize the world around us. For example, how do we know that an ostrich (call it A) is the *same* thing as an eagle (call it W)—that both are birds? Though their surface characteristics are quite different, even to the extent that an ostrich can't fly, we know that both are birds. The answer is: We know that they are *similar* in their deeper, more essential characteristics. Our theoretical knowledge tells us that both are *examples* of the category "bird."

Whenever we classify something or use an example, it's the consequence of the mental processes of comparing and mapping two things and seeing that they are the "same." Thus, reasoning involves assimilating our models of novel situations to our models of familiar situations, that is, seeing things as in some way similar. All thinking seems to be based on a continuum of possible situations of reasoning by similarity. At one end of the continuum is simply *remembering*; in the middle is *generalizing*, being *reminded of*, reasoning by *example*; and at the other end is what might be called analogical reasoning. Most human reasoning is based on these kinds of processes, from simple comparisons to the complex mapping of General Systems theory (see Chapter 10).

One of the things we know about transfer and thinking is that transfer is central to problem solving; we know that learners prepare for transfer by seeing "new" problems not as isolated ones but as instances of a general class of problem. Research indicates that some people tend to solve individual problems as isolated single instances, whereas some treat them as instances of a general class of problems, that is, as a group of similar problems that can be solved by a similar principle. The difference between these two types of people is that those who see each problem as unique tend to be unschooled, with their concrete knowledge base having developed simply out of their own unique experience. People's unique experiences tend to be welded to the particular contexts of those experiences; those using pragmatic reasoning schemas have trouble decontextualizing, or detaching their knowledge base and experience from the concrete situations where they were learned. Again, it's as if we can add two apples and two apples to equal four apples but cannot add the abstraction $2 + 2 = 4$.

Thinking is the reconstruction and application of knowledge from one context to match new contexts; it's a shortcut in mental organization, making it possible to see that new problems are not completely new. In short, it's transfer of learning. In fact, the learning of abstract material and the solving of problems with ideas (that is, reasoning) are the consequence of transfer; it's the ability to transform novel information or situations into something more familiar. Indeed, when we teach problem solving, or reasoning, we are usually referring to teaching people to use (that is, transfer) that learning in new situations to solve new problems.

Thus, contrary to a widely held assumption that people base their decisions on rules and general principles abstracted from experience, increasingly research is showing that people often reason on the basis of a *single* similar instance, using it as a model. Research suggests that when people learn novel behaviors, what they may initially learn is a set of specific examples rather than a general rule. As situations become more complex, people rely even more heavily on single, similar instances in making decisions and predictions. Particular instances become mental models. Experiments also show that people often place as much, if not more, faith in single or similar instances from their own experience as they do in an abstract rule. So much for formal logic in everyday reasoning.

While this concrete mode of thinking may work in many everyday situations, imagine where our knowledge of physics would be if physicists relied solely on such concrete reasoning. However, the same research also shows that when people—even young children—are given sufficient information and theoretical frameworks, they are more likely either to reason on the basis of an abstract rule or principle or to reason on the basis of a single example.

Many people—perhaps most—do not engage in higher-order thinking. This is often true of managers as well. According to Peter Senge, experience and experiments often show that even when some managers have sufficient time for reflection and the opportunity for retrieving relevant information, most do not carefully reflect on their actions, that is, think. Typically, they adopt a strategy; then as soon as the strategy runs into problems, they switch to another, then to another and another, and so on.[18] Most managers tend to be action-oriented people—as they should be. But action should follow, or at least be concurrent with, reflective thinking. Once again, training has tended to create a kind of cookbook approach to thinking. We already saw what happened to General Custer's cookbook approach to knowledge and thinking about battle strategy. In the learning organization, thinking must become more predominant.

Invention often begins with a problem to solve. And solving the problem is often accomplished by using a mental model based on something already known. The problem in the following case was that carbonated beverages could not be put in the plastic bottle that already existed. Why? Because the plastic would expand under the built-up pressure created by the carbonation. In the mid-1970s, Nat Wyeth had been experimenting for a considerable time, trying to engineer a plastic soda bottle that would hold carbonated soda without expanding and blowing apart. Bottles were made out of glass at the time. Meeting with repeated failure, Wyeth continued to show his distorted and misshapen plastic bottles to the director of the research laboratory at Du Pont. He finally succeeded. What kind of reasoning enabled him to invent the process? While arriving at the end product was more complicated, this was the essential transfer breakthrough.

What Wyeth did was to transfer a process used in another area to his own problem. He was aware of the work of Wallace Carothers, the inventor of nylon. Carothers made a strong nylon thread by forcing or squirting the liquid material through a tiny aperture, creating a very thin strand of fiber. Stretching the fibers in such a way made them quite strong because the molecules all line up in one direction. To explain how the strength of the material increased by lining up the molecules, he said, "I like to think of it as the way people line up at a rope in a tug-of-war. If the people on one side are all pulling in different directions, they won't be able to pull as hard as they could if they all pulled in one direction. You get greater force when everybody's pulling in one direction. With nylon Carothers was lining the molecules up so that they all pulled together." With transfer thinking, Wyeth understood that the plastic molecules could be oriented in the *same way* so that "instead of pulling in all directions—making the stuff rather flabby—they can pull together so that it's strong enough to withstand the increasing pressure created by carbonated beverages."[19] Wyeth used the Carothers nylon thread process and the tug-of-war game as mental models.

LEVERAGED LEARNING AND THINKING

The ancient Greek Archimedes is credited with the principle of the lever: Give me a lever, he is reputed to have said, and I will lift the earth. Hence, the principle of leverage. It's transfer thinking that makes possible what I term *leveraged learning*. In developing the term, I have transferred the use of the term *leverage* from systems thinkers like Peter Senge to the learning process. Leveraged learning as it applies to transfer of learning has three aspects.

1. Within a systems thinking framework, the first aspect of leveraged learning is that of a highly focused and concentrated action that produces *significant change with the least amount of effort*. One of the best metaphorical explanations of leveraged action, noted by Senge, is one by Buckminster Fuller: If you are temporarily operating a tugboat and are not familiar with hydrodynamics, how would you go about turning a huge moving oil tanker to the left? Most people might direct the tugboat to the tanker's bow and push. The correct leveraged action, however, is to push on its stern. This is, after all, how the ship's rudder does it. Ships turn because their stern is sucked around. By being turned into the water flowing into the bow, the water flow is compressed, creating a pressure differential

that pulls the stern in the opposite direction as the rudder. Analogical and metaphorical transfer functions as the (leveraged) rudder of thought.

2. The second aspect of leveraged learning is being able to "see underlying structures rather than events," of "learning to recognize types of 'structures' that recur again and again."[20]

A graphic example of this aspect of leveraged learning is the following, where each numbering system while different on the surface is generically or structurally the same.

1.	1	2	3	4	5	6	7	8	9	10	11	12
2.	i	ii	iii	iv	v	vi	vii	viii	ix	x	xi	xii
3.	I	II	III	IV	V	VI	VII	VIII	IX	X	XI	XII

While each of these three numbering sequences is apparently different on the surface, we can nevertheless see that their *underlying structure* is the same.

We recognize this common structure partly by what is called mapping. We map events when *common or similar relations* are compared with the original source. This is what occurred when the atom was conceptualized as being *like* a solar system, example, both the atom and the solar system have revolving objects: electrons and planets. In finding such similarity, new information may be discovered; that is, similarities may be inferred that were not originally apparent when the analogy was first made. In the process of constructing the solar system/atom analogy, for example, it was inferred that there might be a gravitational attraction between an electron and the nucleus, just as there is between a planet and the sun. This is new knowledge.

3. The third aspect of leveraged learning based on analogical transfer is its *economy of thinking function*. In this aspect, when surface differences of events are reduced to their underlying structure, to their similarities, apparently different concepts are compressed into one concept or structure. Continuing the graphic metaphor, the following is a representation of the third aspect of leveraged learning showing an underlying common structure of apparently different events.

1.	1	2	3	4	5	6	7	8	9	10	11	12
2.	.	.	.	.	.	vi	vii	viii	ix	.	.	.
3.	.	.	.	.	.	VI	VII	VIII	IX	X	XI	XII

The use of analogical and metaphorical reasoning, then, is like turning an oil tanker by pushing on its stern instead of its bow.

Analogical transfer makes possible our reducing and transforming the vast amount of *detail complexity* that we have to increasingly deal with everyday; in systems thinking terms, almost by definition, analogical transfer is about reducing detailed complexity to a more manageable *dynamic and structural complexity*. As Senge notes, "[T]he art of systems thinking lies in seeing through complexity to the underlying structures."[21] The real leverage in management situations, he says, is recognizing dynamic complexity. Transfer enables us to accomplish this. It's transfer that makes thinking and reasoning possible.

NOTES

1. "Today's Leaders Look to Tomorrow," *Fortune* (March 26, 1990), p. 30.

2. E. de Bono, "The CoRT Thinking Program," in J. W., Segal, S. F. Chipman, and R. Glaser, (eds.), *Thinking and Learning Skills*, Vol. 1: *Relating Instruction to Research* (Hillsdale, NJ: Lawrence Erlbaum Associates, 1985), p. 368.

3. Ibid., p. 366.

4. M. Pressley, B. Snyder, and T. Cariglia-Bull, "How Can Good Strategy Use Be Taught to Children? Evaluation of Six Alternative Approaches," in S. M. Cormier and J. D. Hagman (eds.), *Transfer of Learning Contemporary Research and Application* (New York: Academic Press, 1987), p. 105.

5. M. Niedelman, "Problem Solving and Transfer," *Journal of Learning Disabilities* 24(6) (1991), pp. 325.

6. W. J. McKeachie, "The New Look in Instructional Psychology: Teaching Strategies for Learning and Thinking," in E. De Corte, H. Lodewijks, R. Parmentier, and P. Span (eds.), *Learning and Instruction*, Vol. 1 (Oxford: Pergamon Press, 1987), p. 447.

7. W. D. Gray and J. M. Orasanu, "Transfer of Cognitive Skills," in S. M. Cormier and J. D. Hagman (eds.), *Transfer of Learning: Contemporary Research and Applications* (New York: Academic Press, 1987), p. 204.

8. D. Kieras and S. Bovair, "The Role of a Mental Model in Learning to Operate a Device," *Cognitive Science* 8 (1984), p. 255.

9. Ibid.

10. S. P. Gott, P. Hall, A. Pokorny, E. Dibble, and R. Glaser, "A Naturalistic Study of Transfer: Adaptive Expertise in Technical Domains," in D. K. Detterman and R. J. Sternberg (eds.), *Transfer on Trial: Intelligence, Cognition, and Instruction* (Norwood, NJ: Ablex, 1993), p. 259.

11. In R. Glaser, "Learning Theory and Theories of Knowledge," in E. De Corte, H. Lodewijks, R. Parmentier, and P. Span (eds.), *Learning and Instruction*, Vol. 1 (Oxford: Pergamon Press, 1987), p. 408.

12. P. M. Senge, *The Fifth Discipline: The Art and Practice of the Learning Organization* (New York: Doubleday, 1990).

13. There are a couple of cognitive theories that take exception to the general cognitive view that our experience is the consequence of abstracting from the data and thus may agree with Senge. The exceptions maintain that organisms "directly pick up" data from the environment. To say much more would take us too far afield.

14. J. Bruner, M. Wallach, and E. Galanter, "The Identification of Recurrent

Regularity," in J. S. Bruner, *Beyond the Information Given* (ed. J. M Anglin) (New York: W. W. Norton, 1973), p. 206.

15. M. Bassok, "Using Content to Interpret Structure: Effects on Analogical Transfer," *Current Directions in Psychological Science* 5 (1996), p. 55.

16. J. F. Voss, "Learning and Transfer in Subject-Matter Learning: A Problem-Solving Model," *International Journal of Educational Research* 11 (1987), p. 619.

17. H. Gardner, *The Mind's New Science: A History of the Cognitive Revolution* (New York: Basic Books, 1985), p. 369.

18. Senge, *The Fifth Discipline.*

19. Kenneth Brown, *Inventors at Work: Interviews with 16 Notable American Inventors*, Tempus Books (Redmond, WA: Microsoft Press, 1988), p. 373.

20. Senge, *The Fifth Discipline*, pp. 65, 73.

21. Ibid., p. 128.

10

Systems Thinking: How to Recognize Generic Structures, System Archetypes, and Transfer of Mental Models

Equivalence categories or concepts are the most basic currency one can utilize in going beyond the sensory given. They are the first steps toward rendering the environment generic.

Jerome Bruner[1]

In his seminal book on learning organizations, *The Fifth Discipline*, Peter Senge discusses at length the cardinal concepts of systems thinking, generic structures, and archetypes and gives numerous practical examples from his work in business and industry. In his fieldbook, he presents a practical guide as to how these structures can be recognized. Senge is one of the few in current HRD management training whose systems model is founded on transfer thinking; he is a person who, therefore almost by definition, possesses a skilled sense of transfer. Unfortunately, he does not address transfer thinking. Senge's systems perspective is, then, an ideal model to use in explaining the importance of transfer for HRD training.

Senge outlines five disciplines involved in learning organizations: (1) the *personal mastery* of our inner goals and visions, (2) understanding the *mental models* we have in our heads, (3) developing *shared visions* with others, (4) *team learning*, and (5) *systems thinking*. Systems thinking is learning to recognize relationships and interconnections among phenomena. Systems thinking involves generic structures, system archetypes. As he uses the term *generic structure*, he refers to recurring patterns of feedback interactions underlying diverse business phenomena. These generic structures may be quite simple, like system archetypes (see below), or more complex, perhaps involving ten to fifteen or more feedback interactions.

A fully developed generic business structure needs to be articulated through a computer simulation model so that its detailed dynamic behavior can be understood properly. So, in this sense, *generic structure* is a general term, which encompasses system archetypes as a specific example. Further, Senge says, "The system archetypes are perhaps the simplest of the generic structures. . . . To use the analogy to a language, the system archetypes are like very simple story lines which could be expressed in a sentence or two. The generic management structures would be more complex stories, which also are less broadly applicable."[2] Although this entire book is on transfer of learning framework for understanding systems thinking and generic structures of thought, this chapter, in particular, is an explicit transfer accounting of the cardinal systems concepts. The reader should be aware, however, that I will not be using the three terms exactly as Senge does; rather, I will be providing an explanation of the psychological underpinning of systems thinking.

Quite understandably, what is missing in systems thinking is a cognitive account and a general psychological framework for how we mentally access, construct, and recognize generic business structures and system archetypes. As Mark Paich pointed out in a 1985 issue of *Systems Dynamics Review*, "[T]he system dynamics method offers no guidance about how to move from a group of case-specific models to generic structures. There are no procedures or methods for synthesizing a mass of case-specific analyses into something more general."[3] Systems thinking and thinking in generic structures and archetypes are a way of reducing detailed complexity to manageable proportions. This mental ability is becoming increasingly necessary for managers who will be working and managing in rapidly changing, diverse, and novel business environments. To succeed at systems thinking requires transfer thinking.

GENERIC STRUCTURES

Generic mental structures are the signatures of transfer. Indeed, as Jerome Bruner and colleagues note, "Much of learning and problem solving can be viewed as a task in identifying recurrent regularities in the environment and this requires . . . the construction of a model of this regularity."[4] In order to recognize generic structures, then, one needs to see through detail complexity to the underlying pattern or template of apparent diverse events. In his book, Senge insightfully chronicles many examples of generic structures and what he calls systems archetypes. He is able to chronicle these archetypes because he is proficient at transfer, as are most systems theorists. We recognize generic structures everyday. They are as common as grass. We could not make sense of our world if we were not all expert in recognizing generic structures, yet most of us are deficient in recognizing such structures where it counts.

In Chapter 2, I pointed out that a rat cannot recognize a triangle if the three sides are presented as a series of dots instead of solid lines. What this means is that the rat was unable to abstract out the underlying generic structure of the idea of triangle. When we recognize an oak, a pine, and a coconut palm as all being examples of the category tree, we are abstracting out their generic invariant structure from their surface diversity. Simple? Yes and no. Once we leave these everyday examples, we often become very much like our fellow rat.

Jerome Bruner wrote extensively on generic structures and what he called equivalence categories. As he says in the display quote to this chapter, equivalence categories are what render the environment generic. The prototype of generic structures is to be found in mathematics: $1 + 1 = 2$. Into this structure, you can plug in apples, peaches, plums, trees, or rats. The detail complexity is ignored; only the essential structure remains. In earlier chapters, I have given examples of technology transfer where a piece of technology developed for one area is transferred to an apparently unrelated area. One of these examples was of modeling (i.e., comparing, transferring) an engineering design schematic to business inventory data and flow charts. Another example was the mapping of microdrilling in one industry to possible microdrilling needs in other industries. Both examples of knowledge transfer required the person doing it to ignore the detail complexity or surface dissimilarities and to abstract out the generic structure. Examples of this kind can be found in business books and magazines. They are usually not presented as examples of transfer, however. In Chapter 6, I outlined many other examples of technology transfer.

One corporate example of "seeing" generic structure and the payoff of being able to think in these terms was cited in *The Teamnet Factor* by Jessica Lipnack and Jeffrey Stamps. While the authors did not present the following example as an instance of generic thinking, this is exactly what the example exemplifies. A few years ago, Erie Bolt Corporation was about to go bankrupt. A new CEO was hired who, from the perspective of this chapter, thought in generic structures. Instead of asking, How can Erie Bolt Corporation make better bolts? he asked a more generic question: What business is Erie Bolt in? That the company makes bolts would have been the obvious answer. Instead, he saw the company as one that (1) forges metal, (2) heat treats metal, (3) does machining of metal, and (4) performs other metalworking functions.[5] In other words, the new CEO "saw" the generic structure of Erie Bolt Corporation. When Erie Bolt was *seen generically*, not just as a manufacturer of bolts, it could then reengineer and reinvent itself. As a result, the company turned its financial losses into profits. Reengineering and reinventing require skill in transfer thinking.

What the new CEO of Erie Bolt did was to create a new concept. In concept formation, the perception of similarity and of generic structure is fundamental. With hindsight, of course, such examples always seem obvious. Once a transfer is recognized, it often appears simple and obvious, even childlike. This is the deceptive nature of transfer. The fact is, however, most people become stuck in the details, in the content activities, in what I referred to in Chapter 2 as functional fixedness. We find this generic style of thinking in those who are highly proficient at what they do. For example, when questioned about their expectations about a general troubleshooting approach that would apply to their new job, more proficient technicians talked in terms of an abstract (or generic) goal structure, whereas less proficient technicians talked in terms of more specific (and concrete) procedural steps as a general approach to troubleshooting.[6] Unfortunately, most learning is welded to the context in which it is learned and not transferred.

It's not at all clear which cognitive processes are responsible when people learn to think generically. For example, they might have an image or mental picture of individual instances, or from many occurrences, they may abstract out a central tendency. Psychologists have developed many excellent theories based on research findings. To review them all here would take us too far afield. In general, however, recent experimental findings indicate that transfer between similar or isomorphic problems (i.e., structurally identical) tends to occur when rules independent of the specific problems are learned during problem solving. Researchers have found that instruction on algebra problems transferred to structurally similar physics problems but that instruction on physics problems tended not to transfer to algebra problems. What these findings suggest is that since algebra is inherently more abstract or generic, more transfer occurs than from instruction in areas that have specific content. The underlying generic structure of specific areas is typically masked by the specific content.[7] Whatever the ultimate explanation, the idea of generic mental structures will undoubtedly figure prominently.

It's the noticing of generic structure that facilitates learning. Experiments have demonstrated that when two stories with the same structure but with different surface appearances are presented to people, it leads to improved learning of the second story—even when the people are not aware that the two stories have the same structure.[8] As Walter Weimer has noted, the only way we have to make "infinite use of finite means," as in generic concept formation, is to employ "grammars" of perception, a kind of syntax or structure of thought itself,[9] that is, transfer. What we learn from particular instances is to see different surface features of events as similar to others in crucial respects. In working with numerous disparate surface features, we tacitly become conscious of the deep structure underlying the particulars. In short, we learn to see patterns, to see connections; we learn to transfer.

Claude Shannon, an electrical engineer at the Massachusetts Institute of Technology (MIT), is typically credited with creating information theory. As a graduate student at MIT in the late 1930s, he had a seminal insight: He saw that the principles of *true/false* propositions in logic could be used to describe the two *on/off* states of electromechanical relay switches. In short, he saw that the structures of these two "different" systems were structurally *similar*, that they constituted a generic structure. This transfer insight provided the initial model for the structure of computer operations.

ARCHETYPES AND MENTAL MODELS

It's probably clear by now that the main concept in this chapter, generic structure, and the main concept of the last chapter, mental model, are integrally related, as is the concept of an archetype, which I will now discuss. As I noted in the previous chapter on mental models, researchers and practitioners in different fields often use the same term differently.[10] Senge suggests, for example, that "systems thinking entails using 'system archetypes' in order to perceive underlying structures in complex situations."[11] Without getting into a war of definition with *Webster* and others, I think it is more useful to reserve the term *generic structure* as the primary structural template upon which mental models and archetypes are based, the skeleton of a mental model or an archetype. Some mental models and archetypes are like apples, peaches, and plums that can be plugged into generic structures like the concept of fruit, or the concept of mammal. Mental models and archetypes have content and represent a mental reality that hopefully corresponds to physical reality in some useful way. Of course, our representations are not perfect representations of reality, as the duckbill platypus clearly reminds us.

Some mental models are closer to generic structures, like mathematical or other abstract models. Archetypes, too, are a kind of mental model—the difference being that they represent some deep, recurring theme, typically, though not necessarily, having to do with life, like a parable. Examples of archetypes are Plato's allegory of the cave, Aesop's fables, stories like "The Emperor's New Clothes," or in Jungian psychology, the idea of Father Time or the Earth Mother. Archetypes are also like story plots. A person familiar with mysteries knows that there is a general schema or script for the plots of mysteries: There is murder, a sleuth, and suspects; the murderer typically has motive, opportunity, and a weapon, with the plot unfolding with both relevant and irrelevant clues; and finally, the sleuth exposes the murderer. The classic Greek myths are archetypal, as the plots are considered ubiquitous and eternal.

In sum, generic structures underlie mental models and archetypes. Put another way, mental models are a subset of generic structures, and archetypes are a subset of mental models. As with most concepts when examined closely, the dividing line between these categories of convenience is often difficult to maintain, especially at the point at which their boundaries meet. As in our personal lives, so too in our organizational life. Senge notes that system archetypes and generic structures hold the key for our learning to recognize the structures in our personal and organizational lives. An archetype that Senge describes, and one that I have used in my social psychology classes for years, is "The Tragedy of the Commons."[12]

As I described it in Chapter 5, in "The Tragedy of the Commons," author Garrett Hardin, a biologist, explained the extinction of many old English pasturelands used by herdsmen for grazing their livestock. The herdsmen could use the commons for all the livestock they owned. It was called a commons because the land was not owned by any individual. As the population of herdsmen and their livestock increased, the commons became overgrazed and turned arid. It became overgrazed because there were no group rules for its use. The herdsmen would not create rules; they saw it as their inalienable right to make use of the commons as they saw fit. Because each individual used the commons for their short-run gain, they lost collectively. This is not a story specifically about an old English commons grazing land; it's a generic story, an archetype. This archetype has been played out—has recurred again and again—all over the world, not just with the specific content of grazing lands but with resources as well.

We can see the *same* dynamics occurring with other commons like air, water, oil, forestation, and other natural resources. The plot remains the same; only the characters change. As Senge aptly recognizes, corporations have their commons, too. They are financial, intellectual capital, customers, and morale. "Individual" may also mean the individual unit of a corporation, where each unit operates on the basis of its short-run interests at the expense of the entire corporation. The essential moral of this archetype is individuals doing their own thing for short-run profit at the eventual expense of the long-run benefit of the group.

One way to recognize archetypes is to consider any story or scenario as an archetype, as one with a generic structure that can be transferred to other situations; you only have to replace the specific nouns or subjects in the story with other possible nouns or subjects. Another transfer method is to replace the nouns with generic notations. The generic structure of the tragedy of the commons is: A common exists if

1. there is a finite X
2. that can sustain only Y amount of Z;
3. it is used by A, B, C
4. without sufficient regulation
5. for short-run gain
6. that exceeds Y amount of Z,

7. leading to the depletion of X,

8. resulting in the long-term loss of X to A, B, C.

The archetypal dilemma exemplified by the tragedy of the commons is the individual versus the group, and the solution to such dilemmas is often counterintuitive. Because our Western mental model of individualism tends to see the causes of events as residing in autonomous individual action, we seek individual solutions to social problems like the commons.

In the commons, or in individual units of a corporation, it will do little good to appeal to the moral integrity of the individual not to graze so many livestock, or not to be so concerned with the department or division unit's monthly bottom line, when the reward structure reinforces the individualistic and short-run behavior. People generally act in their own self-interest. The simple solution, then, is to change the reward structure to reinforce long-term and group interests. If we think we are in environmental trouble now, think what our situation would be like if we had not passed environmental commons laws.

Generic structures and archetypes often take the form of scripts and roles for our personal and professional lives. Such structures and archetypes of which we are unaware keep us conceptual prisoners. When I was a freshman in college, I remember reading Polish anthropologist Bronislaw Malinowski. Malinowski was conducting research in the Trobriand Islands in the South Pacific. He discovered what he called the Kula Ring. The Kula Ring was a kind of economic trade structure. The islanders traded armbands and necklaces. Each Trobriander was only aware of trading with a particular relative each year. In fact, a consistent structure was operating, determining their trading behavior. It seems that armbands always went around the islands in one direction, the necklaces in another. The islanders were not aware of this structure and their part in its perpetuation. I saw Malinowski's Kula Ring as a kind of parable of social life in general.

We, too, have invisible structures that determine our lives; so do organizations, as Senge has demonstrated so well. Being unaware of mental and organizational structures keeps us from inventing, creating, and seeing relationships or connections that could mean profit (see Chapter 5). We recognize these structures and archetypes by abstracting out of apparent diversity *recurring* patterns and *invariant* structures. This is the essence of transfer of learning.

SYSTEMS THINKING

Generic structures are at the conceptual foundation of systems thinking. Both are crucial for learning organizations. Again, Senge recognizes that systems thinking involves learning to see structures that recur again and again. In effect, recognizing recurring and generic structures is, in large measure, systems thinking. Generic structures are also the basis of mental models. In fact, says Senge, "what will accelerate mental models as a practical management discipline will be a library of 'generic structures'. . . . Such a library should be a natural by-product of practicing systems thinking within an organization."[13] Such a library would include a cataloging of archetypes.

One of the most noticeable characteristics about people who write about learning organizations and systems thinking is their facility to reason with models and analogies and to transfer their learning. Jay Forrester, a well-known systems theorist and practitioner, explains how he developed some of his ideas on social systems by comparing and mapping his experience with corporate systems. In 1968 John F. Collins, the former mayor of Boston, became professor of urban affairs at MIT where Forrester was teaching. They discussed each other's work, Forrester's in industrial dynamics and Collins's experience with urban systems and difficulties. Forrester says, "A close collaboration led to applying to the dynamics of the city the *same* methods that had been created for understanding the social and policy structure of the corporation. . . . I had not previously been involved with urban behavior or urban policies. But the emerging story was strikingly *similar* to what we had seen in the corporation" (italics added).[14] Forrester saw that actions taken to fix a corporate problem often lead to making matters worse, that the solution to corporate problems was what he termed counterintuitive. He saw the same counterintuitive dynamics often resulting from attempting to fix urban problems.

In hindsight, this thinking may appear to be a simple example of transfer, but it's not. What Forrester was able to transfer from his experience of corporate dynamics to urban dynamics is not as important here as the transfer by which it was accomplished. On the surface, the transfer was the consequence of seeing corporate and urban dynamics as similar. To think in terms of transfer is not as easy as it would appear after the fact. First, knowledge about both systems had to be present. Second, there had to be cues for accessing the similarities. Since similarities can be drawn between most anything, a systematic search or comparing everything within our purview in order to discover the valid similarities would overload our information-processing capacity almost immediately. Most of the work of transfer is done on a nonconscious level. It's founded on a nonconscious inference process.

At its simplest, systems thinking is thinking relationally, that is, seeing a given thing not as an isolated entity but as being part of a larger whole. Systems thinking involves seeing how different parts of a whole are connected to and reciprocally influence each other through feedback loops. We are all part of a larger system, even in the womb. After birth, we are part of a family system, a city, county, state, national, international, and even cosmic system. A corporation is, of course, a system, and employees are a part of the system, with each influencing the other. Thus, to engage in systems thinking at work, we need to understand how we fit into the larger system, how subsystems fit into each other and to the larger system, along with seeing how we exert influence (either consciously or nonconsciously) on the system, and how it influences us—and what Kula Rings may be operating.

On a more complex level, systems thinking is being attuned to and recognizing the recurrent regularities, the patterns, the generic structures, the archetypes in a system. This level of systems thinking is in fact what is called general systems thinking. General systems thinking is transfer thinking; it's seeing recurrent regularities in systems, be they corporate or cosmic.

The systematic idea of a general systems theory is generally attributed to Ludwig von Bertalanffy, a professor of theoretical biology. The Society for General Systems Research was organized in 1954 for the development of systems structures that are applicable across knowledge domains. According to Bertalanffy, its major functions are (1) to investigate the isomorphy or structural regularities of concepts, laws, and models in various fields; (2) to facilitate transfer from one field to another; (3) to develop theoretical models in fields that do not have them; (4) to minimize the duplication of theoretical effort across knowledge domains; and (5) to promote the unity of science.[15] General systems thinking is applied transfer. General systems thinkers think in structural transfers, in generic structures.

General systems theory is not a search for vague and superficial analogies between physical, biological, and social systems. Such analogies are of little value. General structures, or isomorphic correspondences, are a consequence of the fact that, in certain aspects, abstractions and conceptual models can be applied to different phenomena. This does not mean, for example, that physical systems, cells, organisms, and societies are all the same. It's like when the law of gravitation applies to Newton's apple, to the planetary system, and to tidal phenomena.

A further example of general systems thinking is seeing that the exponential pattern of growth (or decay)—growth like compound interest in a bank account—is applicable to widely different phenomena, from radioactive decay to the extinction of human populations with insufficient reproduction, to the growth of certain bacterial cells, to populations of bacteria, to animals or humans, and to the growth of scientific research in general. While money, bacteria, animals, humans, research output, and so on, are completely different, and governed by completely different causal mechanisms, the mathematical or structural law applying to them is the *same*. This is not a mere metaphor or analogy; it is a formal correspondence, a generic structure. The exponential law could also be called a model.

The existence of laws or patterns of similar structure in different fields, says Bertalanffy, "makes possible the transfer of principles from one field to another, and it will no longer be necessary to duplicate or triplicate the discovery of the same principles in different fields."[16] What this means for the learning organization is exactly what Senge demonstrates: the discovery of general archetypal patterns in the behavior of individuals, organizations, and financial systems. It's also leveraged learning.

General systems patterns, like archetypes (and story plots), appear to be limited in number. Accordingly, says Bertalanffy, "laws identical in structure will appear in intrinsically different fields. The same applies to statements in ordinary language; here, too, the number of intellectual schemes is restricted, and they will be applied in quite different realms."[17] From a generic structures point of view, the world is not as diverse as it first appears. Using general systems thinking reduces detail complexity to a series of templates. Granted, thinking in generic structures is in principle quite easy. We do it everyday. But once we leave the everyday realm, it's more difficult. How to discover and recognize these systems patterns is, again, the problem of the transfer.

In systems thinking, the primary generic structure or equivalence category is called *isomorphism*. It is a kind of analogy, but not a mere literary analogy; it is a formal equivalence—for example, in physics the comparison of heat flow as flow of a substance or the comparison of electrical flow with the flow of a fluid. Another example is Newton's law of gravitation applied to his proverbial apple, to the planetary system, and to tidal phenomena. This isomorphism does not mean that apples, planets, and oceans are the same, only that they are the same in certain important invariant respects. Much of science is the search for such invariance among complex systems.

General systems thinking is generic structure thinking. General systems thinkers tend to think analogically, that is, to see one thing as another, to see sameness underlying apparent difference in everyday life.

GENERIC, GENERAL SYSTEMS, AND ARCHETYPAL THINKING IN CORPORATE AND EVERYDAY LIFE

To think in terms of general systems, you need to see family behavior as small-group behavior and small-group behavior as family behavior; to see a nation's behavior as small-group behavior; or to see corporate behavior as small-group behavior or as a family behavior. There are advantages to thinking of things *as* something else. For example, what we know about family behavior might be useful if applied as a model to corporate behavior. We might find recurring patterns, generic structures, and archetypes. A number of years ago, Harry Levinson, corporate consultant and Freudian psychoanalyst, transferred his knowledge of family dynamics to corporate behavior.[18] Using this model, Levinson saw romantic affairs in the workplace as *equivalent* to family incest, with all of the ensuing problems and behaviors including *denial*. In Freudian terms, a corporation's superego (its conscience) is its value system; its ego (conscious sense of self) is its resources and its style of doing business; its id (primitive unconscious impulses) is its implicit assumptions, folklore, and unrecognized feelings that influence organizational behavior.

To apply what we know of family behavior as a model to corporate behavior, however, we don't have to bring Freud along. Freud has become so much a part of our culture that comparing a boss to a mother or father is typically interpreted as psychoanalysis. Seeing something *as* something else, however, is not necessarily Freudian. While tests show that psychoanalysts are exceptional at transfer, they do not have the corner on the generic thinking market.

From a transfer perspective, corporate life resonates or *reminds* members of *similar* experiences in their family life. It's in the family that we learn our first—and often lasting—social lessons about authority, power, jealousy, rivalry, and peer relationships that we bring with us to corporate life.

As I noted in Chapter 5, archetypes of eternal family behaviors are to be found in the classic Greek myths and in the Christian Bible. Most people in Western culture are familiar with the Greek story of Oedipus, who killed his father and married his mother, or with the biblical stories of Cain and Abel. In more modern vernacular, the (overused) term of dysfunctional family has become a kind of archetype for contemporary families and has been repeatedly applied (none too rigorously) not only to corporate life but to our entire society. Family life and the myriad of classic archetypes seem to be eternal generic structures of social life.

The family model applied to corporate life may explain why different personalities are attracted or repelled by different companies' management styles: They *remind* them of their early family styles. Using a family model, corporate acquisitions are *like* marriages, and mergers are *like* modern two-family (re)marriages where the "kids" from both families must learn to become one new family.

These archetypes are not mere analogies. In general systems terminology, they are isomorphic structures—general laws that are a part of certain kinds of systems, whether they are family systems, small groups and teams, or organizational systems. Thinking in these terms reduces the load on one's memory by creating patterns and categories that are all related in some way. But most of all, perhaps, thinking in these terms leads to insights into, between and among events and situations.

Systems thinkers who study organizational behavior have transferred knowledge of specific areas or used various models for understanding organizations.[19] We can, for example, obtain new insights into organizational behavior by transferring some of what we know about the behavior of nation-states, social movements, or biological populations to understand organizations. Understanding control in organizations has been modeled by transferring what we know about the human nervous system.

For example, a subordinate organizational component (i.e., department, division, etc.) is connected to a superordinate command unit. The command unit can be seen as the spinal cord, collecting information and undertaking low-level coordinative action. The processes of mutual adjustment of the activity level of the system can be seen as the sympathetic and parasympathetic nervous systems of the organization that stimulate and inhibit activity and thus stabilize the production environment of the organization. The output of these adjustments is monitored by a higher system, perhaps the analogue of diencephalon and ganglia in the human nervous system. This relates to the output of the organizational system units to the organizational mission and plans. Finally, the highest level of management, perhaps the analogue of the cortex, clarifies and formulates the organizational mission and plans. The organizational cortex decides on the balance between the requirements for stability and change against the organization's mission.

A further excellent and lucid example of transferring knowledge about the human nervous system to governmental structures has been detailed by systems thinker Karl Deutsch in his classic book *The Nerves of Government: Models of Political Communication and Control*, where bureaucracy is mapped on a model of the human nervous system.[20] To become skilled at transfer thinking, we need to resurrect early general systems thinking prior to its becoming almost entirely mathematical. Reading early general systems thinkers will create the necessary mental set for transfer thinking.

What keeps transfer thinking from generating a nearly infinite number of similarities or mere analogies is knowledge base and theory; they create constraints so that transfer does not become a runaway system. Knowledge base and theory let us know when the transfer is really derived from underlying generic structures and not just from surface similarities. Even then, however, there is no guarantee that it's a valid equivalency. Moreover, occasionally it may not even matter if the similarity is true; it may be more important that the similarity is useful as a heuristic (a kind of rule of thumb) strategy, initially enabling a person to think about something in a way he or she had not thought about it before.

THE MATRIX AND HARMONIC STRUCTURE OF TRANSFER THINKING

General systems thinking sees the universe as an expanding series of isomorphic structures, beginning with atom, molecule, cell, organ, organism, group, society, culture, solar system, and universe.[21] The basic generic form of this expanding series of isomorphic structures is like that of a frequency harmonic. A harmonic is wave oscillation in which each oscillation has a frequency that is an integral multiple of a basic frequency. A similar structure is found in the notion of mathematical progression, as in 2, 4, 8, 16, 32, 64, and so on. A similar (but nonprogressive) structure is also exemplified by the musical concept of an octave, a tone on the eighth degree from a given musical tone. When a melody is played in a different octave, it's still recognized even though what is heard is not the same sound. In playing a melody in a different key, no note is exactly the same as the corresponding note in the original key, yet we recognize the entire melody as the *same*.

Experiments with animals indicate that this kind of transfer may be hard-wired into the nervous system. For example, in experiments with cats taught to respond to a particular tone or frequency, after decortication of their auditory cortex, they no longer responded to the particular tone. They do, however, respond to harmonics of the original frequency. In fact, they respond up to ten levels—or octaves—of the original frequency.

The construction of the Periodic Chart in chemistry is another example of matrix or harmonic transfer. The initial idea of the Periodic Chart was anticipated by Englishman J. A. R. Newland and was modeled on what he called the "law of the octaves." The Periodic Law states that the properties of the chemical elements are periodic functions of their atomic numbers. The chart was developed by the great Russian chemist Dmitry Mendeleyev. Mendeleyev said that if elements are arranged according to the weights of their atoms, then there is one long column. He then demonstrated that the elements fall into a certain analogous periodicity: The first one, lithium, is analogous to the eighth one, sodium, and the second one, beryllium, is analogous to the ninth one, magnesium, and so on, a kind of harmonic progression.

Poet William Blake was intuitively exemplifying generic and general systems thinking in his "harmoniclike" poem "Songs of Innocence" when he wrote:

> See the world in a grain of sand
> And heaven in a wild flower,
> Hold infinity in the palm of your hand,
> And eternity in an hour.[22]

Like Blake, general systems, generic thinking, and transfer thinking all see the world in terms of macrocosms and microcosms, in harmoniclike levels. Thinking *generically* can be a kind of poetry as well as a kind of mathematics. Mathematicians and poets think generically. But there is a difference in the form of their expression. Mathematicians think and write in formal structures and their transformations, whereas poets think in concrete pictures and words. To learn to be a transfer thinker, then, is to apprentice oneself to mathematicians and poets.

NOTES

1. J. S. Bruner, "Going Beyond the Information Given," in J. Anglin (ed.), *Beyond the Information Given: Studies in the Psychology of Knowing* (New York: W. W. Norton, 1973), p. 219.

2. P. Senge, personal communication, August, 1, 1994.

3. M. Paich, "Generic Structures," *System Dynamics Review* 1 (1985), p. 128.

4. J. Bruner, M. Wallach, and E. Galanter, "The Identification of Recurrent Regularity," *American Journal of Psychology* 72 (1959), p. 206.

5. J. Lipnack and J. Stamps, *The Teamnet Factor: Bringing the Power of Boundary Crossing into the Heart of Your Business* (Essex Junction, VT: Oliver Wight Pub., 1993).

6. S. P. Gott, P. Hall, A. Pokorny, E. Dibble, and R. Glaser, "A Naturalistic Study of Transfer: Adaptive Expertise in Technical Domains," in D. K. Detterman and R. J. Sternberg (eds.), *Transfer on Trial: Intelligence, Cognition, and Instruction* (Norwood, NJ: Ablex, 1993), p. 267.

7. See P. A. Klaczynski, "Reasoning Schema Effects on Adolescent Rule Acquisition and Transfer," *Journal of Educational Psychology* 85(4) (1993); J. M. Mandler and F. Orlich, "Analogical Transfer: The Roles of Schema Abstraction and Awareness," *Bulletin of the Psychonomic Society* 31(5) (1993).

8. P. Thorndyke, "Cognitive Structures in Comprehension and Memory of Narrative Discourse," *Cognitive Psychology* 9 (1977), pp. 77–110.

9. W. Weimer, "The Psychology of Inference and Expectation: Some Preliminary Remarks," in G. Maxwell and R. M. Anderson, Jr. (eds.), *Minnesota Studies in the Philosophy of Science: Induction, Probability, and Confirmation* (Minneapolis: University of Minnesota Press, 1975), pp. 430–486.

10. Senge clearly—and rightly so—wants to distinguish his use of the term *archetype* from its use in psychology. Senge, personal communication, August 1, 1994.

11. P. M. Senge, *The Fifth Discipline: The Art and Practice of the Learning Organization* (New York: Doubleday, 1990), p. 373.

12. G. Hardin, "The Tragedy of the Commons," *Science* 162 (1968), pp. 1243–1248.

13. Senge, *The Fifth Discipline*, p. 204.

14. Jay Forrester, "Counterintuitive Behavior of Social Systems," *Technology Review* (January 1971), p. 55.

15. L. von Bertalanffy, *General Systems Theory* (New York: George Braziller, 1963), p. 15.

16. Ibid., p. 6.

17. Ibid., p. 82.

18. H. Levinson, *Organizational Diagnosis* (Cambridge, MA: Harvard University Press, 1972).

19. See examples in H. Tsoukas, "Analogical Reasoning and Knowledge Generation in Organization Theory," *Organization Studies* 14 (1993), pp. 323–346.

20. K. Deutsch, *The Nerves of Government: Models of Political Communication and Control* (New York: Free Press, 1966).

21. See, for example, R. W. Gerard, "A Biologist's View of Society," in L. von

Bertalanffy and A. Rapoport (eds.), *General Systems: Yearbook of the Society for the Advancement of General Theory* (Los Angeles: University of Southern California, 1956), pp. 155–160.

22. W. Blake, *Songs of Innocence and of Experience* (Princeton, NJ: William Blake Trust/Princeton University Press, 1991).

11

Intuition and Decision Making: Transfer of Learning and the Unconscious

Admitting the reality of physical intuition is simply the prelude to demanding an explanation for it. How does it operate, and how can it be acquired?

Larkin, McDermott, Simon, and Simon[1]

There continues to be considerable discussion in management training about decision making based on intuition. Ideally, decision making should not be based on intuition but something more concrete and less irrational. Because of pragmatic workaday time pressures, however, that often preclude the gathering and analysis of an extensive amount of data before making a decision, the idea of the intuitive manager[2] has become an important notion worth careful examination. In 1964 the late pop prophet of the current electronic age Marshal McLuhan, in his book *Understanding Media*, predicted the end of rationality.[3] He foresaw our present electronic age where the rate of change and the explosion of information that we have available to us preclude the careful analysis of data before each decision. By the time we have analyzed the available information, he said, either it would be outdated or the situation we are analyzing or making a decision about would long be past. There's a great deal of truth in what McLuhan predicted.

We know a great deal about the conscious mind. But by comparison, we know less about our unconscious mind. Unfortunately, when we are ignorant about something, we often project our fantasies, needs, and our wildest desires into the void. This has certainly been true for our unconscious mind. Many think that it knows things mystical, that it somehow knows without direct experience or without being taught, or that it can learn while we're asleep. The facts are to the contrary, however—at least for the overwhelming majority of us normal people. In recent years the sale of audiotapes with subliminal messages to the unconscious embedded in them to help us to lose weight, to stop smoking, to increase our motivation, and any number of other habits have sold by the thousands. There is no evidence that they work—beyond what a placebo would accomplish.

Despite a mystical New Age orientation of many people in the HRD field, the intuitive notion of unconscious intuition in decision making is not without its critics. John Sterman, at MIT's Sloan School of Management, for example, is one such critic. In remarking on corporate managers' intuitive capacity to recognize Senge's system archetypes (which originally were discovered by complex mathematical systems analysis), he says, "Predicting the behavior of even the simplest archetype would mean solving a high-order nonlinear differential equation in your head. Human beings do not have the cognitive capacity to do so. Many studies have shown that people's intuitive predictions about the dynamics of complex systems are systematically flawed."[4] While I am more than sympathetic to Sterman's concerns, the question of intuition is complex. It could be argued, for example, that we do in fact unconsciously solve differential equations in our heads. Anecdotally speaking, every time we catch a ball, or when someone throws our car keys to us, our brain has to calculate the velocity and trajectory of the ball so that we can predict exactly where to place our hand to catch the object.

A further anecdotal case of intuitive mathematical calculation is illustrated by Stanford Ovshinsky, the inventor of the amorphous metal semiconductor. He says:

I have many good friends who are much better at mathematics than I am. They've done calculations and shown them to me and I say, "It's wrong." And they say, "But I've spent a whole day on the computer." And I say, "It's wrong. It's just not right." And I was right. Their calculations were wrong. It doesn't mean that I'm better in mathematics than they are. That's ridiculous. But I think it means that I have a physical intuition, a feel that has been right and has been my saving grace. Maybe you can't teach people that, and maybe you can. At least you can sharpen it in people who have it.[5]

For sailing buffs, it's interesting to note here that Joshua Slocum, the famous circumnavigator, hand-hewed his boat directly from the forest and designed it from *feel*. Its lines and proportions were said to have been nearly mathematically perfect.[6]

The great mathematician Henri Poincare (who nearly preempted Einstein's general theory of relativity) said that "to the unconscious belongs not only the complicated task of constructing the bulk of various combinations of ideas, but also the most delicate and essential one of selecting those that satisfy our sense of beauty and, consequently, are likely to be useful." And Garrett Hardin, the great biologist, maintained, "In the thinking that expands the frontiers of knowledge, intuition generally outruns mathematics. No apology need be offered for this fact." Hardin tells the story of Isaac Newton, who was a great believer in intuition. It seems Newton was discussing intuition and the fundamental property of the motion of the planets with his friend and admirer Edmund Halley (the discoverer of the now-famous comet named after him). "Yes," agreed Halley, "but how do you know that? Have you proved it?" Somewhat taken aback, Newton promptly replied: "Why I've known it for years. If you will give me a few days I'll certainly find you a proof."[7] Which he did.

But Hardin correctly warns that us lesser mortals should be wary of proceeding as cavalierly as the great discoverer of gravity and inventor of the calculus. Intuition can be wrong. So what is the truth about intuition? In order to understand intuitive judgment we should look at the pertinent research; otherwise, hard-nosed managers, executives, and engineers will—and correctly so—be somewhat incredulous, to say the least, and those who hold New Age beliefs may claim almost mystical powers for unconscious intuitive judgments, resulting in a kind of organizational gridlock. Moreover, a clear understanding of what we know about unconscious and intuitive processes—and transfer—will enable us to utilize these two abilities more effectively.

At this point, let me briefly state what I will be suggesting about the unconscious and intuition. First, both ideas are based on considerable research; second, many claims for both have been exaggerated; third, both concepts depend on a high level of knowledge base; and fourth, transfer figures prominently into their functioning. In short, does intuition work? The answer is yes and no, and it depends. Sorry. Reality isn't that simple.

As in the corporate culture, in academic psychology, too, the notions of the unconscious and intuition have had a long and controversial past, largely beginning with Freud, of course. Tom Peters and Robert Waterman, in their best-seller *In Search of Excellence: Lessons from America's Best-Run Companies*, point out, that "We 'reason' with our intuitive side [of our brain] just as much as, and perhaps more than, with our logical side." They also insightfully point out, however, the limitations of intuition in business decisions; they note that "as the experiments demonstrate, our collective gut is not much use in the arcane world of probability and statistics. Here is an area in which a little more training on the rational side would help! But the good element is that it probably is only the intuitive leap that will let us solve problems in this complex world. This is a major advantage of man over computer."[8] Perhaps.

Intuition has been the subject of extensive research in psychology. There is no shortage of findings in cognitive psychology clearly demonstrating the flawed nature of clinicians' (read: practitioners') ability to predict and diagnose behavior based on their intuition. Robyn Dawes, a well-known and respected clinical psychologist at Carnegie-Mellon University, has written a very useful book for both the professional and the general public entitled *House of Cards* in which he addresses clinical reasoning by intuition.[9] He compiles the years of research in clinical psychology clearly showing the superiority of statistical formulas in prediction and diagnosis over intuition. And psychologist David Myers concludes, "When you are pushing 90 investigations predicting everything from the outcome of football games to the diagnosis of liver disease and when you can hardly come up with a half dozen studies showing even a weak tendency in favor of the clinician, it is time to draw a practical conclusion."[10] Such research contradicts practitioners' claims to be able to analyze an individual's life in great detail and through a case study decide what caused the individual to behave the way he or she did.

Indeed, we generally expect psychologists to be able to intuitively know and with reasonable probability predict behavior. This expectation stems not only from our intuitive beliefs about the world and how we know it but from professional psychologists and pop psychology books. Studies of medical diagnosis, too, generally show similar findings on diagnoses. The findings on psychological diagnosis and medical intuition are directly transferable to the management field since managers are in fact making diagnoses when they make decisions, when they claim that a system archetype is at work, or when making financial and market predictions. For example, in predicting bankruptcies, some studies show that a statistical formula is quite superior to the intuitive judgment of bank loan experts. Some of these experts are very highly paid by banks for their supposed intuitive judgment abilities.[11] Despite such negative findings, however, they do not tell the whole story of our unconscious processes.

THE REALITY OF THE UNCONSCIOUS MIND

Because of considerable recent experimental research in cognitive psychology, the idea of what is called higher-order mental processes occurring on nonconscious levels is now accepted by many hard-nosed psychologists.[12] It's important to understand, however, that modern psychological research on what is commonly termed the unconscious is not what is popularly understood as our unconscious. Freud, of course, deserves the credit for our general understanding of the unconscious. And we thank him for that. But modern cognitive psychology has gone far beyond Freud in unlocking the workings of what is called the unconscious mind.

Because Freud's notion of the unconscious has become so widespread in Western popular culture, the very idea of mental events occurring outside of our awareness has become synonymous with him. As a consequence, again I should emphasize that modern psychology's notion of the unconscious is quite different from Freud's. First of all, the term *nonconscious* is used instead of *unconscious*. This is not just a semantic difference; it's an important conceptual difference. For Freud the unconscious was an innate, primal set of impulses, largely governed by primitive instincts, and genetically preprogrammed behaviors. Freud came by his ideas basically from his clinical data of working with patients. The modern idea of the unconscious, however, is thought of in terms of neurological structures, of learned behaviors and information. The modern view is based largely on experimental evidence. Because the term *unconscious* is the term in wide use, however, I will continue to use it instead of the term *nonconscious*.

The reason that some people have difficulty in accepting the reality of our unconscious mind is that in Western culture we have the tendency to equate thinking, reasoning, and judgment with our conscious mind only. Even our sense of self, our sense of identity, is based on whom we think we are consciously. We see unconscious events as alien, as not being us. Take, for example, our experience of dreaming. We do not experience that we are responsible for our dreams; instead, we experience dreams as happening to us. The fact is, however, that no one is selecting the subject matter of the dream but us.

The short of it is that we tend to be encapsulated in our conscious experience. It alone seems real. But as important as personal experience is, it should not be accorded the status of the ultimate arbiter of knowledge. Our direct personal experience lives, after all, in a Ptolemaic universe. You may recall that the ancient Ptolemaic model of the solar system was one that viewed the earth as the center of our solar system. Again, we now know that the Ptolemaic view of the solar system is false. Yet our direct everyday experience still tells us that it's correct: We directly experience the sun rising in the East and setting in the West. We experience it (see it) revolving around us. The fact is that we do much, if not most, of our thinking on the unconscious level.

It appears that it may not be at all unreasonable to suggest that in the early history of the human species humans reasoned, spoke, judged, and solved problems but were not conscious of doing so, that much of our thinking and reasoning was done without our awareness. Indeed this is the thesis of psychologist Julian Jaynes, who wrote the acclaimed (yet controversial) and best-selling book *The Origin of Consciousness in the Breakdown of the Bicameral Mind*.[13] A great deal of the so-called right brain/left brain research demonstrates that our hemispheres may, under certain conditions, function relatively independently, with each hemisphere sometimes being unaware (not conscious) of the experiences of the other. Some researchers are speculating that many unconscious phenomena can be equated with our brain's right hemisphere. There are even some who believe that Freud's concept of the unconscious may be equated with the brain's right hemisphere.[14]

A number of experiments and observed neurological phenomena show the existence of nonconscious thinking. Again, we need not invoke a Freudian unconscious. In recent years, there has been an increasing awareness of the reality of such "clinical" entities as fugue states, hypnotic phenomena, and hysterical blindness. Perhaps the exemplar of these unconscious states is the phenomenon discovered by Ernest Hilgard at Stanford University. Hilgard discovered while conducting experiments on the hypnotic control of pain that there is a part of our mind that is always aware of reality. He called this "the hidden observer."

Much less well known is the early work of physician David Cheek who established that surgical patients, while under deep general anesthesia, not only hear but cognitively process certain conversations in the operating room. Through experiments involving tape recorders during an operation, Cheek has later retrieved, by hypnosis, the conversation of operating room personnel. More important, patients have been known to later act on what they heard, just as if they had been given a posthypnotic suggestion. Under general anesthesia, patients are clearly not conscious but are cognitively processing information.[15] Having worked with surgical patients under general anesthesia, I can personally speak for the reality of such unconscious hearing and processing of information.

In a now well-known experiment, a split-brain patient was shown pictures only to the left visual fields, information from which was ostensibly going only to the right hemisphere. One of the pictures was of a nude body. The patient giggled and blushed but did not consciously have any idea why he or she giggled. The explanation was that since the information went only to the right hemisphere, which does not appear to have an adequate language function (at least for about 95% of people), the patient could not report it. Here we have an example of felt—or intuitive—meaning, of nonconscious cognitive processing on a meaningful level but no conscious awareness of it. There are a host of other experimental findings showing a fully functioning unconscious mind. Similar unconscious effects have been found in the reasoning of patients with what used to be called hysterical or functional disorders. Unlike the above neurological deficits, hysterical or functional disorders are purely psychological. No physical cause for their blindness, deafness, or paralysis can be found.

Functionally blind subjects, like the neurological subjects cited earlier, often can guess—intuitively know—what is present. Further, similar deficits can be reproduced with hypnotic subjects who are given a posthypnotic suggestion for blindness, deafness, or paralysis. Now consider a more everyday example of unconscious functioning: the case of language learning and use. Most of our use of language is carried out on an unconscious level. How many of us are aware of the multitude of grammatical rules that we correctly use when we speak or write—especially when speaking? More than this, how many of us ever consciously learned most of the thousands of grammatical rules of our language? The answer is virtually no one. Yet we use them every day. We unconsciously learned them through interaction in our language community.

For present purposes, the significance of this research is twofold: first, that information is cognitively processed, not just perceptually received, on nonconscious levels; second, that nonconscious information influences conscious awareness and responses in clearly distinct ways. Conscious and unconscious processes are often qualitatively different modes of mental functioning, with each being separate or dissociated from the other. As some research shows, the unconscious, at least under certain conditions, like our conscious mind, can reason, judge, think, and evaluate.

UNCONSCIOUS INTUITION, KNOWLEDGE BASE, AND EXPERTISE

Now that I have outlined some of the basic issues and the scientific reality of our unconscious mind, what are the pragmatic, hard realities of its use in everyday thinking, reasoning, predicting, and decision making? The first hard reality is that unconscious intuition requires the same rigor that our conscious mind requires in order to make valid diagnoses, perceptions, predictions, and decisions: (1) a large, valid base of information and (2) continuous practice. I stress a *valid* knowledge base, not just any knowledge base. What I mean by this is a knowledge base made up of the most valid data as possible. Any other type of knowledge base will lead to distortions in our intuition, just as a nonvalid knowledge base does in our conscious reasoning. Herbert Simon and his associates maintain, "In every domain that has been explored, considerable knowledge has been found to be an essential prerequisite to expert skill. . . . This knowledge includes sets of rich schemata [and patterns] that can guide a problem's interpretation and solution and add crucial pieces of information. This capacity to use pattern-indexed schemata is probably a large part of what we call physical intuition."[16]

On a perhaps more concrete level, how would a successful business magnate like Ross Perot describe the development of his own sense of intuition? In an interview with Perot, he described the basis of his intuition in three words: It means "k-n-o-w-i-n-g y-o-u-r b-u-s-i-n-e-s-s," slowly drawling out and heavily emphasizing the three words.[17] And knowing your business, continues Perot, means having a large knowledge base.

Building on the work of Herb Simon and his colleagues at Carnegie-Mellon University, Beryle Benderly has found that intuitive people share one common and essential trait: They are all experts in a field of knowledge.[18] Contrary to much everyday thinking, people are not experts because they are intuitive, rather, they are intuitive because they are experts in some field, an achievement that, as I noted in Chapter 8, requires hundreds and thousands of hours of learning, experience, and practice. Thomas Peters and Robert Waterman comment on Simon's work in their book *In Search of Excellence*, "When we start to dwell on the implications of Simon's research, we are struck by its applicability elsewhere. The mark of the true professional in any field is the rich vocabulary of patterns, developed through years of formal education and especially through years of practical experience."[19]

In Chapter 8 I noted that when knowledge about or experience in an area increases, it is not just added onto the areas; it changes how we think. Our information base not only becomes larger, but the very structure of our knowledge base changes. It becomes structured more generically, more abstractly, and becomes more organized for application and transfer. The larger our knowledge base becomes, however, the less we have conscious control over it. Our attention span and working memory are limited by the number of different pieces of knowledge we can consciously process at a given time. Cognitive research clearly shows that our conscious "channel" is a limited one in terms of processing information; it's our unconscious channel that is superior in processing and correlating large amounts of data. The Zen masters understood this.

The expert perceives the relevant pattern behind the details because of the size of his or her knowledge base and how it is organized. Chess masters have been shown to recall the layout of chess boards not as separate pieces but as functional clusters, with individual chess pieces used in developing specific strategies. Expert readers see whole words and even phrases, not the letters in a word; expert musicians recall passages, not separate menu items. This ability to see meaningful patterns does not reflect a generally superior perceptual ability. Rather, it reflects the organization of one's knowledge base. Verbally communicated problems often contain words that act as cues for access. Most of the time this ability is carried out nonconsciously. Obviously, the larger the knowledge base, the more cues we have for finding generic patterns. People who do not develop the ability to notice relevant generic features of new situations are at a disadvantage not only in terms of transfer but in terms of intuitive perceptions.

On a more action-oriented level, procedural knowledge is usually tacit or unconscious in the sense that the reasoning processes used to reach sound judgments cannot be specified consciously. We know, for example, that for skilled performances like driving a car, athletic activities, and other job tasks that require sequences of action, a great deal of practice is required—over and over and over again. One doesn't become a great musician or an Olympic star by relying on one's innate or mystical unconscious or intuitive knowledge. That direct knowledge and practice are required for unconscious-based skills has been known for some time. The practice of Zen archery requires (tutored and reflective) practice until the motor sequences become automatic, that is, performed unconsciously. The same is true for mental skills as well.

Constant practice with a given knowledge base (be it motor or mental) enables us to react faster than our bodies can physically react to an isolated stimulus. For example, the time it takes to respond to a stimulus even after extensive training is often between 0.5 and 1.0 seconds, which is too slow to account for a return of a hard tennis serve, a goalie's catching a hockey puck, or extreme speed in motor activities like typing or playing a musical instrument. Research on the return of a tennis serve shows that experts do not wait until they can see the ball approaching them. Instead, they carefully study the action of the server's racquet and are able to predict approximately where the tennis ball will land even before the server has hit the ball. While practice does not necessarily make perfect, the critical role of practice for anticipation (i.e., intuitively predicting) in expert performance in many areas clearly shows its importance.

For example, expert typists are looking well ahead at the text they are typing. The difference between the text visually fixated upon by a typist and the specific letters typed in a given instant (eye-hand span) increases with a typist's speed. The high-speed filming of an expert typist's finger movements shows that his or her fingers are simultaneously moved toward the relevant keys well ahead of when they are actually struck. When the typing situation is experimentally changed to preclude looking ahead at the text to be typed, the speed advantage of the expert typists is nearly eliminated.[20] The same is true for psychological processes (I do not call them skills) that require constant acquisition and practice with a large knowledge base. But it's not foolproof.

In the study I mentioned involving predicting bankruptcies, a statistical formula was found superior to the intuitive judgment of bank loan experts. There are situations, however, where intuition is superior. In a study predicting sales, managers outperformed the statistical formula. In the bank loan prediction study, the predictions of both the actuarial formula and the bank loan experts were based on the same information; but in the sales study, where the managers had other information in addition to the information used in a statistical prediction package, intuitive judgment won out.

Similarly, the predictions of a statistical formula have been found inferior to predictions by doctors who were board-certified in internal medicine who had seen patients, obtained their history, and conducted a physical examination, as well as reviewed the pertinent laboratory data. Thus, in both the medical and the business contexts, exceptions to the general superiority of actuarial judgment are often found when people have access to more (and valid) information than the statistical formulas used.

Perhaps, however, if the added information had been incorporated into the formulas, they would have again been superior to individual judgment. In fact, this is what is (unfortunately?) found. Statistical formulas, for example, outperform doctors in predicting death within 24 hours of people in an intensive care unit. Nevertheless, the pragmatic realities are that in the workaday world statistical prediction formulas are more often than not unavailable; so this leaves us with our unconscious and intuitive judgments. For our purposes here, the implications seem clear: Our unconscious and our intuition are only as good as the information they are based upon.

INTUITION AND TRANSFER OF LEARNING

So what does transfer of learning have to do with intuition? The short answer is: A great deal. Well-known cognitive researchers Mary Gick and Keith Holyoak, from the University of California at Los Angeles, summarize the internal workings of what I am calling the unconscious transfer process. "When subjects operate in an implicit learning mode," say Gick and Holyoak, "they may rely on a *generalization process* that develops multiple rules based on similarities among instances (italics added)."[21] Research supports an interpretation of our unconscious thought process as functioning on the basis of similarity relations. The similarity of instances is what transfer is all about (see also Chapter 9 on leveraged learning and transfer). The longer answer, of course, is more involved.

One explanation supporting my transfer theory of intuition comes from the work of neuroscientist Karl Pribram.[22] As a part of his holographic explanation of how the brain works, Pribram suggests that our brain functions as a spectral frequency analyzer. It's in the nature of a holographic image that an entire three-dimensional picture can be reproduced from only a part of the original picture. Likewise, Pribram's theory suggests that information in the brain is distributed everywhere, not just localized in one place. His research indicates that individual cells and ensembles of cells conform to certain mathematical functions (Fourier and Gabor Transforms), where on one side of the transform lies the space-time order of our phenomenological or everyday perception and on the other side lies a distributed, enfolded holographiclike order constituted by a frequency or spectral domain. According to Pribram, holographic brain perceptions are selected from a primitive mental matrix in which frequency conjunctions abound. By analogy, perhaps we can think of the strands of our genetic DNA code (the enfolded order) that when unfolded result in our total everyday physical being.

Our everyday categories and objects are constructed by mathematical operations on this primitive mental matrix. Largely responsible for these operations that convert the frequencies to our everyday perceptions are microbrain processes that function as cross-correlational devices. A correlation between two things is simply the degree to which two or more things have a tendency to vary together. Now, "Cross correlations," says Pribram, "are a measure of similarity of two original images." More important, he says, "a measure of similarity is precisely what is required for recognition (italics added)."[23] Once again, we see that similarity is fundamentally involved in how the brain works.

Presumably, our primitive frequency matrix is constituted by an enfolded array of "information" from everywhere in the organism; hence, it's holonomic and holographic—that is, all information is stored everywhere, and each part contains the information of the whole (though to a different order of resolution, or grain). Cross correlations and transformations are carried out on this spectral information pool, resulting in our everyday perceptions. From a holographic perspective, our initial perceptions are transformational, not elementaristic. That is to say, our sensory processes are not built from discrete elements but rather consist of the reordering of a distributed enfolded spectral array that forms the content of our sensory apparatus.

Thus, discrete elements (and concrete things) that we appear to see in the world are in fact emergent or built from a more fundamental frequency order in our brain. According to Pribram, a cell's response is defined by manifold frequency averages, not simple elements. The sum of the manifold is constituted by that which remains *invariant* across the various processing stages or levels involved in perception and thinking. Gerald Edelman, who won the Nobel Prize in physiology and medicine, in his book *Bright Air, Brilliant Fire: On the Matter of the Mind*, essentially says the same thing when he notes, "The properties of association, inexactness, and generalization all derive from the fact that perceptual categorization, which is one of the initial bases of memory, is probabilistic in nature."[24] In discussing his holographic theory of the brain, the interesting and difficult problem, says Pribram, is specifying the transfer functions, the transformations involved in correlating one code (read: area or subject) or one level to another.

The implication of such a theory of invariance for analogical reasoning and transfer of learning is that improving our ability to apprehend *equivalence* or *invariant* transformations is increased to the extent that our primitive spectral matrix is provided with a wide spectrum of knowledge/information/experience. Such a base would increase the ability of the system to more accurately disregard irrelevant information and similarities and/or to cancel out irrelevance in an averaging process. The richer our mental matrix, the more robust the cross-correlational thought processes.

Peter Senge advances a similar explanation of learning based on the work of Cambridge physicist and philosopher David Bohm. In Senge's terms, unconscious and intuitive learning is deep learning, a level of learning that draws from a fundamental source similar to Pribram's frequency or spectral matrix. In extending what he terms a "deep learning cycle," Senge relates it to Bohm's theory: "There is a level still more subtle than the deep learning cycle. This most subtle level is, however, also the most difficult to talk about. In fact we may only infer its presence, since there is no tangible evidence of its existence. But ultimately it may prove vital to a full understanding in the deep shifts in awareness and capabilities of learning organizations."[25] Says Senge, "Bohm proposed a 'new notion of order' to describe this deeper reality, the implicate order,' where 'everything is enfolded into everything.' In Bohm's view, the implicate order is continually unfolding into what we experience as the manifest world, the explicate order."[26] Pribram's view is similar to Bohm's view of what he calls the implicate order of the universe. Now, whether this deeper level of reality advanced by Pribram and Bohm is correct remains to be seen.

On a more concrete level, Herb Simon's work on artificial intelligence and intuition demonstrates that intuition is quite understandable and not mysterious at all. Using computer simulation programming, Simon has created at least what we might term a *virtual intuition*. Whether real intuition is different remains to be seen. In any event, Simon's work offers insights into the working of what we call intuition or insight. Says Simon, "On the basis of these models and experiments, it would appear that the process named 'intuition' by Gestalt psychologists is none other than our familiar friend 'recognition,' and that recognition processes are readily modeled by computer programs."[27] Simon suggests that intuition is in fact just another term for what we call *recognition* and for what Gestalt psychologists have called *insight*. Thus, intuition and recognition can be seen as functionally the same thing. Enter transfer of learning again. Recall in the preceding paragraphs that Pribram noted that similarity is exactly what is required for recognition.

Moreover, what is required of Simon's artificial intelligence programs to model intuition is a robust network of relations among the elements of a situation that are built on a large database of knowledge. A further requirement is for the programs to have a sufficient capability for drawing *inferences* from the knowledge. The database is often organized as a set of if-then statements that recognize appropriate cues in the problem situation and retrieve from the database relevant information associated with these cues. The components are highly related to each other in many ways and contain data structures and addresses that "point" to other components in the system, thus linking them together.

It's by this method that computer data structures can represent complex ideas. These systems, says Simon, all have varying degrees of understanding and insight. Simon and his associates have demonstrated this virtual intuition (or recognition process) by programming information available to scientists at the time an insight or discovery is made by them and have been able to reproduce the intuitive insight.[28] From Simon's perspective, the unconscious nature of intuition is a red herring. An unconscious view of intuition simply notes that information is simply not available to the conscious awareness of the person. A belief in the unconscious nature of intuition does not imply that the process is fundamentally different from other processes of recognition.

Granted, Simon's work on discovery and intuition has been largely in physical science, where the data and ideas are concrete in comparison to many areas like psychology. Simon himself recognizes that his programs may not work with soft areas like psychological discoveries, but in principle, there is no reason to suspect that the mental processes are qualitatively different in the soft science areas.

CONCLUSION

Our unconscious, intuitive, and transfer processes are constructed in a way that demands that we accumulate large amounts of valid information and repeated practice over a considerable length of time. Ironically (and unfortunately) this situation leads to behaviors that must resist a basic law of learning: that of having immediate reinforcement (i.e., payoff or reward). From all that we know about learning theory, the probability that a behavior—in this case, continued learning—will continue is determined by whether it's reinforced. Thus, when we do not receive immediate feedback or reinforcement of learning, the probability is that we will extinguish that behavior.

As Senge points out, however, deep learning, as opposed to training, often involves a fairly lengthy time before a payoff is recognized. I say "recognized" as there are internal mental developments (unconscious payoffs) constantly occurring, but we may not recognize it consciously until much later. Senge explains the unrecognized deep learning with an analogy from R. Buckminster Fuller's work. It seems that Fuller talked about the principle of recession, a principle that can be transferred to deep learning or learning that takes considerable time to develop.[29]

When a toy top is spinning, the primary characteristic of the movement is rotation around its axis. As time goes on, however, a secondary mode of movement develops: The top begins to *precess* as the axis gradually begins to move around its original position. This precession appears mysterious to a casual observer because there is no visible relation to the obvious rotation of the top. Unless we understand the dynamics of the top as a system, we might not even notice the precession, and we certainly wouldn't tend to connect this subtle movement to the spinning.

So it is, says Senge, with the deep process of learning. For a long time it may appear that there is nothing going on. Yet deeper changes are occurring. Just as with the precession of the top, when deeper changes begin to become evident, many people will not notice them. Those who may notice them will often not connect them with the new learning, even though the two are connected in many developmental and subtle ways. Deeper changes are brought about only by sustaining the surface movement. If the rotation of the top ceases, so too will the precession. The moral of this story being: If we cease learning about something, the deeper learning cycle, based on nonconscious transfer connection, will cease as well.

Despite the sophistication of our unconscious mind, like our conscious mind, it's hardly infallible. Our unconscious mind may have wisdom of which we know not, except by intuition, but we can't always count on it.

NOTES

1. J. Larkin, J. McDermott, D. Simon, and H. A. Simon, "Expert and Novice Performance in Solving Physics Problems," *Science* 208 (1980), pp. 1335–1342.

2. R. Rowan, *The Intuitive Manager* (Boston, MA: Little, Brown, 1986).

3. M. McLuhan, *Understanding Media* (London: Routledge & Kegan Paul, 1964); see also P. Levinson, "McLuhan and Rationality," *Journal of Communication* 31 (1981), pp. 179–188.

4. In P. Senge, C. Roberts, R. Art, B. Smith, and R. Keiner, *The Fifth Discipline Fieldbook: Strategies and Tools for Building a Learning Organization* (New York: Doubleday, 1994), p. 178.

5. Kenneth Brown, *Inventors at Work: Interviews with 16 Notable American Inventors*, Tempus Books (Redmond, WA: Microsoft Press, 1988), p. 163.

6. J. Slocum, *Sailing Alone Around the World* (1900; New York: Dover Publications, 1956).

7. G. Hardin, "Intuition First, Then Rigor," in G. Hardin and J. Baden (eds.), *Managing the Commons* (San Francisco: W. H. Freeman, 1977), pp. 31–33.

8. T. J. Peters and R. H. Waterman, *In Search of Excellence: Lessons from America's Best-Run Companies* (New York: Harper & Row, 1982), p. 61.

9. See R. R. Dawes, *House of Cards: Psychology and Psychotherapy Built on Myth* (New York: Free Press, 1994).

10. D. G. Myers, *Social Psychology*, 4th ed. (New York: McGraw-Hill, 1993), p. 160.

11. See W. H. Beaver, *Empirical Research in Accounting: Selective Studies* (Chicago: University of Chicago, Graduate School of Business, Institute of Processional Accounting, 1966); E. B. Deacon, "A Discriminant Analysis of Prediction of Business Failure," *Journal of Accounting Research* 10 (1972), pp. 167–179.

12. For selected literature on nonconscious processing, much of it experimentally generated, see K. Bowers and D. Meichenbaum (eds.), *The Unconscious Reconsidered* (New York: Wiley-Interscience, 1984); A. Marcel, "Conscious and Unconscious Perception: Experiments on Visual Masking and Word Recognition," *Cognitive Psychology* 15 (1983), pp. 197–237; also see S. Freud, *Jokes and Their Relation to the Unconscious*, Standard ed., Vol. 8 (1905; London: Hogarth Press, 1960); J. Piaget, "The Affective Unconscious and the Cognitive Unconscious," *Journal of the American Psychoanalytic Association* 21 (1973), pp. 249–261.

13. J. Jaynes, *The Origin of Consciousness in the Breakdown of the Bicameral Mind* (Boston, MA: Houghton Mifflin, 1976).

14. D. Galin, "Implication for Psychiatry of Left and Right Cerebral Specialization," *Archives of General Psychiatry* 31 (1974), pp. 572–583.

15. D. B. Cheek, "Unconscious Perception of Meaningful Sounds from Careless Conversation during Surgical Anesthesia as Revealed Under Hypnosis," *American Journal of Clinical Hypnosis* 6(3) (1959), pp. 237–280; see also H. L. Bennett, "Preoperative Suggestions Reduce Blood Loss," *Human Aspects of Anesthesia* (January–February 1985), pp. 1–3.

16. Larkin et al., "Expert and Novice Performance in Solving Physics Problems," p. 1342.

17. Rowan, *The Intuitive Manager*, p. 9.

18. B. L. Benderly, "Every Day Intuition," *Psychology Today* 29(9) (September 1989), p. 36.

19. Peters and Waterman, *In Search of Excellence*, pp. 66–67.

20. In K. A. Ericcson and N. Charness, "Expert Performance: Its Structure and Acquisition," *American Psychologist* 49(8) (1994), p. 736.

21. Mary L. Gick and Keith J. Holyoak, "The Cognitive Basis of Knowledge Transfer," in S. M. Cormier and J. D. Hagman (eds.), *Transfer of Learning: Contemporary Research and Applications* (New York: Academic Press, 1987), p. 28. Italics added.

22. See K. H. Pribram, "Brain Organization and Perception: Holonomic and Structural Determinants of Figural Processing" (Stanford University, 1988, mimeographed); Karl Pribram, *Languages and the Brain: Experimental Paradoxes and Principles in Neuropsychology* (Englewood Cliffs, NJ: Prentice-Hall, 1971).

23. Karl Pribram, M. Newer, and R. Baron, "The Holographic Hypothesis of Memory Structure in Brain Function and Perception," in D. Krantz, R. Atkinson, R. Luce, and P. Suppes (eds.), *Measurement, Psychophysics and Neural Information Processing*, Vol. 2 (San Francisco: W. H. Freeman & Company, 1974), p. 429.

24. G. M. Edelman, *Bright Air, Brilliant Fire: On the Matter of the Mind* (New York: Basic Books, 1992), p. 104.

25. In Senge et al., *The Fifth Discipline Fieldbook*, p. 46.

26. Ibid., p. 240; see D. Bohm, *Wholeness and the Implicate Order* (New York: Ark Books, 1983).

27. H. A. Simon, "The Information Processing Explanation of Gestalt Phenomena," *Computers in Human Behavior* 2 (1986), p. 244.

28. See P. Langley, H. A. Simon, G. L. Bradshaw, and J. M. Zytkow, *Scientific Discovery: Computational Explorations of the Creative Processes* (Cambridge, MA: MIT Press, 1987).

29. In Senge et al., *The Fifth Discipline Fieldbook*, p. 47.

12

The Transfer Consultant: How to Begin Implementing Transfer and Save Your Training Dollar

> The challenge faced by those involved in the provision of training is to find methods of instruction which retain flexibility, and therefore provide efficient transfer of skills.
>
> Hesketh, Andrews, and Chandler[1]

In an age of the learning organization, corporate downsizing, budget reductions, and a consequent trend to outsource much of the training function, ironically, the role of the transfer consultant becomes an increasingly important one. Not only does the transfer consultant become generally important to business and industry, but he or she becomes important as a consultant to other training consultants, both in-house and to the traditional HRD consulting firm that designs and delivers HRD training. The bottom line is that learning in the workplace, technological conversion, product development, and therefore our competitive edge depend on the development of our ability in the transfer of intellectual capital.

Corporate management often seems to treat the training function as a kind of ritual. And when budget cuts are imminent, the training budget is frequently the first one cut. To use a cliché, this is penny wise and dollar foolish. Two assumptions seem to underlie this attitude. The first is that when push comes to shove, learning can take place by functioning on the job. While this is true to a degree, it is often inadequate for today's needs. The second assumption is that training is considered an expense, not as capital accumulation. But as we saw in Chapter 4, increasingly knowledge, and its acquisition, is considered intellectual capital, with corresponding titles like director of intellectual capital and director of intellectual asset management to reflect its importance. It has been one of the goals of this book to justify switching the column under which training has been found in the corporate ledger.

In this chapter, I will (1) outline the unique roles of the transfer consultant, (2) outline the requirements for reducing the time and economic costs of transfering evaluation research, and (3) conclude by summarizing the necessary requirements of reengineering the corporate transfer of learning function. Taken together, these areas constitute an outline of how to implement transfer in an organization.

REDUCING RELIANCE ON CONSULTANTS

In the learning organization literature, there continues to be talk and action about reducing reliance on outside consultants. In keeping with the "learning organization philosophy," the idea is to make members of the organization consultants and not "shift the burden" to external consultants who, through no fault of their own, often render the organization dependent on them. The move toward this goal is both philosophically and fiscally sound. Indeed, it could be maintained that most corporate training should not require an outside consultant—at least ideally.

But we don't live in an ideal world. The fact is, few organizations will be able to have all requisite knowledge reside within the organization. This is especially true of transfer. If I may be permitted an analogy to the classical ideal of the Renaissance Man (the eighteenth-century idea of a person able to encompass all knowledge), just as it's no longer possible to be a renaissance person, so, too, it's no longer possible for an organization to encompass all the knowledge and expertise they require. No single organization is a World Bank of intellectual capital.

Thus, in practical terms, most organizations require outside consultants. At the risk of appearing self-serving, people who are not trained in an area often think they may have sufficient knowledge or expertise to carry out the activity without a consultant. At this point in time, expertise in program design and instruction for transfer is not within the repertoire of most trainers. If it was, there would be no need for this book. Thus, while it is an ideal for organizations to reduce their reliance on consultants, in most corporate situations, transfer expertise will require a transfer consultant. I might note here, however, that "transfer consultant" refers to any training firm or in-house person who has acquired in-depth knowledge of the transfer research.

Nowhere is the dubious assumption by in-house personnel of having the requisite knowledge as true as it is in the "soft" human resources area of training. A recent article entitled "Self-Directed Team Building without a Consultant"[2] is an example. It's interesting that the content area of this article is teams. There continues to be a tendency to think that most anyone can effectively facilitate a team or small group. They can't. Let me somewhat embarrassingly illustrate from my own early experience.

When I left graduate school for the first time with a master's degree, I was hired by a federal agency to conduct crisis intervention–type counseling groups. The thinking of the administrator who hired me was, "Oh, you have a master's degree in psychology and sociology, Rob, so you know how to run groups." The fact was I had one course in group dynamics. Since I, too, thought I knew about groups (and needing a job), I agreed with their assessment of my potential skills. After all, aren't groups just a bunch of individuals? I was hired. Looking back on it, the groups I first conducted were disasters in terms of effectiveness. Worse yet, they may well have been counterproductive. But everyone thought I was doing a "great job." But what did they know about whether I was doing a great job or not? Enough said.

THE TRANSFER CONSULTANT

Where the consultant of transfer and intellectual capital fits into this new era of learning organizations, downsizing, and outsourcing is to enable organizations to learn in a more transfer-leveraged manner, to learn how to learn and to think, to facilitate both the individual development and organizational transfer of both minor and major stores of intellectual capital by creating a foundation that will be a continual source of transfer.

The transfer consultant, of course, must have extensive knowledge in transfer. Being thoroughly and specifically grounded in the transfer research is crucial. I say specifically grounded in transfer research, not just in the literature on learning, because as we have seen, instructing for transfer is often not the same as instructing for learning. As we have also seen, not being specifically grounded in the transfer research can lead not only to counterintuitive methods but to *counter*productive instruction.

You will note that I used the phrase *knowledge in* transfer, not just *knowledge of* transfer. This distinction means that the transfer consultant should be one who does not just have knowledge *of* the transfer literature but, in addition, has *demonstrated* expertise *in* transfer, not only on an abstract level but in actually being proficient *at* transfer, either on a general level or within a specific area. It goes without saying, however, that no consultant can have expertise in all content areas. And as we have seen throughout this book, most transfer is dependent on knowledge of the specific area in which transfer is to occur.

This leaves the transfer consultant in a precarious place. Thus, there are two basic roles for the transfer consultant. The first role is that of general instruction about transfer. The second is instruction in applying transfer in a particular content area. In the first role, transfer becomes a content area, just as any other area of expertise. The second transfer role requires the specific areas of expertise of those being instructed. This makes the second role of the transfer consultant largely a team process. This means that when working with other professionals who have specific content knowledge that they would like to transfer, the consultant must be a "quick study," as it were. Of course, the transfer consultant may also have specific content areas of expertise as well. For example, one of my content areas is groups/ teams. Let me now outline what I consider to be the new transfer consultant roles.

NINE TRANSFER CONSULTANT ROLES

The nine transfer consultant roles are (1) the general transfer seminar role, (2) the transfer application role, (3) the team transfer role, (4) the cross-function transfer role, (5) the systems transfer role, (6) the transfer program–design role, (7) the detailed programming role, (8) the collateral consultant role, and (9) the transfer research role.

1. *General transfer seminar role.* This role involves instruction to employees, managers, and trainers about transfer of learning. It includes seminars or talks on (a) what transfer of learning is, (b) why transfer is important, (c) the research findings about transfer, (d) how to acquire expertise in transfer thinking, and (e) approaches to applied transfer thinking and performance. These areas are prerequisite to the implementation of all other transfer consultant roles. In keeping with the distinction between *training* and *learning*, this first level of instruction in knowledge about transfer is extremely important. Given sufficient instruction about transfer through seminars and talks and specifically designed hands-on workshops, employees, managers, and trainers should be able to generally increase the level of transfer performance in a corporation.

2. *Transfer application role.* This role involves actually generating or applying transfer to a specific job or function. Since most transfer requires a knowledge base in the particular job, the consultant will likely not have this content expertise. In most cases, then, the role of the consultant is to work with individuals who have the content knowledge. This is where it's crucial for the consultant to have the concrete ability to engage in transfer thinking and to be a quick learner. With this expertise, the consultant is able to understand, relate, and help facilitate an individual's transfer thinking.

3. *Team transfer role.* This role involves the facilitation of transfer ideas directed at a particular job or issue. In this situation, members of a specifically selected team explore and brainstorm around the particular transfer problem. Other people often have valuable insights into areas in which they do not have expertise. In fact, this can be a benefit, as sometimes experts

in an area are blocked by their expertise from considering certain ideas or options. In addition to facilitating transfer thinking within the team, the consultant should have knowledge in group and team processes.

4. *Cross-function transfer role.* This role is similar to the team transfer role in that it is a group or team activity. The difference is that the transfer problem is a common one to the team's everyday functioning, involving a common knowledge base of all the cross-function team members. In this role the transfer consultant would also need to have group expertise.

5. *Systems transfer role.* This role involves integration of departmental and other functional roles within the organization. It may take the form of seeking out the similarity of functions, knowledge, or tasks shared by the different organizational systems.

6. *Transfer program–design role.* This role involves designing instructional programs for transfer. The design of transfer programs should be based on the level of transfer that the job requires. In Chapter 2, I outlined six levels of transfer: Level 1, nonspecific transfer; Level 2, application transfer; Level 3, context transfer; Level 4, near transfer; Level 5, far transfer; and Level 6, displacement or creative transfer. The level of transfer is often overlooked when designing instructional programs.

7. *Detailed programming role.* This approach is the standard instructional approach. It involves a very concrete, sequential, step-by-step method of instruction. It's similar to the "programmed text" approach to learning, leaving little or nothing to inference by the learner (see Chapter 3). The difference between this standard design and mine is that my detailed approach to instruction is framed in transfer of learning findings, with specific transfer enhancing strategies and examples. A detailed programming design is based in more of a training than a learning approach. As such, like most training approaches, the emphasis—though not exclusively—is on instructional method and design, rather than on the learner as the central cause of learning. This role basically is relevant to lower-level, more concrete and detailed tasks. Job or knowledge bases that involve detail and that are technical are often best taught with this approach. It can also be used as a base approach to Levels 4, 5, and 6.

8. *Collateral consultant role.* The transfer consultant role is an overarching one. Since transfer undergirds all learning, the transfer consultant becomes collaterally important to all HRD consulting. This means that the transfer consultant can provide valuable information about transfer to all HRD consultants in applying their content-specific areas.

9. *Transfer research role.* To know whether any training is instructionally effective and cost-effective requires research. Research provides feedback and the means for correction and improving learning. Let me say that I know there are often economic and time pressures connected to doing evaluation research. I will suggest some possible remedies for these pressures in a moment.

Before I outline the possible remedies for reducing the costs of research, however, first I'd like to outline these five instruction-related research roles. I didn't entitle this section "The Transfer Evaluation Research Role" because there are five basic instruction-related roles for research in any HRD instructional program. To reasonably ensure that instructional programs transfer into performance, programs should be preceded by

- a detailed research rationale or outline of pertinent research findings on the instructional content area and the best methods of delivering that instruction (this is essentially what researchers do when writing a research proposal—the history section serves a number of purposes; this review of the research delineates the instructional problems and its themes and also prevents reinventing the wheel and faddish approaches to instruction);
- a job analysis outline of how to tie in the instructional program specifically linked to job tasks;
- an evaluation of general instructional effectiveness;
- a determination of the cost effectiveness of the instruction; and
- an assessment not only of whether the instruction was effective but of whether it was the least costly of other effective programs.

These five research roles are continuous and additive. Finally, smile sheet research doesn't count.

REDUCING THE TIME AND ECONOMIC COSTS OF EVALUATION RESEARCH

The time and costs involved in research can be considerable. I should note, however, that in the long run research is always less expensive than not doing research. There are ways of reducing this cost, however.

1. Instead of hiring an outside research firm, hire or train someone within the corporation to conduct the research. Depending on the size of the business, the research role can be full-or part-time. Keeping the research function in-house can reduce the costs in three ways. First, the general salary of such a person is typically lower than the rate of a consulting firm. Second, the in-house person provides a cost savings by being familiar with the ongoing nature of the research, reducing the redundancy that is typically created by starting anew each time research is conducted. And third, this continuity often provides the opportunity for insights and linkages within such an ongoing research program that is typically missed when such continuity is not a part of research.

2. Instead of hiring an expensive consulting firm to conduct research, hire university professors who have expertise in research. University professors, especially young professors, can typically be retained relatively inexpensively. Many are intrinsically motivated to do research. It's what they

are educated to do. Moreover, they need research publications for promotion and tenure, so they are extrinsically motivated. In addition, many have access to either undergraduate or graduate students who are looking for research experience. Students get rewarded by the experience, being given internship credit, and can put this experience on their resumes.

3. Whether university professors or outside consulting firms are retained to conduct research, if it's possible, it is efficient to try to maintain a constant relationship with the same researchers. Just as with the in-house person, such continuity provides a cost savings via familiarity with the research, again reducing redundancy and providing the opportunity for insights and linkages within an ongoing research program.

THE REQUIREMENTS FOR REENGINEERING CORPORATE TRAINING TO TRANSFER OF LEARNING

In transfer terms, it is appropriate to end this book where it began. In responding to a Department of Education survey regarding educational quality and the workforce, Robert Tucker, in his article "Revisiting the Role of Higher Education in Workplace Competence," writes:

Rapid acceleration in the development of technologically intensive goods and services has shifted the means of production from steel and sweat to software and greymatter-wetware. Wrong were the futurists who predicted that technological advancement would displace "thinking" careers with an endless variety of no-brainer menial jobs. . . . Technology has created jobs that are insatiable consumers of knowledge. But there is more to it. Today's jobs are insatiable consumers of rapidly evolving knowledge. Where the life cycle of a cluster of job-related knowledge was once quite long, perhaps spanning an individual's career, it is now quite short, often recycling in a few years.[3]

What this quote means is that we need a workforce that's capable of generic learning and of generalizing that learning. In summary, this is how transfer of learning is accomplished:

Preconditions for Implementing Optimal Transfer

1. Mastering *a large primary knowledge base or high level of expertise in the performance area of transfer* (see Chapter 8). This means:

• mastering the information that's part of the task or tasks to be performed by

• reading pertinent material and

• involving yourself in active experiencing and working with the material.

2. Acquiring *some level of knowledge base in subjects outside the primary performance area* (see Chapter 8). This means:

• reading related material and
• reading what may be considered useless knowledge (see Chapter 8).

3. Acquiring *an understanding of the history of the transfer area(s)*. This means:

• mastering the past knowledge of the pertinent area, including
• how the area to be transferred developed (see Chapter 6).

4. Acquiring *motivation or, more specifically, a "spirit of transfer"* (see Chapter 7). This means:

• connecting knowledge closely to your sense of self-mastery and personal development,
• developing an emotional relationship to the material, and
• involving yourself in a team or social support network for the learning.

5. Understanding *what transfer of learning is and how it works*. This means:

• mastering the concept of transfer, including
• the different kinds and levels of transfer
• as well as its strategies and methods.

6. Develop *an orientation to think and encode learning in transfer terms* (see Chapter 9). This means:

• thinking in generic terms, using
• analogies, metaphors, examples, and archetypal models and
• decontextualizing the material learned (see also below).

7. Involving yourself in *cultures of transfer* (see Chapter 7). This means:

• creating or finding concrete social situations that support transfer, and
• becoming mentally a part of an abstract community of those interested in the task or area (e.g., published writings, Internet discussion groups).

8. Understanding *the theory underlying the transfer area* (see Chapter 8). This means:

- familiarize yourself with the deep and overall connections and
- the relationships among the concepts and data in the transfer that tie them all together into a system.

9. Engage in *practice and drill* (see Chapter 8). This means:

- hours of reviewing and practicing the material to mastery by
- reflective, not rote, practice.

10. Provide *time for the material to mentally digest or incubate* (see Chapter 11). This means:

- allowing time for conscious reflection and
- "downtime" for the nonconscious processing of the material.

11. Observe and read *the works of people, both in and out of the performance field, who are exemplars of transfer thinking.* This means:

- immersing yourself in accounts of scientific discoveries, of invention, of innovation, and
- in the works of others, like poets, who think in transfer terms

Methods of Access

The primary problem of transfer is accessing the linkages that connect material. In addition to the eleven general principles that I've outline above and throughout this book, there are specific methods to facilitate transfer. (in a subsequent volume, I'll more extensively outline a series of methods that I've developed based on the transfer research findings.)

Transfer Access Questions
- The basic transfer access question is: What do I know that I've learned in the past that I can apply to this present situation?
- The second, corollary set of access questions are: What is it like? How is it equivalent to? What is it akin to? How is this the same as? What are the similarities? Does this remind me of anything? How does it resemble something in the past? Is this comparable to something that I already know?

Thought Extensions or Generalizing
- using analogies, metaphors, archetypes, and models
- using analogies of experience
- using microworlds
- substituting one noun for another

Generic Thinking
- decontextualizing or deconcretizing the learned material
- systems thinking
- mapping information and knowledge
- recurrent pattern recognition

Examples of Transfer Exercises

As a simple transfer exercise for developing transfer ability, consider the following three examples. These examples can be considered instances of product development (recall also Chapter 6). For each example, the reader has the basic knowledge to solve the transfer exercise.

Transfer Exercise # 1

Question: How did the idea for the product known as Velcro originate?

Description: Velcro is the self-fastening material used as a fastener on garments. It is made of opposing pieces of nylon fabric, one with minute hooks, the other with dense piles that interlock with each other when pressed together.

Think: What is Velcro like?

1. _____
2. _____

Answer:[4]

Transfer Exercise # 2

Question: How did the idea of barbed wire originate?

Description: Wire with sharp barbs at intervals (invented to keep livestock penned in).

Think: What is barbed wire like?

1. _____
2. _____

Answer:[5]

Transfer Exercise # 3

Question: What does the following abstract description describe?

Description: (1) There is an abundance of a consumer resource (2) that can be sustained by only a certain amount of usage; (3) the resource is utilized by multiple consumers, (4) without regulation, (5) leading to a short-term gain for each consumer (6) but exceeding usage limits of the resource, (7) leading to the depletion of the resource, (8) resulting in long-term loss of the resource to consumers.

Think: What is this like?

1. _____

2. _____

Answer:[6]

What Else Reengineered Corporate Instructional Programs and Transfer Consultants Need to Know

- detailing the importance of the eleven transfer principles

- how transfer can increase performance

- spirit of transfer: motivation for transfer

- importance of transfer for organizations that need to learn constantly

- intellectual capital and transfer of learning

- how knowing and learning a lot create transfer expertise

- unconscious, and transfer thinking

- transfer of learning versus training: a corporate and educational merger

- how to recognize systems thinking, generic structures, and archetypes

- how to practice for transfer ability

- reading for transfer

- teaming with transfer: experiencing team and small-group functioning through transfer

- designing and creating cultures of transfer

- understanding the different kinds and levels of transfer

- individual development and empowerment through transfer

- intuition in decision making: how to make it work

- use of examples, and specific instances in developing transfer ability

- how to decontextualize material learned so it's generalizable

- exploring similarity relationships

- using analogies, metaphors, and parables in acquiring transfer thinking

- role of differences in seeing similarities

- how to design instructional programs for transfer

- how to redesign existing programs for transfer

- transfer strategies for promoting transfer performance

- specifically designing transfer exercises to fit the corporate need

- institutionalizing transfer in the organizational structures and staff

CAUTIONARY POSTSCRIPT: RESEARCH BIAS AND INSTRUCTIONAL "*MIND*FIELDS"

Bias in research is always a problem. Without getting into methodological intricacies, one serious precaution to reduce bias is not to have the same people who are delivering an instructional program also conduct the evaluation research on that program. At best, no matter how well intended, we know that there are pressures and unconscious bias that can slant the research seriously. We saw in the opening chapter that an unfortunate aspect of OD research is that nearly all published cases report the success of the intervention. At worse, it's like having the fox guarding the chicken coop.

In the shift to a learning approach by organizations, and with a shift in how to instruct for transfer, there are *mind*fields to be negotiated. While we don't know where all the mindfields are, some will certainly be found in new learning fads that are not directly performance related but that will be offered under the guise of long-term benefits to performance. There is no end to general education or general knowledge–type programs that could theoretically be seen to relate to performance.

Promises of *learning* and *long-term* benefits, then, can be like black holes, sucking in all available instructional resources within their gravitational reach and never emerging into a future performance universe. Such instructional trekking—however enjoyable—may lead to exploring deep intellectual space where no one has gone before, but its return on transfer of learning performance will be earthbound.

NOTES

1. B. Hesketh, S. Andrews, and P. Chandler, "Training for Transferable Skills: The Role of Examples and Schema," *Education, Training, Teaching International* 26 (1989), p. 156.

2. E. Glassman, "Self-directed Team Building without a Consultant," *Supervisory Management* 37 (1989), pp. 6–7.

3. R. W. Tucker, "Revisiting the Role of Higher Education in Workplace Competence," *Adult Assessment Forum* 5(1) (Spring 1995). Available at: http://www. intered.com/edv5nl.htm

4. The invention of the Velcro material was transferred from the natural fastening mechanism of the burdock. Nature's buttons: A burdock is a coarse, broadleaved weed bearing prickly heads of burs. Pressed together, they stick to each other very tightly. In *like* manner, Velcro is made of opposing pieces of nylon fabric, one with minute hooks, the other with dense piles that interlock with each other when pressed together. This was in fact a conversion from a natural technology to a human technology. (Incidentally, CEO Victor Kiam of electric shaver fame reportedly turned down the opportunity to purchase the Velcro patent, thinking it would not have widespread use. Oh, the wonders of hindsight.) See R. A. Postiglione, "Velcro & Seed Dispersal," *American Biology Teacher* 55 (January 1993), p. 44.

5. Before barbed wire, various materials were used as fences, including briar and mesquite, cactus species of thorny plant growth. The most effective was Osage orange. It is a short tree with pronounced thorny branches. It became widely cultivated into "live fences," or Nature's fences. In 1868, Michael Kelly patented his barbed wire, describing it as approximating a thorn hedge but preferring to call it a "thorny fence." Just as the Osage orange twig had thorns about one-half inch long and spaced fairly evenly apart, so did Kelly's barbed wire. The Osage orange tree is Nature's barbed wire, just as burdocks are Nature's Velcro.

6. You will, I hope, recall that this archetypal or generic dilemma is the *tragedy of the commons*, outlined in Chapter 10. If you didn't recall correctly, this is an excellent example that just having knowledge is not sufficient to ensure access to transfer.

Appendix A: Kinds of Transfer

An important ingredient in understanding something is to know where it belongs in the scheme of things and to become familiar with its parts. Knowing what kinds of tools are available for a particular kind of job, for example, not only allows us to select the tool that will do the best job but provides us with a framework and a plan for how to do the job. It follows that tools create (and limit) the possibilities for what and how a job can be done. The same is true with concepts and the words that we describe them with. The more extensive vocabulary we have, the more ways we have for seeing, describing, and doing something. In the same way, having categories of the kinds of transfer allows us to recognize how, when, and where transfer occurs.

Transfer can be classified into two basic categories: (1) the type of knowledge that the transfer is based on and (2) the specific kinds of transfer. The first category corresponds to the five types of knowledge that I described in Chapter 8 (declarative, procedural, strategic, conditional, and theoretical knowledge); the second category is based on transfer itself. I should point out that none of the kinds of transfer are necessarily mutually exclusive.

Content-to-content transfer is making use of what we know in one subject area in the learning of another area. Content knowledge is what I describe in Chapter 8 as declarative knowledge. Declarative-to-declarative transfer occurs whenever existing knowledge of some content area facilitates or interferes with simple learning. It also refers to learning new knowledge that may be somewhat different from the original learning. Knowledge about proteins, fats, and carbohydrates from chemistry, for example, will be useful in health education. Knowing about how small groups work will help in understanding business meetings. Content or declarative knowledge may provide us with a general framework, it may help us to elaborate, or it may provide an analogue for the second content area.

Procedural-to-procedural transfer, or what is also known as *skill-to-skill transfer*, refers to using the procedures learned in one skill area in another skill area. For example, skills used in riding a bicycle transfer to driving a motorcycle or driving a car. Procedures are sequences of actions. Sequences learned operating one computer program may transfer to operating another similar program.

Declarative-to-procedural transfer occurs when learning *about* something helps in actually doing something. For example, knowledge about computers enables us to learn programming procedures, or knowledge about stocks enables us to play the stock market more proficiently.

Procedural-to-declarative transfer is when practical experience in an area helps us to learn more abstract knowledge of the area. Practical experience in constructing electronic circuits, for example, will help in learning theoretical knowledge of electronics; knowledge of programming may help in learning computer theory.

Strategic transfer involves knowledge about our mental processes, such as how we learn or remember; it is knowledge gained through monitoring our mental activities during learning. Knowledge of how we solved one problem may transfer to the solving of another problem.

Conditional transfer occurs when knowledge learned in one context is seen as be appropriate for transfer to another context.

Theoretical transfer is understanding deep-level relationships of cause and effect in one area that can be transferred to another area. Recognizing that a spark and lightning are the same, that combustion and rusting are the same, and that the inverse square law applies to planets and the tides are all examples of theoretical transfer.

General or nonspecific transfer occurs when previous knowledge that is not specific to the training situation transfers to other situations when no apparent similarities exist between the old and the new situations and therefore speeds up learning. The first kind of content-to-content knowledge described above is an example. General transfer is often described under the concepts of "learning to learn" and "warm-up effects."

Near transfer occurs when previous knowledge is transferred to new situations that are closely similar but not identical to previous situations. A person's experience in roller skating when transferred to ice skating is an example of near procedural transfer. Learning to calculate the amount of floor tile needed for a living room by using your prior classroom experience in figuring the area of rectangles is another example of near transfer. As obvious as this may seem, many people do not make this simple kind of transfer.

Far transfer takes place when previous knowledge is transferred to new situations that are quite different from previous knowledge. Elie Mechnikoff's transferring the behavior of the mobile cells in the transparent larvae of starfish when confronted with thorns, *reminding* him of what happens when a human finger is infected with a splinter, can be seen as an example of far transfer.

Literal transfer is using knowledge or a procedure directly in a new learning situation. In studying about the American Revolution, you might learn that wars are caused by competition to control natural resources. Then in studying World War I, you might look for competition to control natural resources as an explanation of the cause. Literal transfer is near transfer.

Vertical transfer refers to prior learning transferred to new learning that is higher in a hierarchy, or learning that presupposes the prior learning. Learning in which prerequisite skills are necessary requires vertical transfer. For example, to calculate percentages, you must already know how to divide and multiply.

Lateral transfer occurs when previous learning is transferred to new learning at the same level in a hierarchy. The example of transferring roller-skating skills to ice skating is an example of lateral transfer, as is transferring the known laws of the flow of a liquid to a theory of heat conduction.

Reverse transfer, sometimes called *backward transfer*, occurs when existing (prior) knowledge is modified and re-viewed in terms of its similarities to the new information. Typically, transfer is defined as old or existing knowledge impacting on new knowledge. Backward transfer reverses this.

Proportional transfer is a more abstract transfer. Recognizing a melody played in a different octave or key is an example.

Relational transfer can be illustrated by mathematical analogies. In biology, this kind of structure is called a homology, a correspondence in form of external appearance between two species as with the wing of a bird and the fin of a fish, even though the underlying causal mechanisms are different. Both share a similar structure, but there is no underlying causal relationship. Relational transfer is seeing the same structure between two things.

Structural or *isomorphic transfer* is also seeing similar structures, but unlike relational structure, structural transfer is based on the two things being compared having similar underlying causal mechanisms—such as the law of gravitation, which can be applied to Newton's apple, to the planetary system, and to tidal phenomena, although the surface similarity or appearance between the phenomena is almost entirely absent. The transferring of what is known about racial prejudice to gender prejudice is another example of structural transfer.

Appendix B: Transfer of Learning and the Development of Computer Competencies

David A. Allie

Over 71 million computers were sold worldwide in 1996, representing almost an 18 percent increase from the previous year, indicating tremendous usage and exposure. It's now a safe assumption that all people in modern societies will need to interact, either directly or indirectly, with computers during their professional and personal lives. Accordingly, businesses have been implementing courses with the goals of teaching specific, concrete computer and word processing skills.

As admirable as many programs and courses are, the majority fall short (see Chapter 1) in that their focus is too narrow, limiting training to specific software applications. Mastery of specific software applications is important, yet the wealth of different programs within any given area (e.g., word processing) makes it more important not merely to strive for the training of discrete tasks but, rather, to aim for the development of computer competencies through a *transfer of learning* paradigm. A *transfer of learning* goal is more productive to the corporation, individual, and society in that learners will be capable of adapting—*transferring, generalizing* their skills—to new programs and applications with a reduction in retraining time.

It is surprising why so little emphasis in training is placed on a *transfer* or analogical method of teaching computer competencies. For example, computer-assisted instruction (CAI) brings a diverse and increasing array of computer technologies to assist the teaching and learning process, including guided drill and practice exercises, computer visualization and manipulation of complex objects, and computer-facilitated audio-visual communication between even geographically distant learners and instructors.[1] While the effectiveness of CAI may not be widely disputed, it must be remembered that the focus of CAI has been upon discrete actions with little to no regard for the development of a "whole," whereby learners learn to *transfer* an understanding of one kind of software application to another. What is needed is a sound method for assisting not only the specific learning (as opposed to training) of how individual programs may be used to fulfill a task but also a general understanding and appreciation for the program's generic structure (see Chapter 10), built upon a series and practiced set of basic skills and transfers.

To illustrate: The Macintosh computer and Microsoft Windows operating systems both embody a graphical user interface that utilizes *common skills* and tasks for performing similar actions among different software applications. One of the goals in the design of Microsoft Windows[2] is to reduce the learning curve dramatically whenever a user is faced with the prospect of a new software application. I have taught introductory through advanced-level courses and have developed a method for learning that aids the learner in mastering specific skills but, more important, a method to develop the learner's ability to *transfer* learning from one application to another (and from one type of program to another). This is achieved, first, through conceptual understanding versus training for only discrete specifics, although specific skills are acquired in the process, and second, through emphasis on the development of a knowledge base versus teaching just specific procedures.

Leading the learner to this discovery and learning must be subtle, because if the learner is resistant to a true learning approach, preferring what I've called a "Just show me" attitude, the likelihood of achieving positive *transfer* (and accruing the benefits of increased speed, efficiency, and productivity) will be threatened. My own teaching experiences have consistently shown that adult learners tend to place more intrinsic value on learning than their school- and college-age counterparts.

BASIC LEARNING AND PRIMING FOR TRANSFER

Windows 95 includes a number of small programs or applets in addition to the core operating system (the operating system is the most elemental software that controls the computer by coordination and manipulation of hardware, file organization on various storage media, and management of hardware errors and data loss). Notepad is one of these applets and is analogous to the traditional paper notepad. WordPad, another of the included programs, is a miniature word processor with slightly increased usefulness. Very simplistic in their nature and capabilities, most users totally ignore the existence of both Notepad and WordPad and choose to use more complex word processors such as WordPerfect for all forms of written notes and documentation. Claims of *unfamiliarity* with Notepad and WordPad are frequently heard as the primary reasons why a relatively huge program like WordPerfect will be used instead when making the simplest

Figure B.1
Exploring the Common Elements through Notepad

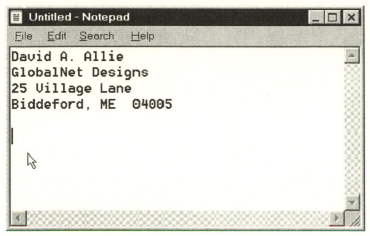

Microsoft Notepad, Windows 95, Copyright © 1981–1995, Microsoft Corporation.

of notes, even though in the paper/hardcopy world these same users typically would use a small notepad or even a torn scrap of paper to jot down
a grocery list—not a large notebook.

In my introductory course the goals are:

• to familiarize learners with the computers on campus,
• to provide detailed instruction on the use of WordPerfect and Quattro Pro, and
• to provide basic information on computer history and terminology.

Learners come to the course with a variety of skills and experiences and
leave not only with the ability to use these specific word processing and
spreadsheet programs but with an enhanced ability that enables them to
use previously *unfamiliar* applications. The key to their procedural skills is
an increased knowledge base and emphasis on *transfer*.

Just as children begin formally learning language from phonics and repeated practice, learning how to use a word processor should begin with
rudimentary elements. Notepad is used since it is the simplest of text editors
and does not include any formatting capabilities, thereby forcing the user
to focus on the programs' basic functions.

Learners are first shown that Notepad (see Figure B.1)[3] corresponds to
all other Windows 95 programs in that it *likewise* possesses a resizable
window, a title bar, borders, a menu, a set of control icons (minimize,
maximize, and close), and a set of scroll bars. The learners are shown
through a number of miniexercises that they can (1) control the size and

shape of the Notepad window, and (2) minimize and reaccess (versus re-opening) the program from the Windows 95 task bar, reinforcing that any changes in size won't negatively impact any data they may enter. Emphasis is placed upon *similarities* as their knowledge base is expanded and rein-forced by repeatedly emphasizing these similarities.

Learners then are asked to simply type in their name and address, in mailing label fashion, in the document editing portion of the window. As they type, it is reinforced that the action of typing in Notepad is

- similar to a typewriter in that the ENTER key is pressed at the end of each line and
- different from a typewriter in that they can simply use the backspace key to wipe out previously typed characters in error. Next,
- learners are asked to watch the mouse pointer change shape as it moves over different regions of the window, noting its two distinct shapes of arrow or I-beam.

Further reinforcement is provided as the mouse is repeatedly moved back and forth over the different parts of the Notepad window. Once the shape distinctions of the mouse pointer have been noted and explained, learners are instructed

- to highlight their entire name and address,
- individual words, and
- entire lines, then
- back to highlighting their entire name and address using the mouse.

The knowledge base is expanded, and motor skills are sharpened as learners perform these simplest of manipulations.

With their name and address highlighted, learners are shown various ways to copy the selected text, using both the menu and keyboard shortcut (see Figure B.2). Keeping the Edit menu open, they are asked to notice the relationship between the assigned keyboard shortcuts for the elements Cut, Copy, and Paste and their keyboard, wherein they discover that

- the keyboard shortcuts are sequential on the keyboard as they are in the menu, and
- the keyboard shortcuts can be executed solely with the left hand, while the right hand (assuming right-hand dominance) maneuvers the mouse for text selection.

It is noted that combined use of both hands when performing any of these actions will allow them to improve their speed, efficiency, and productivity.

After copying the material using both the menu and keyboard shortcut,

Figure B.2
Learning to Cut-Copy-Paste in Notepad

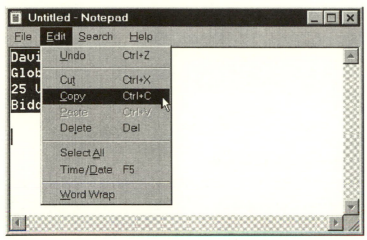

Microsoft Notepad, Windows 95, Copyright © 1981–1995, Microsoft Corporation.

learners are given the opportunity to play with pasting in the text multiple times within the same document—also using both the menu and keyboard shortcut—which allows them to

• increase the length of the document (thereby activating the vertical scroll bar) and
• realize that both actions (menu versus shortcut) achieve the *same* results.

As learners play with increasing the copy and paste commands, it is explained that once the copy (or cut) command is executed, the selected material is placed on an invisible clipboard—ready for use with the paste command until replaced by using the cut or copy commands again or until the computer is rebooted or shut down.

Learners are then taken step-by-step through the remaining menu actions, including

• the process of saving the document to disk,
• closing and opening files,
• changing the page setup and printing the document,
• searching for a specific word within a document, and
• using the Undo command.

It's important to emphasize repeatedly that virtually every single action they learn now—and the associated understanding of how/why it works—can be *transferred* to most new programs they encounter.

Figure B.3
Learning to Learn More through the Notepad Help File

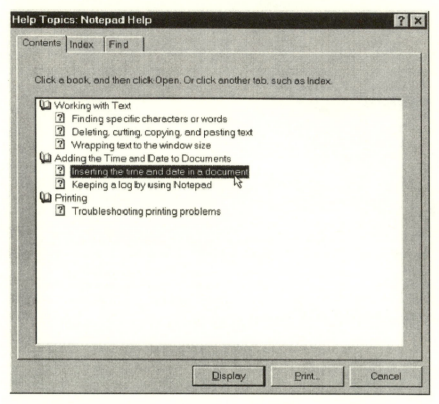

Microsoft Notepad, Windows 95, Copyright © 1981–1995, Microsoft Corporation.

Next, learners are shown how to learn more by using the Notepad Help system (see Figure B.3). Learners are walked step-by-step through the process of learning how to insert the time and date in a document. At the same time, it's noted that most software now comes with very small user/reference manuals—if any at all—and that this is an industry-wide trend toward reducing production costs, saving natural resources, and making the manual more accessible by placing it on the computer. Finally, I mention that the Notepad Help system is *common* to all Windows 95 programs as well as being the underlying concept for navigating and browsing the World Wide Web—with the goal of showing that understanding how the extremely simple Notepad Help system can lead to easier *transfer* when working with other programs as well as the Internet.

Subtle emphasis is given to the fact that an increasing amount of information will be (and become) accessible through hypertext files and systems throughout their professional lives. The phrase "subtle emphasis" isn't necessarily a contradiction in terms but reflects that, through phrasing and intonation, I'm "setting the stage" for them to learn later that both the WordPad and WordPerfect help files work the *same* way. In essence, I'm priming them to begin their first serious *transfer of learning* in computer competencies.

The learners should have a solid foundation now that they've mastered Notepad and are now asked to minimize the program to an icon on the Windows 95 Task Bar. It's mentioned that just as a craftsman has an array of tools—some with a general and others with a specific purpose—learning when to use any given tool is the result of

• the specific knowledge of the tool and its intended actions and
• experience of using the tools under varying conditions.

TRANSFER

Learners now open the WordPad program (see Figure B.4), which, like Notepad, is a text editor but possesses some basic and rudimentary word processing features as well. Learners are urged to ignore the *differences* temporarily and initially focus on and indicate the *similarities* between Notepad and WordPad, including the presence of

• a resizable window,
• a title bar,
• borders,
• a menu,
• a set of control icons, and
• a set of scroll bars.

Therefore, if those elements allowed learners to control the size, placement, and active state (minimized or not) and perform specifics actions with Notepad, these elements will allow learners to control exactly the *same* characteristics within WordPad. Learners should note that scroll bars are not immediately visible within WordPad. This may lead to *negative transfer* unless it is specifically noted that scroll bars (vertical and/or horizontal) will appear as soon as there is sufficient text within the document to justify their display. This can be proved by the simple action of having them type their name and address, copying it multiple times below the original, selecting the text and deleting it, and finally restoring it with the Undo command.

The recognition of this positive *transfer of learning* should be reinforced because while advanced computer users may be cognizant of this fact (an

Figure B.4
Learning by Comparison the Similarities of WordPad to Notepad

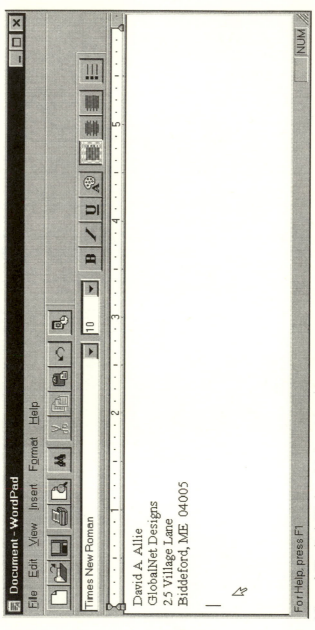

addition to their knowledge base), most novice—and even intermediate—computer users fail to recognize this until either someone explicitly points it out or they discover it after considerable inter-program experience. Inter-program experience is simply the experience of working with multiple applications, both sequentially and in parallel (via multitasking). A majority of business job positions are restrictive in that employees are required to use only a very limited number of programs when there may be other programs available that may help the employee to

- increase their productivity directly and/or
- enhance their knowledge base and conceptual understanding of programs in general, leading, under the right conditions, to the *transfer of learning* (which again will increase their speed, efficiency, and productivity).

Once again, learners should type (within WordPad) their name and address as they did in Notepad. They are then walked step-by-step through the process of copying all of the text (using both the menu commands and keyboard shortcuts) and pasting it multiple times as they did previously, noting the *similarities* in commands (menu or keyboard) for performing these *same* types of actions. This recognition of more transfer of learning (and the associated addition to their knowledge base) should be positively reinforced.

Another series of miniexercises, *identical* to those performed when using Notepad, should be done in WordPad, including

- the process of saving the document to disk,
- closing and opening files,
- changing the page setup and printing the document,
- searching for a specific word within a document, and
- using the Undo command.

When learners attempt to use the "Search" command for locating a specific word, they may falter when they don't see a "Search" item from the main menu. Without allowing them to search the remaining menu items, I ask them to identify reasons why there isn't a "Search" menu in WordPad, forcing them to think about the two programs. Here, one of the goals is to have them identify that

- WordPad is a more enhanced text editor (versus Notepad),
- it would be very unlikely that Microsoft (who designed both programs) would include a feature in the smaller, less capable program (Notepad), yet remove it in the larger, more enhanced program (WordPad), and therefore,

- the commands for "Find" must simply be relocated to another menu (see Figure B.5).

Once this is acknowledged and learners locate the "Find" command on the "Edit" menu, several items should be pointed out while the item is high-lighted on the menu (see Figure B.5). First, the "Find" and "Find Next" commands simply changed location, placing them in conjunction with the familiar cut-copy-paste commands and the new "Replace" command—all commands relative to editing text. The learner can achieve more *transfer* now and later understand that the command was moved for a conceptual reason (i.e., to place it in close proximity to other editing and text selection commands) rather than simply memorizing the commands' locations within this specific program.

Second, the "Find" and "Find Next" commands retain their keyboard shortcuts, thus providing another opportunity for positive transfer of learn-ing. Hopefully, learners will begin to suspect that Notepad commands will have their equals or counterparts in other programs, with corresponding menu commands (occasionally relocated when conceptually appropriate to a program) and keyboard shortcuts (which should remain *identical*, no matter what program it's used in).

Third, a status bar now exists at the bottom of the WordPad window; and as each menu item is highlighted, a brief description of the item's function is displayed in the status bar. This is a good opportunity to men-tion

- that this is one of the enhancements available in WordPad, thereby making it easier for them to know what each command does (without prior knowledge, experience, or trial and error) and, more important,
- that virtually all other Windows 95 programs will likewise have a status bar.

Several other points should be made clear. Notepad, while useful, is very limited in scope and functionality. As a result, the number of *common* elements it requires and possesses is minimal. WordPad is larger and has much more functionality, thereby requiring more common elements, in-cluding

- a status bar,
- scroll bars that dynamically appear/disappear as the need exists,
- new menu commands for print preview, text replacement, setting program op-tions, and setting various font attributes,
- a tool bar using icons with balloon help,
- a format bar with character and document formatting options, and
- a ruler bar.

Figure B.5
Identifying the New Location of the "Find" Command and Recognizing the Existence of the Status Bar

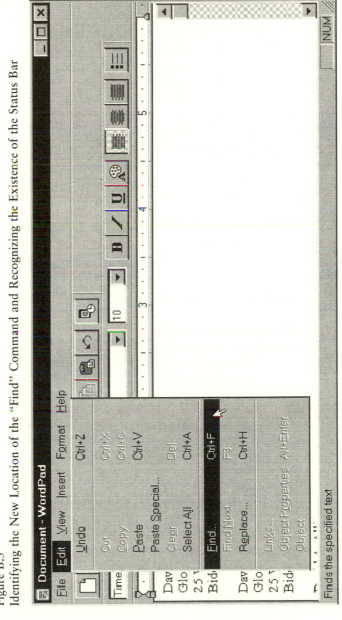

Microsoft WordPad, Windows 95, Copyright © 1981–1995, Microsoft Corporation.

Subtle emphasis is placed on the fact that

- virtually every other (larger) Windows 95 program will contain these *common* elements;
- while other programs may contain the same elements, there may be subtleties due to each program's specific needs; and
- WordPad is to WordPerfect (which will be explored soon) as Notepad is to WordPad.

A useful *analogy* here is to look at this from the historical perspective of

- going from a manual typewriter to an electronic one (with features for easily correcting or centering text and the addition of font attributes such as boldface and italics)—and then
- from an electronic typewriter to a word processing program on a computer.

I've discovered that the use of more analogies to other concepts, facts, and disciplines serves multiple goals of providing additional opportunities for achieving *transfer* and time to let the material "sink in."

Confronted with both changed and new elements, learners should be reassured that virtually all Windows 95 programs that use tool bars will use the same icons to describe, for example, saving to disk (an icon/picture of a disk), and so on. The paradigm to strive for is that of building blocks— all of the elements in Notepad contributed to the design, layout, and functionality of WordPad—and will do so in the WordPad-to-WordPerfect (WordPad-to-Works, WordPad-to-Word, etc.) transition.

Once again, it's important to emphasize that the *differences* between Notepad and WordPad are simply extensions and enhancements; the *differences* are minor and related only to the performance of specific, discrete actions rather than the general concept of text editing. In the instances of the tool bar and formatting bar, each item on these bars has a corresponding menu item (and maybe even a keyboard shortcut), yet the conceptual idea behind the tool bar (formatting bar, ruler bar) was to place the most frequently used commands one step closer to the user—thereby allowing the user to focus more on the content of the document.

Finally, before performing the transition to WordPerfect, I have the learners open a new document in WordPad, giving them a blank page. Next, they're shown how to use the Alt-Tab key combination to switch from program to program (versus using the mouse to click on each minimized icon on the Windows 95 Task Bar). Once they're comfortable with this new skill, they're asked to switch to Notepad, where they should still have their original document visible, and copy their name and address to the clipboard. Then, they switch to WordPad and paste in the information, which demonstrates that it's possible to cut-copy-paste information with the clipboard from/into virtually any other document. What's important is that information is no longer "chained" solely to any specific, individual program but can be moved from document to document.

For example, what if a learner needs to jot down some ideas for a new research paper, yet he or she is not at his or her own computer and has to use another computer that doesn't have the same word processing program he or she normally uses? Every computer has some form of plain text editor, like Notepad. He or she can easily jot down ideas and an outline in Notepad and save the file for later work. Later, the notes may be copied from Notepad using the clipboard or simply opened as a file in whatever word processing software is preferred (all of which support ASCII text). Therefore, what may begin as a simple outline of ideas in Notepad can be pulled into WordPad, where the full article is created.

FURTHER TRANSFER

Learners should now be ready for the next transition[4] to WordPerfect (see Figure B.6).[5] Using another set of mini-exercises *identical* to those done when performing the Notepad to WordPad transition, remembering to keep the initial focus on *similarities*.

The learners should now be able

• to start identifying *common elements* on their own and
• be encouraged to list as many *common elements* as they can find.

Having gone through both Notepad and WordPad very carefully, taking the time to assemble the building blocks,[6] and having completed several out-of-class exercises using these smaller programs, they should begin to make a number of positive *transfers* of learning on their own. As encouraging as this is, many learners tend to stray from the conceptual, knowledge-base approach as soon as they get into WordPerfect, focusing back on whatever report is due currently. As a result, my role as instructor and *transfer* facilitator continues.

Once learners have recognized and identified the common elements, both conceptual and specific, they should look at the *differences*. At first, the items they list will all tend to pertain to specific, concrete actions and commands. Then, without looking at the screen, they should rearrange their list into a set of smaller, conceptual groups (e.g., formatting commands, graphics commands, supplemental tools, etc.). In most cases, they'll later see that these groups correspond to the menu headings and groupings of icons on the various tool bars and formatting bars. To assist, I have the learners consider how actions and commands were grouped in both Notepad and WordPad—and transfer those ideas to WordPerfect.

Figure B.6
The Next Transition to WordPerfect 7.0 Reveals Common Elements, as Well as Additional Features and Enhancements

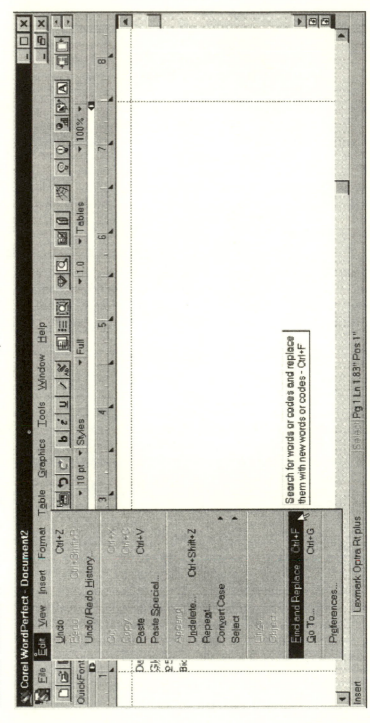

Once the two transitions have been made, I have learners demonstrate copying material from Notepad/WordPad and pasting it into Word-Perfect—and vice versa—noting the effects of the formatted material when copying back (from WordPerfect). Since you're going from a more specific program with more complex formatting, have learners note what happens to the formatting when going to WordPad or Notepad.

Finally, I return to more strongly emphasize concepts and ideas that I've been subtly emphasizing up to now. Learners should

- understand that all the key skills that were learned in Notepad apply to WordPad and WordPerfect,
- realize that differences are primarily conceptual, so by understanding what each program is designed to do, one can effectively choose the program appropriate for each task,
- access specific, concrete information accessible through hypertext files,
- understand that virtually every other Windows 95 program will contain a number of *common elements*,
- understand that while other programs may contain the *same* elements, there may be subtleties due to each program's specific needs,
- accept that learning is a lifelong cycle, and
- be capable of moving to entirely new programs with minimal effort/maximum *transfer*,

thereby proving the efficacy and productivity gains achieved as a result of learning, by discussion and example, how to achieve *transfer of learning*.

HIGHER-ORDER TRANSFER

These methods have proven quite valid and reliable in the corporate setting. In addition to providing learners with a set of skills, they leave the course with a solid foundation, knowledge base, and conceptual under-standing of computers and software that enable them to use the various pieces of software they may use and encounter more effectively and pro-ductively. For those who become responsible for aiding their co-workers in the use of new software, a higher-order *transfer* is required that enables them (the new instructor) to aid their learners more successfully and prof-itably.

I often use a real-world example I experienced to demonstrate how im-portant *transfer of learning* truly is. A colleague had bought a new flatbed scanner. The installation guide was very simple to read, well phrased, and seemingly complete. This particular scanner even included a short videotape to walk me through the installation of SCSI interface card, scanner, and software. The steps were brief and clearly defined, and after completing the installation, everything worked perfectly.

The next time the computer was rebooted, he turned on the scanner and opened the scanning software. However, the software reported that it didn't recognize the scanner! After repeated attempts to contact the scanner and OCR software manufacturers were in vain, I rebooted the computer and reinstalled the software. Everything worked again. However, the process repeated itself.

The solution lay in another, totally "unrelated" experience (see Chapter 8) I had several weeks prior to this incident. I was trying to access the embedded diagnostics on my own computer, yet the system kept hanging partway through the diagnostics recognition of SCSI devices. None of the components were damaged. I had, though, recently installed an external SCSI Zip drive.[7] Sitting back in my chair, I looked at the Zip drive. Why weren't the diagnostics recognizing (and hanging) the Zip drive? While the Zip drive was on (power is continual unless you unplug it from the wall socket), I noticed that the Zip disk was not inserted, so I pushed the disk in and the diagnostics began working again. This solution required that the disk be inserted in the Zip drive!

Coming back to the scanner problem, there was no disk that needed to be inserted. However, both my Zip drive and my colleague's scanner were external SCSI devices. In the case of my diagnostics "problem," the Zip drive needed to be on and a disk needed to be inserted so the computer could access the disk (if the Zip drive was unplugged, diagnostics ran fine, simply not acknowledging what it thought wasn't there).

After going through the process of reinstalling software and getting the scanner to work several times, I then shut the system down and watched my colleague repeat what was thought to be the *same* exact steps in using the scanner. I noticed that he turned the scanner on only after he turned on the computer and was into Windows 95, a process that I would have considered logical (no need to keep the scanner on all the time if it's not in use). However, if the scanner was turned on when the system was booted up, all of the various scanning and OCR software worked perfectly.

The important question here is, How did I know that turning the scanner on before booting up would result in success? In the case of the diagnostics and my Zip drive, the diagnostics software needed to have the drive on and with a disk in, in order for the diagnostics software to complete its recognition phase. In the case of the scanner, the scanner needed to be turned on before Windows 95 started to load, because that's when Windows 95 does its recognition of devices attached to the computer system. In both cases, there was a recognition phase being conducted by the computer, albeit at different times, yet the similarity exists and was valid— resulting in positive transfer. The next point was to adapt the Zip drive incident to the scanner problem, which was achieved not by mapping out specific, concrete facts about each device but by looking at the problem *conceptually* and seeing how the recognition phase interacted with each device.

The current trends of corporate downsizing and increasing employee productivity are achieved most effectively when emphasis in training is placed on a *transfer* or analogical method of teaching computer competencies. Also undisputed is the fact that the number of computers purchased and the types of software applications in use will increase, thereby necessitating a thorough understanding and wholehearted endorsement of *transfer of learning* principles. The most successful companies will be those that discover the long-term value and, hence, realize the profits from embracing a *transfer* paradigm for all learning experiences.

NOTES

1. New developments in hardware and software have expanded the ways in which CAI is now being used, to include specific course/topic tutoring, manufacturer and corporate training, and even the instruction of entire academic programs.

2. For brevity, examples will be phrased in terms of the Microsoft Windows 95 operating system and applications. However, all concepts apply equally to the Apple Macintosh Finder and OS/2 Presentation Manager operating environments.

3. All screen shots are reprinted with permission from Microsoft Corporation, and all mentions of Microsoft Windows 95, Notepad, WordPad, the Microsoft Windows 95 Help system, and any other components of the Windows 95 software are trademarked by Microsoft Corporation.

4. I try to avoid saying "final transition" since (1) software is in constant flux and change and (2) people may need to perform a transition and *transfer* from, for example, WordPerfect to Microsoft Word. I prefer to describe the paradigm of learning software as a circle, since once one program is learned, knowledge, conceptual understanding, and skills can be applied to another program.

5. This screen shot is reprinted with permission from Corel Corporation Limited, and all mentions of Corel WordPerfect and any other components of the Corel WordPerfect software are registered trademarks by Corel Corporation Limited in Canada, the United States, and/or other countries.

6. I typically spend up to four-and-a-half hours (about three 90-minute classes) from the moment we boot up the computer into Windows 95 until the point where we even run WordPerfect. My classes, however, cover more concepts and material than I've included in this appendix and, more important, consistently are resulting in more examples of positive transfer.

7. The Zip drive mentioned here is a product of the Iomega Corporation.

Index

About the Author

ROBERT E. HASKELL is Founder and Director of TransLearn Associates, a consultancy in Old Orchard Beach, Maine, that specializes in the design of business training and educational courses. He is also Professor of Psychology at the University of New England. With expertise in learning transfer and team/small group processes, he has published four books, numerous chapters, and research articles in national and international journals. He is also Associate Editor of *The Journal of Mind and Behavior*.